INTELLECTUAL PROPERTY RIGHTS, EXTERNAL EFFECTS AND ANTI-TRUST LAW

LEVERAGING IPRs IN THE COMMUNICATIONS INDUSTRY

INTELLECTUAL PROPERTY RIGHTS, EXTERNAL EFFECTS AND ANTI-TRUST LAW

LEVERAGING IPRs IN THE COMMUNICATIONS INDUSTRY

ILKKA RAHNASTO

OXFORD

UNIVERSITY PRESS

OXFORD
UNIVERSITY PRESS

Great Clarendon Street, Oxford OX2 6DP

Oxford University Press is a department of the University of Oxford.
It furthers the University's objective of excellence in research, scholarship,
and education by publishing worldwide in

Oxford New York

Auckland Bangkok Buenos Aires Cape Town Chennai
Dar es Salaam Delhi Hong Kong Istanbul Karachi Kolkata
Kuala Lumpur Madrid Melbourne Mexico City Mumbai Nairobi
São Paulo Shanghai Taipei Tokyo Toronto

Oxford is a registered trade mark of Oxford University Press
in the UK and in certain other countries

Published in the United States
by Oxford University Press Inc., New York

The moral rights of the author have been asserted
Database right Oxford University Press (maker)

First published 2003

British Library Cataloguing in Publication Data

Data available

Library of Congress Cataloging in Publication Data

Data available

ISBN 0–19–925428–1

1 3 5 7 9 10 8 6 4 2

Typeset in Times by
Cambrian Typesetters, Frimley, Surrey

Printed in Great Britain
on acid-free paper by
Biddles Ltd., Guildford and King's Lynn

PREFACE

This book provides an analysis of intellectual property rights and their usage in the communications industry. The topic turned out at the same time to be highly interesting, dynamic and difficult. My writing has greatly benefited from the insight into some of the key developments derived from my daily work. My intention is that this book provides an overview of this fascinating framework of technology, economics and law.

I wish to thank all those colleagues and friends who have supported, guided and challenged my thoughts, particularly Bengt Domeij, Niklas Bruun, Annette Kur, Mikko Tulokas, Martti Castren and Esko Friman. Gary Smith has provided valuable comments during the final editing of the manuscript. Finally, I wish to thank my wife Jaana and my children Johanna and Tuomas for their flexibility during the intensive writing process.

Further, I wish to thank Paulon Säätiö, Niilo Helanderin Säätiö, Suomen Lakimiesliitto, the Fulbright Foundation and the Nokia Corporation for the financial support that enabled the preparation of this work, and Oxford University Press for publishing the book. The writing process was greatly influenced by being able to spend time at the George Washington Law School, the Franklin Pierce Law Center and the Max Planck Institut für gewerbliche Rechtschutz und Urheberrecht.

The coverage of case law and legislation is up to date to early 2002, and I have also been able to incorporate a good number of more recent developments during the editing and proofing process.

Espoo
Ilkka Rahnasto
January 2003

CONTENTS

TABLE OF CASES

European Court of Justice (in alphabetical order)

Other European Cases (in alphabetical order)

United States Federal Courts (in alphabetical order)

TABLE OF LEGISLATION

EU Legislation

International Conventions and Agreements

ABBREVIATIONS

ANSI	American National Standardization Institute
ARIB	Association of Radio Industries and Businesses
CMLR	Common Market Law Reports
DOJ	US Department of Justice
ECJ	European Court of Justice
ECR	European Court Reports
EIPR	European Intellectual Property Review
ETSI	European Telecommunications Standardization Institute
FTC	US Federal Trade Commission
GRUR	Gewerblicher Rechtschutz und Urheberrecht
IETF	Internet Engineering Task Force
IIC	International Review of Industrial Property and Copyright Law
IPR	Intellectual Property Rights
KHO	Finnish Supreme Administrative Court
KKO	Finnish Supreme Court
NIR	Nordisk Immateriellt Rättsskydd
PLI	Practising Law Institute
SDMI	Strategic Digital Music Initiative
SOU	Statens Offentliga Utredningar (Sweden)
TRIPS	Trade-Related Aspects of Intellectual Property Rights
UCC	Uniform Commercial Code
WAP	Wireless Application Protocol
WIPO	World Intellectual Property Organisation
WTO	World Trade Organisation

INTRODUCTION

Background

This is a book about the external effects of patents and copyrights in the commu-   **1.01**
nications industry. External effects or externalities are impacts caused by patents
and copyrights on others than the rights holder.[1]

If the Linux operating system is less attractive for users because copyright owners manufacturing DVD movies with technical protection means allowing them to be played only
on Windows operating system, the exercise of copyright has an external effect on the
market of software operating systems.

If the cumulative patent royalties for the combination of all technically necessary patents
for standards-compatible cellular phones are higher than the average expected operating
profit, a single manufacturer is less likely to allocate her resources to that business. The
royalty request of a single patentee has an external effect on the market of complete cellular phones.

Samuelson and Nordhaus provide a widely used definition of external effects:[2]   **1.02**

An externality or spill-over effect occurs when production or consumption inflicts inci-
dental costs or benefits on others; that is, costs or benefits are imposed on others yet are
not paid for by those who impose them. More precisely, an externality is an effect of one
economic agent's behavior on another's well-being, where that effect is not reflected in
dollar or market transaction.

The internal effects of patents and copyrights have long been studied. Internal   **1.03**
effects are impacts of the protection on potential inventors and authors.
Consequently, it has been established that patent and copyright protection
increases incentives to allocate more resources to inventive and creative activities. Such protection also encourages inventors and authors to publish their

---

[1] Also the terms 'social costs', 'social benefits' or 'spill-over effects' are sometimes used.
[2] P A Samuelson and W D Nordhaus, *Economics* (12th edn, New York, 1985) 712.

inventions[3] and works, to identify and record inventions and works, and effectively to make use of such inventions and works. While some ambiguity exists on
the issue as to whether competition alone would provide the same encouragement, it is almost universally accepted that unlimited free copying is not socially
and economically desirable. These internal-effect justifications have in recent
years been the primary reason for the expansion and enhancement of patent and
copyright protection: it has been necessary to strengthen protection against imitators and 'free-riders'.[4]

1.04 External effects of patent and copyright protection have attracted substantially
less interest among policy makers and researchers. Apart from the traditional

---

[3] In this book, the word 'invention' is used in the meaning of patent laws. The term 'innovation' is
largely used as a synonym since patent laws grant protection for both inventions and those innovations
that fulfil the requirements of patent laws. It is recognized that economists sometimes distinguish between
innovations and inventions. Under economic terminology, the term 'invention' is most frequently used
solely to identify the creation of new products or discovery of production techniques. The term 'innovation' has primarily been used to describe the introduction of such techniques or the act of bringing them
onto the market. While there is a difference between successful discovery and introduction onto markets,
for this book, the distinction is largely arbitrary. See E Mansfield, *Technological Change. An Introduction
to a Vital Era of Modern Economics* (New York 1971), 74–77 (introducing some examples of time differences between initial inventions and the first introduction of commercial products).

[4] See for general overview about discussion F Machlup, *An Economic Review of the Patent System*.
Study No 15 Subcommittee of the Judiciary of the US Senate (Washington 1958) 79–80 (concluding
that even though there is no conclusive evidence of the benefits of the system as a whole, there is
usually evidence to support or oppose any proposed changes in the system); P A David, 'Intellectual
Property Institutions and the Panda's Thumb: Patents, Copyrights and Trade Secrets in Economic
Theory and History', in *Global Dimensions of Intellectual Property Rights in Science and Technology*
(Washington DC 1993), 5 (concluding that strong intellectual property laws serve the promotion of
technological progress at the expense of technology diffusion); F M Scherer, *Industrial Market
Structure and Economic Performance* (1980), 444; M A Lemley, 'The Economics of Improvement in
Intellectual Property Law' (1997) 75 Texas Law Review 989–1084, 993; P Demaret, 'Patent, Territorial
Restrictions, and EEC Law. A Legal and Economic Analysis', IIC Studies Vol 2 (Weinheim 1978), 3;
G Inge, *The Use and Abuse of Intellectual Property Rights in EC Law* (London 1996), 2 (criticizing
that this conceptual change was by 1995 not yet fully understood in Europe); Ibid at 18–19; W F
Baxter, 'Legal Restrictions on Exploitation of the Patent Monopoly: An Economic Analysis' (1966) 76
Yale Law Journal 267, 268–271 (without proper protection private investment in innovation would stop
at the point where gains from alternative investment targets yield the gains from innovation); W M
Cornish, *Intellectual Property: Patents, Copyrights, Trademarks and Allied Rights* (4th edn, London
1999), 129; R C Nordhaus, *Invention, Growth and Welfare: A Theoretical Treatment of Technological
Change* (Cambridge, Mass, 1969), 86–90 (establishing the basic thesis that incentives for inventors
should be strengthened); F K Beier, 'The Significance of the Patent System for Technical, Economic
and Social Progress' (1980) 11 IIC 563, 580–584 (listing incentives for R&D, promotion of dissemination and international transfer of technology); P K Haarmann, *Tekijänoikeus & Iähioikeudet*
(Helsinki 1999), 11 (listing studies on the economic importance of copyright industry); see also U
Bernitz, G Karnell, L Pehrson and C Sandgren, *Immaterialrätt* (7th edn, Stockholm 1998), 142 (intellectual property rights granted to private inventors and authors are effectively slowing down the
concentration of economic decision-making); *BIE Paper* (1995), 77–92 (introducing empirical data);
E W Kitch, 'The Nature and Function of the Patent System' (1977) Journal of Law and Economics, 265
(patent system increases output from resources used for technological innovation); T Saarenheimo,
Studies on Market Structure and Technological Innovation (Helsinki 1994) (spill-overs may affect willingness to patent); P Esala and S Manni-Loukola, *Tekijänoikeuden Merkitys Suomen Kansantaloudessa
Vuonna 1998* (Helsinki 1991) (empirical evidence in Finland).

discussion focusing on the proper length and 'breadth' of protection,[5] the discussion has been led primarily by US economists focusing on the impact of network externalities on anti-trust analysis. Other externalities have been either dealt with under theories focusing generally on 'public interest' (eg on the free benefits gained by a single consumer when being able to record movies from television or music from radio, on imitations and 'free-riders') or they have not been taken into account.

Some fairly recent cases such as *Magill*[6] in Europe and *Kodak*[7] in the US, or **1.05** policy debates involving interfaces, intermediary copies or technical protection mechanisms of copyrighted materials, are difficult to understand and analyse if the focus is solely on the imitation argument. Rather, those cases involve examples in which external effects of patents and copyright are an integral part of the analysis and discussion. However, the inherent difficulty that courts and commentators have in analysing and interpreting these cases and policy discussion reveal the lack of proper legal tools to take such effects into account systematically.

This book analyses externalities, categorizes them and identifies their impact on **1.06** intellectual property and anti-trust policy and enforcement. The need for a study on external effects is reinforced by two ongoing developments.

Firstly, patents and copyrights are increasingly treated as property with the same **1.07** constitutional protection as any other privately owned property. Consequently, analogies from externalities of tangible property, such as real estate, are increasingly appropriate.

Secondly, the method of producing and distributing new inventions and works **1.08** has been changing. Up until the 1990s, individual companies developing proprietary technologies created most of the technical advances in information technology. Since the early 1990s, it has been increasingly difficult for any individual company to claim authorship or status as an inventor of any new successful technologies. The result has been an increasing interdependency between companies. The development can be characterized by the shift from the 'serial model' to a 'simultaneous model of innovation'.[8]

Innovation in the 'serial model' is based on the idea that innovation occurs as a **1.09** series of small steps. After the initial innovation, subsequent improvements are made to the technology. It is primarily a vertical process. The model has largely been based on information in the public domain and on information created by universities.

---

[5] See T Takalo, *Essays on the Economics of Intellectual Property Rights* (Helsinki 1999) for an overview of the discussion.

[6] *Radio Telefís Éireann (RTÉ) and Independent Television Publications Ltd (ITP) v Commission (Magill)* [1995] 4 CMLR 718.

[7] *Eastman Kodak Co v Image Technical Services Inc*, 504 US 451 (1992) (*Kodak II*).

[8] T M Jorde and D J Teece, 'Innovation Co-operation and Anti-trust', *Anti-trust, Innovation and Competitiveness* (Jorde and Teece, eds, New York 1992), 48–50.

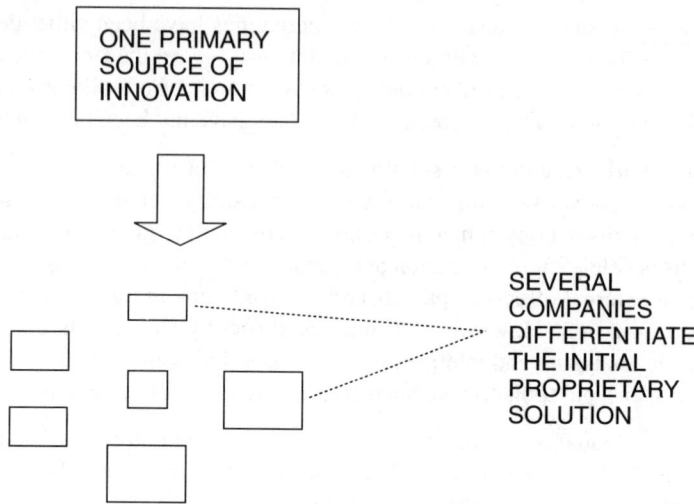

An example of a product resulting originally from a serial model of innovation is the personal computer. IBM developed the concept of a personal computer and other companies have developed it further. It is typical for industries in which the serial model of innovation is the dominant concept that companies claim, for marketing or other purposes, to be the sole inventors of their product concepts. Particularly in the pharmaceutical industry, the serial model is still frequently used when individual companies develop their own pharmaceutical products.

1.10 In the 'simultaneous model of innovation', the same innovation happens at the same time in various places. It is not necessarily based on any initial innovation that others then advance. Rather, the innovation is increasingly based on any available information source. The simultaneous model of innovation has been characterized as 'incremental and cumulative activity that involves building on what went before, whether the knowledge is proprietary or in the public domain'.[9] Any new innovation is increasingly based on information that has been developed by private companies.

1.11 In the case of such simultaneously developed information, the 'basic' information is increasingly proprietary.[10] It is only accessible to authorized persons and only

---

[9] Jorde–Teese, n 8 above, 49.

[10] According to Thurow, some fairly recent studies suggested that 73% of private patents were based on knowledge generated by public sources such as universities and non-profit or government laboratories. L C Thurow, 'Needed: A New System of Intellectual Property Rights' (1997) Harvard Business Review, 95, 98 (suggesting this as evidence that privately developed secret knowledge does not generate the next generation of knowledge).

SIMULTANEOUS MODEL OF INVENTION

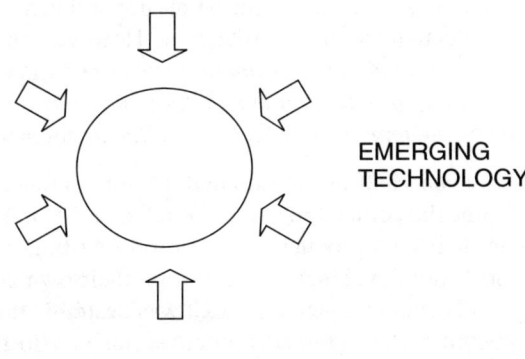

EMERGING
TECHNOLOGY

SEVERAL PRIMARY SOURCES
OF INNOVATION

those who have the appropriate authorization to do so can use it. At the same time successful products require a combination of various complementary innovations.[11] Therefore, one of the key success factors of a company is increasingly the way it secures its access to relevant 'basic' information. Such access to basic or 'state-of-the-art' information is thus vital for a company's own innovative activities.

Development of Linux and other open-source software products is largely dependent on the contributions of their users. Most communication products are also the results of standardization. During standardization, ideas from a number of contributors are combined in order to secure interoperable advanced systems. Even multi-media and entertainment industries are combining efforts of a number of authors. **1.12**

The challenge is that these individual contributions are largely privately owned. In order to enable the use of open-source software, communications products or advanced entertainment products, one has to find an effective way of treating the various motivations, interests and practices underlying the use of patents and copyrights on which these contributions are based. **1.13**

This book also covers leveraging intellectual property rights. The term 'leveraging' is used here to identify business strategies that actively aim to control the external effects of patents and copyrights in order to maximize business **1.14**

---

[11] In respect of the discussion involving complementary assets, see Jorde–Teece, n 8 above, 53.

benefits.[12] One of the traditional views is that intellectual property rights are necessary for individual companies in order to protect their investment and to exclude imitations. That may still be an important reason for business firms to rely on intellectual property protection. However, this book is based on the presumption that *intellectual property rights are strategically important because with patents and copyrights it may be possible to control other firms' behaviour and influence the manner in which they allocate their resources.*

1.15 During the second half of the twentieth century, intellectual property rights were for a long time the cornerstone of the serial model of innovation. Companies were developing their own products, authors were writing their own books and more recently, software developers were writing their own computer programs. From the social and economic perspective, it was desirable that those who were first in doing something were granted limited exclusivity to their results. It was even concluded that it was desirable to encourage such activities, so it was clear that one should not deliberately copy what others were doing. Unless your strategy was based on copying of others' products, this conclusion was not particularly interesting for anyone engaged in the development of business strategies.

Consequently, companies adopted either passive or active intellectual property strategies. A *passive intellectual property strategy* meant that the company adopted a strategy of investing in intellectual property rights as little as possible. An *active intellectual property strategy* meant that the company was actively organizing the detection of new innovations, was patenting its innovations, protecting its trade marks, clearing new products against prior rights and attacking imitators.

Since most of this had seldom any direct impact on the success of the company, it was not surprising, as one commentator identified, that patents were long considered to be an uninteresting subject for study and business strategy.[13] In many countries, copyright was similarly seen as only being a part of cultural policy, as the legislation was relevant only to the experts of collecting societies and media houses.[14]

1.16 The approach has changed. Intellectual property rights have gained new popularity as ingredients of industrial policy. At the same time, entirely proprietary product concepts are giving way to products and services that combine various technical and creative components. A successful business strategy is increasingly based on intellectual property rights because through intellectual property rights it is possible increasingly to control the activities of other companies.

---

[12] See *Integraph Corp v Intel Corp*, 3 F Supp 2d 1255 (ND Ala 1998) ('leveraging' occurs when a firm uses its market power in one market to gain competitive advantage in another market other than by competitive means), vacated 195 F 3d 1346 (Fed Cir 1999).

[13] K G Rivette and D Kline, *Rembrandts in the Attic—Unlocking the Hidden Value of Patents* (Boston 2000).

[14] SOU 1984:5, 49 (identifying cultural politics as the driving force for copyright legislation in Sweden); P C Grindley and D J Teece, 'Managing Intellectual Capital: Licensing and Cross-Licensing in Semiconductors and Electronics' (1997) 39 (2) California Management Review, 8 (intellectual property management used to be a backwater).

Accordingly, companies are adopting either offensive or defensive intellectual property strategies.

An *offensive intellectual property strategy* is based on strategic planning of the **1.17** use of intellectual property rights in the business, proactive litigation of intellectual property rights and active lobbying for new intellectual property legislation. A *defensive intellectual property strategy* is aimed at minimizing any effects the intellectual property strategies of others may have on the business of the company.

Research problem

In this book the external effects of patents and copyrights are analysed using the **1.18** legal doctrines developed to respond to such external effects. The main problem analysed is the conflict between competing interests of rights holders and those who are affected by the external effects. How do legal theories respond to this conflict and how should they respond? Based on the categorization of external effects and the resulting rules for solving potential conflicts, the theory is applied to the most frequent external effects in the converging communications industry.

Traditionally, any conflict involving the use of patents or copyrights has been **1.19** solved by modifying the scope of the protection of intellectual property rights or by applying anti-trust laws to a particular practice. In the US the traditional doctrine of misuse of rights has occasionally also been applied to patents and copyrights. Consequently, the application of intellectual property rights and anti-trust theories in the network economy of converging telecommunications, media and information industries are a central part of this book. These industries are in this book referred to as 'the communication industry'. Traditionally, there has been some tension and interaction between intellectual property laws and anti-trust laws. Are these theories still fully applicable to the externalities in the network economy? How should these theories be adopted in the network economy? What influence, if any, do these theories have when analysing the acceptability of particular leveraging practices?

Essentially, leveraging practices are aimed at having an impact on the behaviour **1.20** of others. Even if intellectual property rights were not intentionally used to harm others, they may have such effects. These externalities, or social costs, have not been popular targets for anti-trust law enforcement. The popular slogan suggests that 'anti-trust laws do not protect competitors, they protect competition'. This book analyses whether external effects of intellectual property rights in the communication industry should be targets for intervention.

In brief, this book analyses the principles that are used to identify lawful from **1.21** unlawful leveraging practices in the use of intellectual property rights. It also analyses possible strategies that may be used to respond to leveraging. Finally, this book suggests theories and principles that could be used more effectively to identify desirable practices from undesirable practices in the network economy. In particular, this book proposes the integration of the concept of external effects into the legal doctrine involving intellectual property rights.

1.22 Traditionally, intellectual property rights were held to provide monopolies.[15] The existence of patents and copyrights were considered to be evidence of market power. In the modern analysis, this view has been rejected. It is now popular to argue that both intellectual property rights and anti-trust laws promote the same goal, consumer welfare. Only the means used to promote this goal are different. Intellectual property laws encourage innovation and creativity. The resulting innovative and creative products are presumed to increase welfare. Also competition may encourage innovation. Therefore, anti-trust laws focus on structural safeguards ensuring that the benefits for consumers are maximized through the increased innovation and creativity. This increased competition is presumed to increase welfare.[16]

1.23 The remaining practical problem in the interface between intellectual property rights and anti-trust laws is finding a proper balance. The balance may be achieved through two alternative routes. Firstly, balancing factors may be incorporated into intellectual property laws. This means that when enacting new laws and interpreting the scope of existing intellectual property rights, the effects of the chosen interpretation on competition are taken into account. Alternatively, intellectual property arguments may be incorporated into anti-trust doctrines. Thus as a part of the proper investigation into the relevant market, it may be asked whether the existence of intellectual property rights somehow changes the relevant market. Also, when evaluating a particular practice, one may ask whether the existence of intellectual property rights justifies an otherwise condemned practice or whether an otherwise justified practice should be condemned because of intellectual property rights.

1.24 As an alternative, it may also be argued that no balancing is necessary because the most effective result is achieved through private negotiations. In the discussion in the late 1990s, there was a view that primarily intellectual property owners

---

[15] See G W Stocking and M W Watkins, *Monopoly and Free Enterprise* (New York, 1991), 84: 'As the patent system has actually developed, it has in various ways provided legal cover for practices that undermine a competitive economic system' (proposing in 1951 additional safeguards to stop misuse of patent system); D D Chisum and M A Jacobs, *Understanding Intellectual Property Law* (New York 1992 (rep 1999), 1–6; P E Areeda and H Hovenkamp, *Antitrust Law. An Analysis of Antitrust Principles and Their Application.* Volume III. Revised edition (Boston, 1996) § 704a (suggesting that much of this tension is caused by the lack of interaction between specialized intellectual property experts holding intellectual property rights as some sort of 'natural' rights and others who consider that some kind of restrictions are 'inherent' in any intellectual property rights).

[16] S W Bowman, *Patent and Anti-trust Law. A Legal and Economic Appraisal* (Chicago 1973), 1–2 ('Both anti-trust law and patent law have a common central economic goal: *to maximize wealth by producing what consumers want at the lowest cost.*').

advocated their rights as property rights allowing them the sovereign control of the use of their exclusive rights. This book discusses both these balancing methods and the property theory in connection with leveraging practices.

Limitations[17]

This book focuses on the identification of leveraging practices in the communication industry, on the external effects caused by patents and copyrights, and on the proper methods of balancing exclusive rights provided by intellectual property rights with justified concerns of those whose activities are affected by such external effects. **1.25**

This book analyses the strategic use of patents and copyrights in the communication industry. It recognizes that while some overlapping principles may apply, the underlying economics may be different in other industries. Further, this book does not analyse potential interaction between trade marks and competition. The nature and function of trade marks as primary indicators of origin and marketing tools may justify somewhat different treatment. Therefore, this limitation has been made. Also, any protection provided by *sui generis* laws for databases, music performers, producers and semiconductor manufacturers or by virtue of utility models has not been discussed. Again, this does not mean that the results of the analysis would not be applicable to such rights. **1.26**

The analysis and discussion focuses on the law and policy in Western Europe and North America. Only limited references are made to Japanese law or to the laws of other countries. This limitation has not been made because the topic is relevant only in Western Europe or North America. Rather, it is for practical reasons relating to the availability of and accessibility to the relevant theories and materials. It is presumed that the conclusions of this book may be applied universally. A reader familiar with or interested in Scandinavian law will find references and comparisons with the Scandinavian tradition. However, this book aims to be primarily the author's input to the international discussion and not a description of the Scandinavian legal framework. **1.27**

This book does not discuss the externalities that have an impact on international trade. Therefore, any wealth transfers caused by particular solutions between different nations are beyond the scope of this book. It is recognized that some of the international implications may affect allocation of resources between nations. However, such effects would be the topic of another study. Consequently, issues such as territorial nature of intellectual property rights and the related controversy between territorial or global exhaustion of intellectual property rights is not discussed or analysed in this book in any depth. **1.28**

---

[17] Any ideas or opinions of this book reflect solely the ideas and opinions of the author.

1.29 This book does not analyse intellectual property rights to the extent they have significance in merger control. It is recognized that acquisition of intellectual property rights through mergers may sometimes be a significant motivation to or an effect of a merger. However, since this book focuses on the strategic exercise of intellectual property rights and not on the acquisition of such rights, the issues involving mergers are not discussed.

The methods used in the discussion are focused on the impact of external effects in the legal doctrines. Consequently, the analysis focuses on general trends and main developments. Individual issues are identified in order to identify the treatment of external effects or a lack of such treatment. This book is not intended as a comprehensive study of the case law and doctrine of any individual legal questions.

1.30 Finally, a deliberate choice has been made not to describe the current basic legal frameworks covering intellectual property rights and anti-trust. It is presumed that the reader has a general understanding of such basic issues as patent and copyright systems or anti-trust frameworks in Europe and in the United States. If the reader is not familiar with those basic principles, there are a number of excellent textbooks and treatises available.

1.31 A simple starting point to serve as the initial framework for those readers who are not experts in the field follows. Patents and copyright provide their owners exclusive rights. These exclusive rights allow the owner to request that a court of law issues an injunction and monetary damages against anyone that makes unauthorized use of a patented feature or the protected work. This may become strategically important if this right is used without any need to balance it against potential consequences which such an exercise may have.

1.32 Anti-trust laws in the US and in Europe protect consumers against practices that limit competition. The focus of the control is on the contractual arrangements between two or more entities. Anti-trust laws may exceptionally also interfere with the unilateral conduct of even a single business entity, if that entity is deemed to have market power.

Source materials and methodology

1.33 The analysis in this book is based on a combination of case law, legal doctrines and economic studies. The research method is reflected in the text itself. The structure of the book provides an analysis of existing legal theories and their criticism and introduces an alternative theory in the following framework:

Chapter 2: Introduction of traditional legal theories and their criticism.
Chapter 3: Introduction of external effects analysis as an alternative theory.
Chapters 4–6: Application of external effects analysis.

Even though the aim is not to focus on the discussion of legal research methods   **1.34** as such, it is recognized that legal research always reflects traditions. The method used for interpreting primary and secondary sources of law potentially affects the results of the research.[18]

The analysis has taken the potential external effects of intellectual property rights   **1.35** as a starting point. In the beginning two initial questions were identified.[19] These questions also provide a starting point for the methodology of this book. This starting point is reflected against case law, legal doctrines and economic theory. Chapter 2 ties the legal tradition and various methods to the research problem. That chapter discusses and explains alternative methodologies traditionally used to explain the interface between anti-trust laws and intellectual property rights. The doctrines, methods and traditions relevant to the topic of this book are described and analysed in detail. The result is a mixture of various methods and explanations.

There are a number of alternative ways to interpret the results of Chapter 2. This   **1.36** book relies on three main traditions when implementing the results of Chapter 2 into selected practical business strategies and legal doctrines in Chapters 3–6.

Firstly, this book relies on the theory of law and economics to explain and inter-   **1.37** pret the results of Chapter 2. When introducing theories containing economic arguments, it is possible either to treat the economic arguments as a normative source of information or to treat economic arguments as only one element affecting the outcome. According to the normative approach, the interpretation chosen should be the one that leads to the most efficient outcome.[20] The interpretation should be chosen irrespective of whether it causes distribution of wealth between the parties affected by the interpretation.[21] According to a descriptive approach, the knowledge of the underlying economic effects is useful for the decision-maker or policy-developer. Economic arguments are essential elements of the analysis but there may also be other arguments that affect the outcome. Therefore, even though it may be presumed that no decision or policy should deliberately lead to effects that are not efficient, the efficiency argument may still compete

---

[18] Consequently, it is relevant whether one emphasizes individual case law over the legislative history of a particular statute, effectiveness over fairness, individual reward over social values, anti-trust over intellectual property rights, competition over exclusive rights, or simply property rights over government intervention.

[19] (1) What are external effects and how could they be categorized and treated under intellectual property laws and anti-trust laws; and (2) what means does one have to utilize external effect for one's benefit and what limitations does the law impose on such utilization.

[20] A R Posner, *Anti-trust Law, an Economic Perspective* (Chicago and London, 1976), 112–13; R H Bork, *The Anti-trust Paradox* (Chicago 1978, rev edn 1993)), 91; M Hemmo, *Vahingonkorvauksen Sovittelu ja Moderni vahingonkorvausoikeus* (Helsinki 1998), 27 (pointing out that the efficiency argument does not necessarily provide answers to the issue to whom should the benefits resulting from the increased efficiency be allocated).

[21] A M Polinsky, *An Introduction to Law and Economics* (Boston and Toronto, 1989), 7–10.

with other arguments, such as the distribution of wealth resulting from the increasing efficiency.[22] This book uses the latter approach.

1.38 Secondly, conclusions can be based on legal doctrines alone or be based on the analysis of the underlying rationality of a rule and the discussion of its suitability in particular circumstances. Formal conclusions from legal doctrines were a part of legal theory in the early twentieth century but the use of this method almost disappeared in the latter part of the century.[23] Surprisingly, this method has reappeared in the legal theory involving external effects of intellectual property rights.

1.39 The issue relates closely to the method used when deriving legal conclusions from particular facts.[24]

1.40 If in a particular jurisdiction legal conclusions may only be based on legal doctrines or categorizations, there is a risk that the application of the doctrine leads to a legal conclusion that is not rational or efficient.

1.41 As is discussed in more detail in Chapter 2, the mere existence of intellectual property rights has sometimes been interpreted as establishing market power under anti-trust analysis. Similarly, the refusal to license has sometimes been considered as *per se* lawful. Finally, it has been popular to argue that because an author has an exclusive right to reproduce the work, that exclusive right covers, without any finding of particular circumstances, automatically all interim copies that are caused by new digital technologies.

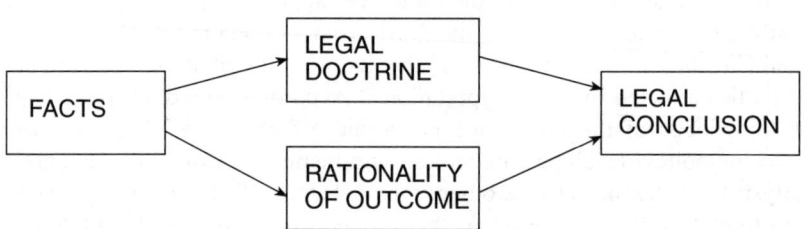

---

[22] The recent Scandinavian doctrine has largely relied on the descriptive use of economic arguments. See Hemmo, n 20 above, 30 (discussing the lack of proper economic argumentation in the traditional legislative history); P Timonen, *Määräysvalta, hinta ja Markkinavoima* (Helsinki 1997), 70; Haarmann, n 5 above, 4–10 (discussing economic goals and other goals in terms of copyright laws); M Levin, *Formskydd* (Helsingborg 1984), 465 (economic arguments an essential part of design protection); P L Aro, *Ennakkokäyttöoikeus patentinhaltijan yk sinoikeudon rajoituksena* (Vammala 1972), 26; Bernitz n 5 above, 13; B Domeij, *Läkemedelspatent* (Stockholm 1998), 31–41 (concluding that even when one uses economic analysis, policy decisions cannot be based solely on efficiency arguments). See also P E Areeda and L Kaplow, *Anti-trust Analysis. Problems, Text, Cases* (Boston 1988), 38–39 (a proper policy is accepting a certain amount of market power but is also driving low entry barriers).

[23] See analysis in M Helin, *Lainoppi ja metafysiikka* (Vammala 1988), 396–422 (identifying the development in Scandinavia from the era of legal categorizations of the 1920s and 1930s into the acceptance of justifications based on rationality in individual cases or so-called 'realistic arguments').

[24] Op cit, 399.

This book urges judges and policy-makers to rethink some traditional doctrines 1.42
and make 'reality checks' whenever traditional doctrines are applied to new facts.
It may be recognized that the value creation and complexity of the communication industry is different from the value creation in some more traditional industries. Since most intellectual property doctrines have been created and established
to reflect the value creation in the more traditional industries, it may be appropriate to adjust these doctrines to reflect the value creation in the communication
industry. It may be further recognized that some business methods justify a different interpretation of the same legal doctrine when compared with some other
business methods. Finally, circumstances may be identified which justify a different legal treatment depending on the market in which the effects of particular
activities are most visible.

Consequently, this book criticizes methods of intellectual property law and anti- 1.43
trust law that base legal conclusions on doctrines alone without justifying such
doctrines in particular circumstances. At the same time, this book recognizes that
without legal doctrines, uncertainty would increase and legal decisions would
potentially be tailor-made for each circumstance. In order to avoid this, this book
suggests in Chapters 3–6 some typical circumstances in which conclusions from
legal doctrines alone may be appropriate whereas in other circumstances a more
detailed analysis should be preferred.

At the level of legal theory, the issue relates to a traditional discussion on the 1.44
proper object of protection or protected subject matter. In terms of real property
or tangible property, rights and obligations are frequently tied to the concrete
physical appearance of such object. In the field of intellectual property laws, the
basic object is intangible. Consequently, aspects other than the mere physical
appearance have to be relied on.

One alternative is to extend the intellectual property protection to the creative or 1.45
inventive idea of the author or inventor. This theory would give protection to any
idea of the author or inventor that is original. In order to encourage inventive and
creative activities, the protection should be easily available and extend to all relevant uses of such protected subject matter.

The creation of even the simplest computer code requires that the developer make 1.46
at least a minimum number of choices between alternative methods. According to
this theory, copyright should protect such code in order to encourage its creation.
Further, there is an increasing tendency to grant patent protection for the underlying algorithm in order to provide further incentives to the computer industry.

As discussed in more detail in Chapter 2, recent legislative developments support 1.47
the strengthening and expansion of rights to cover elements that, according to this
traditional approach, would have been categorized as subjective ideas of the
author or inventor. The traditional criticism of this theory relates to its subjective

nature. Even though appropriate as a general policy concept, without relying on any concrete facts, the conclusions using this theory are not likely to give any concrete guidance to the decision-maker.[25]

1.48 A second alternative is to emphasize the fixation of the work or the invention, or its crystallization in a particular form. The protected subject matter is the fixation of the work or the invention in the form claimed in the patent application. This theory emphasizes the abstract nature of the work or invention. It is essential to compare the fixation of the work or claimed invention with previous fixations of works and inventions in order to find out whether something is inventive or original. Similarly, it is necessary to compare the fixation of the work or invention to later fixations of works or inventions in order to determine whether they are within the exclusive rights of an author or an inventor. Under this theory, the abstract nature of works and inventions is recognized. The exclusive right covers generally all forms into which the fixation may be brought.

A copy of a movie is protected by copyright in all its forms. The protection does not depend on whether the movie is fixed on a film, videotape, DVD disk, broadcasted by a television network or cable network or distributed as a digital file through the Internet.

1.49 The contemporary intellectual property statutes largely reflect this theory. However, the theory is not free from criticism. If the abstract nature of a work or an invention is emphasized this involves a risk that the connection between the fixation and the underlying ratio justifying the protection of a fixation is lost.[26] Further, as discussed in more detail in Chapters 3 and 4, it should not be self-evident that the fixation of a work or invention justifies the same protection in all circumstances. In the network economy and in the digital world, the relative importance of protection may depend upon circumstances.

The need to protect rights holders against economic losses may be substantial when consumers download unauthorized digital copies of music from the Internet. There is potentially no such need for protection if consumers only make back-up copies of lawfully downloaded digital copies for their own use.[27]

---

[25] For a Scandinavian overview, see M Koktvedgaard and M Levin, *Lärobok i immaterialrätt* (6th edn, Helsingborg, 2000), 34; T M Kivimäki, *Tekijänoikeus* (Porvoo, 1948), 74–76; T Lund, *Ophausretsloven* (Copenhagen 1961), 46–48.

[26] For a Scandinavian theoretical discussion, see Koktvedgaard–Levin, n 25 above, 34–36; Haarmann, n 5 above, 38; Kivimäki, n 25 above, 64–65 (copyright has never been absolute and limitations are justified by the fact that external factors always affect the creation of the work); J Rosen, *Förlagsrätt* (Stockholm, 1981), 104–105 (both individual and objective aspects of a work are relevant); B Godenhielm, *Patentskyddets Omfattning i eurospeisk och nordisk ratt* (Helsinki, 1994), 47–48; B Godenhielm, 'Verksbegreppet inom upphovsrätten', in *Uppsatser i immaterialrätt* (Lund 1983); S Bergström, *Uteslutande rätt att Förfoga över verket* (Uppsala 1954); M Helin, *Immateriaalioikeuksien kohteesta* (Lakimies 1978).

[27] Except for the potential need to ensure that such back-up copies are not distributed further without any payment to the rights holder.

Similarly, the need to protect an inventor or an author is potentially different as the fragmentation increases. Discussed in more detail in Chapter 5, the importance of a single patent or copyright diminishes when fragmentation of the value chain increases. Fragmentation means that in order to manufacture and distribute complete products, one is increasingly relying on multiple intellectual property rights and the contributions of multiple parties.

This book relies on the third frequently used theoretical approach. Under this, it **1.50** is relevant to analyse various factual circumstances and relationships.[28] The conclusions reached under this method are made only after careful study into the rationality of a particular conclusion.

According to the traditional scientific method, a theory that cannot provide a **1.51** rational outcome in individual cases would not be acceptable. In legal reasoning, legal doctrines that do not provide a rational or efficient outcome have greater acceptance.[29] Typically, arguments that rely on economic theory, fairness in individual cases or other similar arguments have gained the most acceptance if the outcome they provide can be justified by using particular doctrines.

VCRs can technically be used for home taping of broadcasted movies. If one concludes that such taping does not really decrease the income of rights holders since it only allows the consumers to view the movie in the most convenient time and place for them, thereby also allowing the broadcaster to maximize the number of viewers and the related advertising revenue, the required legal reasoning may be different in various jurisdictions. It may be concluded that since the rights holders have exclusive rights to any reproduction of their works, they still need to be compensated merely because of the doctrine.[30] Another possibility is to use the doctrine of fair use or private copying as a justification for economic arguments allowing such activity.[31]

Finally, an important choice is made between case law and legislative history as **1.52** the primary source of legal authority. This book uses the European Union and US federal case law as its primary source for legal authority in the field discussed. This is because the recent tendency to harmonize laws and practices has led national case law within particular European territories, such as Germany, the UK or Scandinavia, to lose some of its importance. This development has also caused legislative history to lose some of its relative importance. Under traditional Scandinavian doctrine, legislative history of intellectual property laws enacted as a result of inter-Scandinavian legislative co-operation used to have an important

---

[28] For Scandinavian views, see A Aarnio, *On the Legal Reasoning* (Turku, 1977), 122–123; M Koktvedgaard, *Konkurrencepraegede immetrialretspositioner* (Copenhagen, 1965), 117; M Koktvedgaard and M Levin, *Lärobok i immaterialrätt* (6th edn, Helsingborg, 2000) 36; Haarmann, n 5 above, 38 (the relationship of an author to parties affected by copyright is essential).

[29] Helin, n 23 above, 405–406.

[30] In Europe, in some jurisdictions there are particular fees or levies imposed on the sale of blank VCR tapes, or even on the sale of VCR hardware equipment.

[31] *Sony Corp v Universal City Studios, Inc*, 464 US 417 (1984).

role.[32] However, the flexible wordings of intellectual property and anti-trust laws have, perhaps more than in other fields of law, caused case law to have a central role in the development of practical decision-making.

1.53   Quite recently, case law has expanded and new problem areas have been identified. However, in some areas, case law still remains vague in terms of theory and practice. While it is recognized that some potential external effects have been taken into account within intellectual property laws, pure intellectual property cases discussing the interface between anti-trust, exclusivity and external effects are few in number. US case law, with its traditions of flexible doctrines, provides generally more in-depth analysis of various issues. However, also the adverse is true. Some doctrines, such as compatibility of software or markets for spare parts, were discussed and solved in Europe a number of years ago. US practice still continues the debate on those issues.

1.54   Legal and economic scholarly works increased significantly in volume during the 1990s. This book discusses the most prominent contributions while others, those on which this book does not rely, are not discussed at any length. Some patterns are useful to recognize. It can be recognized that several fundamental studies and commentaries have influenced discussion in this field for decades. Internationally, Machlup's study on the economic impacts of the patent system is frequently cited and relied on as one of the basic works in the field. The works of Coase, Demsetz, Calabresi and Melamed established the basic structure for external effects in general. The studies on network effects owe a lot to scholars closely connected to the University of California in Berkeley. In Europe the influence of the Max Planck Institut in Munich on the development of European intellectual property doctrines is undisputed.

1.55   There have been close links between anti-trust treatment of intellectual property rights and the development of general anti-trust doctrines. The dialogue between Chicago School and Harvard School theories contributed significantly to the change from basic hostility against intellectual property rights to the recognition of intellectual property rights as the basic building blocks of prosperity. In Europe the creation of the common market has long been behind European anti-trust doctrine. This is also reflected in the available source materials. Finally, this book provides an overview and analysis of external effects and their legal treatment under intellectual property and anti-trust laws. Consequently, the source materials involving individual issues, such as and especially exhaustion and licensing, do not aim to be exhaustive.

---

[32] In the field of copyright law, see KM 1953:5, 4–5 (overview of early history of cooperation); SOU 1956:25; NU 1973:21. In the field of patent law, see NU 1963:6; B Godenhielm, *Patentskyddets omfattning i eurospeisk och nordisk rätt* (Helsinki 1994) 33–38. See also M Salokannel, *Ownership of Rights in Audiovisual Productions* (The Hague, 1997) 2–4 for the recent use of this method.

The Scandinavian intellectual property tradition is taken into account in selected **1.56** chapters. Even though this is not a book about Scandinavian intellectual property law, the Scandinavian tradition provides several useful viewpoints for the international discussion. The Scandinavian sources have been used for this particular purpose.

HOW THE TENSION BETWEEN INTELLECTUAL PROPERTY PROTECTION AND ANTI-TRUST LAWS IS BALANCED

Introduction

The rationality of the rules and principles applicable to the interface between **2.01** intellectual property laws and anti-trust laws may be difficult to identify. This is simply because such rules reflect different underlying theories. The rules have been created as a response to particular effects of intellectual property rights in different times. The prevailing theory at the time the rule was initially created may simply have been different from the one prevailing at another time. The understanding of proper control methods, priorities in society or even the effects caused by particular practices may have been different.

These different theories have sometimes been identified to reflect the battle between (1) incentives and competition, and (2) property and monopoly.[1]

Limited exclusive rights have long been seen as desirable and useful rewards for **2.02** the inventors and creators. However, over the centuries, the idea of what should be rewarded has changed. It was once argued that the act of making the invention or work of authorship public should be rewarded. In modern intellectual property laws, the primary driver for reward is the necessity to encourage innovation and creativity through incentives. This is reflected in the most contemporary balancing theories that primarily deal with the problem of incentives and imitation. In these theories, a set of factors that involve the rights holder, end-user or licensee, competitor and some contract practice that affects these parties is considered.

---

[1] D D Chisum and M A Jacobs, *Understanding Intellectual Property Law* (New York 1992 (rep 1999)) 1–6.

2.03   The history of intellectual property rights has always had a close connection to the development of the business environment.[2] The entities implementing intellectual property laws have at various times tried to solve the problem of external effects caused by such rights. There has always been an issue whether a holder of an exclusive right may somehow use it to exclude others or cause others additional costs.[3] The following table illustrates the development:[4]

TIME PERIOD	TYPICAL LEVERAGE SITUATION	SOLUTION USED
Venice 1474	Printers, craftsmen and architects excluded others as suppliers to the City.	The City reserved the right to use the invention without compensation.[5]
England sixteenth century	Foreign craftsmen excluded England as a primary place for their business.	New inventions were protected and inventions made in England were favoured.[6]
England 1624	The legal monopoly of a patent was used to raise prices.	Patent was not allowed to be used to be contrary to the law, mischievous to the state, by raising prices of commodities at home, or hurt trade, or be generally inconvenient.[7]
England seventeenth century	The unlimited exclusive rights of printers reduced the availability of books.	The Act for Encouragement of Learning (1709 Statute of Anne) reduced the term of protection.

---

[2] M Koktvedgaard, *Konkurrencepraegede immetrialretspositioner* (Copenhagen, 1965) 7.

[3] F Machlup, 'An Economic Review of the Patent System', Study No 15, Subcommittee of the Judiciary of the US Senate (Washington, 1958), 22 ('If one always cites only the "first and true inventor" of an argument concerning the patent system, one will rarely be able to cite an author of the 20th century').

[4] The topic of a reward and its development has induced a number of commentaries. This does not intend to be a comprehensive study of those studies but merely an overview of some basic trends.

[5] G Mandich, 'Venetian Patents (1450–1550)' (1948) 30 Journal of the Patent Office Society, 166, 179–180.

[6] R P Merges, 'The Economic Impact of Intellectual Property Rights: An Overview and Guide' (1995) 19 Journal of Cultural Economics, 103, 196; the English protectionist example has been followed by other countries; in respect of the United States, see D S Chisum, 'Foreign Activity: Its Effect on Patentability under United States Law' (1980) 11 IIC 26, 26.

[7] Great Britain, Statutes at Large (1624); Merges, n 6 above, 106; Koktvedgaard, n 2 above, 53; W M Cornish, *Intellectual Property: Patents, Copyrights, Trademarks and Allied Rights* (4th edn London, 1999) 111.

TIME PERIOD	TYPICAL LEVERAGE SITUATION	SOLUTION USED
		Common Law Literary Property debate during the eighteenth century.[8]
Industrial society	Intellectual property rights are used to control the traffic of goods.	Anti-patent movement 1850–1873: limiting patent protection.[9]
		Only acts that are inherent to protection have immunity from anti-trust and competition law enforcement.
Network economy	Intellectual property rights are used to control activities of various parties.	Solution not yet implemented.

Some of the current tension arises from the fact that the traditional discussion was **2.04** focused on the relationship between the inventors or authors and the general public. The public interest was considered as an argument not to unreasonably restrain the activities of competitors for an unlimited period of time or to extensively abuse the right against the general public.[10] The current tension is also created primarily because patents and copyright may affect activities that are beyond the reach of the traditional discussion: the role of the parties or activities affected by particular practices may be entirely different than the traditional 'public interest' discussion.

Supremacy of anti-trust laws

Introduction

It is not uncommon to argue that intellectual property rights should be subject to **2.05** the same rules as any other property. If the main purpose of anti-trust laws is seen as the promotion of free competition, the tension between such laws and intellectual property laws is obvious. Intellectual property rights provide exclusive rights to inventors and authors. These exclusive rights may cause the prices of

---

[8] For a good detailed overview, see B Sherman and L Bently, *The Making of Modern Intellectual Property Law. The British Experience, 1760–1911* (Cambridge, 1999), 19; also G Davies, 'Copyright and the Public Interest' (1994) IIC Studies, vol 14, 7–10, 19–23; *Copinger and Skone James on Copyright* (12th edn, London 1980), 10–11.

[9] Machlup, n 3 above, 4; U Bernitz, *Marknadsrätt* (Stockholm, 1969), 125–129.

[10] See Davies, n 8 above, 139 for a good overview of this traditional debate in respect of copyright.

such products to be higher and the output lower than without the existence of such rights. From the short-term economic point of view, potentially higher prices and lower output may be seen as market failures when compared against the model of perfect competition. This is sometimes supported by the argument that monopoly is the reward the intellectual property owner is being given through the ownership of intellectual property rights. According to the supporters of this theory, such market imperfection justifies intervention in the practices of the intellectual property owner.[11]

2.06 In its most extreme use, the theory emphasizing the supremacy of anti-trust laws over intellectual property laws would nullify any intellectual property laws since the mere enforcement of one's patent or copyright would involve monopolization or abuse of dominant position.[12] In its more pragmatic application, the relationship would not be as straightforward. It is usually recognized that intellectual property rights may have beneficial effects since they encourage innovation and the production of new useful features.[13]

The key argument by the proponents of this theory is that even without intellectual property protection, the entity that introduces its product first is likely to maintain a high market share. The market share remains high even without the protection by intellectual property rights because of other benefits the early introduction of products may provide over later competitors.[14]

---

[11] See for an overview of discussion, P A David, 'Intellectual Property Institutions and the Panda's Thumb: Patents, Copyrights and Trade Secrets in Economic Theory and History', in *Global Dimensions of Intellectual Property Rights in Science and Technology* (National Research Council, Washington DC 1993) 19, 34.

[12] L Kaplow, 'The Patent Anti-trust Intersection: A Reappraisal' (1984) 97 Harvard Law Review, 1815, 1818, n 10; S F Anthony, 'Anti-trust and Intellectual Property Law: From Adversaries to Partners' (2000) 28 AIPLA Quarterly Journal, 1, 5; W K Tom and J A Newberg, 'Anti-trust and Intellectual Property: From Separate Spheres to Unified Field' (1997) 66 Anti-trust, 167, 172 (the concept of 'limited monopoly' was not referring to the market power but to the scope of the patent grant); P E Areeda and H Hovenkamp, *Anti-trust Law. An Analysis of Anti-trust Principles and their Application* (Vol III, revised edition, 1996) § 704a at 150–151 (anti-trust decisions traditionally expressed hostility towards patent practices, often regarding the Patent Act as a body of rules creating only the narrowest exceptions to anti-trust enforcement, and treating any enforcement activity by the patentee as almost inherently monopolistic); *Zenith Radio Corp v Hazeltine Research, Inc*, 395 US 100, 135 (1969) (patents are 'lawful monopolies'); *Crown Dye & Tool Co. v Nye Tool & Mach Works*, 261 US 24, 35–36 (1923) ('a patent confers a monopoly').

[13] G W Stocking and M W Watkins, *Monopoly and Free Enterprise* (New York, 1991), 447; M Handler *et al*, *Patents and Anti-trust* (Mineola, 1983), 2.

[14] Such reasons include, in addition to eventual network effects, (1) the possibility by early introduction to recoup development costs before competitors enter the market, (2) the fact that even competition will not necessarily drive prices down but it can even increase the success of the feature as 'lock-in' risks are less significant, (3) some innovation is always necessary for survival in the competitive market, and (4) some innovation will always continue even if the possibilities to have costs covered are reduced. See P E Areeda, E Elhauge and H Hovenkamp, *Antitrust Law. An Analysis of Antitrust Principles and Their Application*, Vol X (Boston 1996) §1780a; see also Justice Brandeis in his dissent to the US Supreme Court decision in *International News Service v Associated Press*, 248 US 215, 250 (1918); F M Scherer, *Industrial Market Structure and Economic Performance* (1980), 444–446 (imitation lags behind innovation because of secrecy, incompleteness of information,

According to the pragmatic approach, the core of this theory is the proposition **2.07**
that the holders of intellectual property rights do not have any absolute privileges
under anti-trust laws. This means that the scope and enforceability of intellectual
property rights would be subject to regular anti-trust scrutiny.[15] How would this
scrutiny then be carried out?

Essential elements of this theory are various legal presumptions and '*per se*' rules **2.08**
involving intellectual property rights. These legal presumptions may relate either
to the definition of the relevant market or to particular business practices involving intellectual property rights.

Presumption of market power

There is a well-known presumption that products covered by intellectual property **2.09**
rights are presumed to have market power or a dominant position.[16] This legal
presumption has practical consequences in the definition of relevant markets. In
its most extreme application, it has sometimes been presumed that any product
covered by intellectual property rights has market power. Therefore, any further
study of the relevant product market or geographic market is irrelevant.

In *Loew's* the US Supreme Court held that in tying cases, the necessary market **2.10**
power may be presumed by the existence of intellectual property rights.[17] Still,
as late as 1984, in *Jefferson Parish*,[18] the same court refused to overrule that
presumption. Analysis of that presumption reveals deficiencies such presumptions frequently have. Even though the case is specific to the US, the analysis
illustrates generally the problems that may be faced when defining the relevant
product market where there are intellectual property rights. Both in the US and in
Europe, the law treats intellectual property owners with market power differently
from the rights holders that do not possess any significant market power.

need of additional know-how and first-to-market benefits); 1 FTC Report 1996, chap 1, 25 (referring
to studies according to which in consumer goods markets pioneers had 29% market share, early
followers 17% and later entrants only 12% market share); see also 1 FTC Report 1996, ch 6 (citing
studies that only chemical and pharmaceutical industries considered patent protection as highly relevant and 86% of all innovation would have been developed even without any patent protection); C T
Taylor and Z A Silbertson, *The Economic Impact of the Patent System. A Study of the British
Experience* (Cambridge, 1973), 201 (in the UK electronic industry, the dependency on patent protection was found to be negligible).

[15] Koktvedgaard, n 2 above, 26–27 (one may compete but not fight).

[16] See generally, Cornish, n 7 above, 38–40.

[17] *United States v Loew's*, 371 US 38 (1960). *Loew's* involved blockbooking of films.
Blockbooking is a practice in which one film is licensed to a theatre only if it also books another film
or a number of films.

[18] *Jefferson Parish Hospital District No. 2 v Hyde*, 466 US 2 (1984). See, however, *Abbott Labs.
v Brennan*, 952 F 2d 1346, 1354 (Fed Cir 1991) (possession of patent does not establish market
power) and the Patent Misuse Reform Act of 1988 (no illegal tying unless 'in view of circumstances,
the patent owner has market power in the relevant market for patent or patented product') 35 USC §
271 (d) (1988).

2.11   In the US, tying two products together violates the Sherman Act if one has market power in the market of the tying product. In *Loew's* the defendants were in the business of licensing films to movie theatres. They licensed single movies only on the condition that one also licensed a number of other movies. The case was initiated on the grounds that this practice involved illegal tying. The defendants in *Loew's* argued that the tying arrangement should be subject to the market power analysis of the relevant market.[19] Since the market share of the films sold by defendants was only 8%, they relied on the notion that films were reasonably interchangeable with other types of programming materials. Therefore they were not supposed to have the prerequisite market power. The Supreme Court held the market power analysis to be the correct standard but was unwilling to overrule the well-established rule of *per se* illegality related to patents and copyright. Justice Goldberg, writing the opinion for the Supreme Court, solved the controversy by interpreting the previous case law to support the presumption of market power whenever the tying product is patented or copyrighted.[20]

2.12   It is reasonable to argue that the market power theory used in *Loew's* is not consistent with contemporary anti-trust theory and that the holding is therefore no longer a valid precedent. However, it has not yet been formally overruled. In *Loew's* the definition of market power was not based on market conditions but on the existence of copyright protection. Contemporary anti-trust theory rejects non-market-based definitions of market power. They generally lead to the finding of market power in cases where there is little or no *actual* market power. Therefore, in order to avoid presumptions of market power that are too broad, analysis based on the actual market conditions is the only acceptable theory considered.[21]

2.13   The situation could be illustrated by the following simple table:

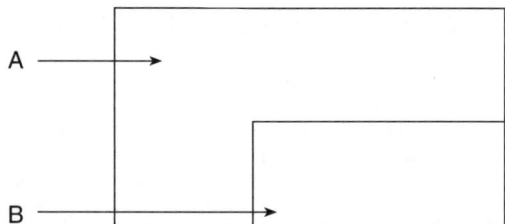

Table. The assumption of the market power theory A was in *Loew's* supposed to reflect the actual market power of the defendants (B). The problem is that the presumption could be and has in some cases been extended to cases in which the defendant has little or no market power. The presumption is in those cases too broad.

---

[19] *Loew's*, 371 US, 47–48.   [20] 371 US, 45–46.
[21] P E Areeda *et al*, *Antitrust Law. An Analysis of Anti-trust Principles and their Application* (Vol IIA, Boston 1995) 130–132.

In the case law following *Loew's* the presumption of market power has been **2.14** discussed, followed and criticized. Areeda has pointed out that market power can be protected or reinforced by intellectual property, but it cannot be inferred merely from the existence of such property.[22] According to Posner, it is arbitrary to condemn the tie-ins involving intellectual property rights when the owners of intellectual property rights are lawfully allowed directly to discriminate.[23] Bork and Stigler have indicated that condemnation was not based on the economically viable theory.[24] Turner's criticism has focused generally on the fact that the prohibition extends to tying arrangements with no significant anti-competitive effects.[25]

The presumption of market power doctrine has been criticized because it appar- **2.15** ently does not rely on any viable economic theory. It is alleged that the mere existence of a patent or copyright does not create demand for the product. If there are adequate substitutes, supernormal profits for the patented or copyrighted product are impossible to sustain.[26]

Presumption of market power criticized: market-based analysis

Patents and copyright may have an effect on several economic factors. In a **2.16** number of cases the discussion has focused on the actual attractiveness of the patented or copyrighted product.[27] The attractiveness of the product refers to demand elasticity. If the product is attractive, the decisions of the customers are less likely to be affected by the price increase of the tying product. In that case the market power of the tying product may be higher. The problem is that

---

[22] Ibid, 132. The copyright forbids copying but does not itself create any value. Similarly, a patent protects a particular product (or a process) from duplication, but not from competition.

[23] R A Posner, *Anti-trust Law, an Economic Perspective* (Chicago and London 1976), 178. Posner characterizes the tying arrangements as a form of indirect price discrimination.

[24] R H Bork, *The Anti-trust Paradox* (Chicago 1978 (rev edn 1993)), 373–374; G Stigler, 'United States v Loew's Inc: A Note on Block Booking' (1963) Supreme Court Review 152, 152–153. Stigler uses an example: Why condemn a tie-in of *Gone With the Wind* and *Getting Gertie's Garter* if the producer could lawfully sell only *Gone With the Wind* for the price of the package and throw the other film away? See also E W Kitch, 'Patents: Monopolies or Property Rights?' (1986) 8 Research in Law and Economics 32 (discussing competitive pressures on patents: substitutes, existence of traditional technologies and entry of new firms by the end of the patent life).

[25] D F Turner, 'The Durability, Relevance and Future of American Anti-trust Policy (1987) 75 California Law Review 797, 805–806.

[26] S Addanki and K Anderson, 'The Relevant Market in Intellectual Property Anti-trust: An Economist's Overview' (1995) 414 PLI/PAT 557 (separating substitutes for complete products and substitutes for technology).

[27] See *Loew's*, 371 US, 48 (*Gone with the Wind*), *Digidyne*, 734 F 2d, 1342–1343 (RDOS software), *Metromedia*, 611 F Supp, 424–425 (*Fame*), *Outlet Communications*, 685 F Supp, 1577 (*Wheel of Fortune*), all finding market power because copyright blocked competitors from copying the attractive product. See also *A.I. Root*, 806 F 2d, 676–677 (copyrighted operating system), *Virtual I*, 957 F 2d, 1327 (PDGS software), *Olsten*, 506 F 2d, 663–664 (trademarked franchise business), *UNIQ*, 73 F 3d, 762 (effects of refusal to satisfy customer needs), all finding that the attractiveness did not support the existence of market power.

customer preferences are not permanent. The costs of creating and maintaining customer preferences must eventually be repeated for every product.[28] Therefore, attractiveness is necessary for the product to have market power but attractiveness does not always raise anti-trust concerns.

2.17   Demand elasticity is only one factor relevant in market power analysis. To find market power merely on the basis of attractiveness is incorrect. Supply elasticity of the product or service has always to be considered.[29] Patents and copyright may have an impact on supply elasticity.[30] If a patent protects a product, competitors are excluded from producing the products covered by the patent protection. There may still be effective substitutes available but the supply elasticity is always lower than for a product not protected by a patent. This means that the actual market power derived from the same market share is higher if the product is protected by a patent. If the product is protected by copyright, this effect is less likely but still possible. The amount of this effect depends on the capacity of existing competitors. Existing competitors may have the capacity to provide the supply of substitute products to serve the previous customers of the patent or copyright owner where there is a price increase. In that case the effect of the patent or copyright protection on market power is minimal.[31]

2.18   It has sometimes also been presumed that patents and copyright form barriers to entry.[32] If the starting point of market analysis is the patented or copyrighted product, it may be possible by using such a presumption to maintain that the rights holder may raise the price and, because of the exclusivity provided by intellectual property rights, other producers are legally barred from entering into the market with identical substitutes. This would lead to a finding of market power even if there were not any alleged presumption of market power.[33] This demon-

---

[28] P E Areeda *et al*, *Anti-trust Law. An Analysis of Anti-trust Principles and their Application* (Boston 1995, Vol IIA) 69.

[29] P E Areeda *et al*, *Anti-trust Law. An Analysis of Anti-trust Principles and their Application* (Boston 1996, Vol X) 124–125 (mere product differentiation within the market presumptively insufficient), *Virtual II*, 11 F 3d 660, 664–665 (market power cannot be defined without considering the supply side of the market), *Rebel Oil, Inc v Atlantic Richfield Co*, 51 F 3d 1421, 1436 (9th Cir 1995) (defining a market on the basis of demand considerations alone erroneous).

[30] The ability of competing suppliers to provide substitutes in the case of a price increase. See *Rebel*, 51 F 3d 1421, 1436 (supply elasticity measures the responsiveness of producers to price increases).

[31] Areeda, n 27 above, 262 (products can be near-perfect substitutes even when their prices and qualities differ); Posner, n 23 above, 127; OECD Report, 16; *United States v Microsoft Corp*, 253 F 3d 34, 54 (DC Cir 2001) (the current market share may be misleading if competitors can enter the market in the near future).

[32] Most cases did not discuss the question of the new entry since the initial inquiry already showed that there was no actual market power.

[33] Therefore legislative initiatives abolishing the alleged presumption of market power do not make much sense. Unless there is no presumption of entry barriers caused by copyright or patents, analysis may easily end up with the outcome condemning the tie. The court in *Digidyne* might have come out with a similar decision condemning the tie-in between a superior operating system and CPU just by relying on the actual market power created by the technically advanced software and copyright

strates two problems relating to widely used market definition practices. The first is that the analysis starting with the market of one producer's product may not be appropriate whenever there are patents or copyright involved. The second involves the proper use of the term 'a barrier to entry'.

Firstly, the eventual entry barriers caused by patents and copyright are presumed **2.19** to be based on superior creativeness. Therefore the existence of formal entry barriers due to patents and copyright should not be relevant in anti-trust analysis. Secondly, a patent may cover the entire commercial product or just a component of a product. The most common product patents relate to the components of commercially sold products. A product patent may cover for instance one specific component of a product that contains hundreds of components. Unless the patent covers a key element of the commercial product, the barrier to entry (and impact on supply elasticity) caused by the patent is minimal.

If the patent is an improvement patent, traditional market power analysis may **2.20** face difficulties.[34] The easiest way to explain the problem is in the form of a simple diagram.

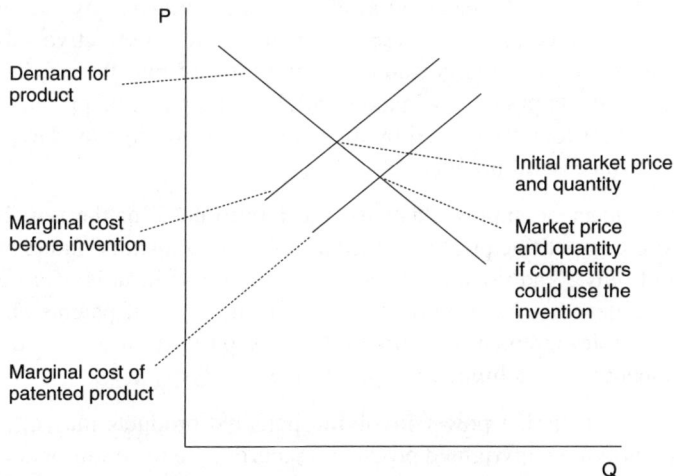

Table. If an invention lowers marginal costs of production, then it has the potential to reduce price and increase output. If it is patented, the patentee may choose not to lower its price to the full extent of the cost saving, but to make a super-normal profit.

protection as a legal barrier to new entry. In *Virtual II*, 11 F 3d 660, the court, referring to the holding in *Kodak*, came to the conclusion that the possibility of the relevant market consisting of only one product could not be precluded whenever the supply was restricted by the copyright protection at the same time the demand was restricted (by Ford's requirements for its suppliers).

[34] E W Kitch, 'Patents: Monopolies or Property Rights?' (1986) 8 Research in Law and Economics, 31, 35.

2.21 If the patented product were cheaper to produce than other similar products, in the competitive market the product would generally be sold at a substantially lower price than other products. If the invention is patented, this is not necessarily the case. Therefore, if market power is defined as a power to earn supra-competitive profits, the patentee may have market power since competitors cannot replicate its process. According to Areeda, an individual's ability to produce an identical product at a lower cost and to prevent others from matching that cost advantage is market power in economic terms. This has, however, not been a concern in anti-trust laws. The rationale lies in the difficulty of comparing costs across firms.[35] The other limitation is that generally it is not necessary that substitutes have to be perfect substitutes to be recognized as relevant substitutes.[36]

2.22 It is further easily recognizable that only a small number of patents granted each year relate to commercially successful products.[37] This is generally due to the fact that a patent application has to be filed in the early stages of product development. It often turns out that there is either no market demand for the patented subject matter or the commercialization of the patented subject matter is for some reason not successful. If the patented product is not commercially successful, it does not generally have market power even if there are no effective substitutes available. This is because the customers simply do not buy the product if the manufacturer raises its price. If demand elasticity for a patented product is high, the potential barrier to entry caused by the patent does not give market power to an otherwise unsuccessful product.[38]

2.23 The ultimate impact on supply elasticity, barriers to entry or the possibility of charging supra-competitive prices are furthermore of a transitory nature and for a limited period only. Traditionally, if the effect on competition is of a transitory nature, its treatment has been more flexible.[39] In the case of patents and copyright, more flexible treatment is supported by the purpose of the protection: to provide an incentive for a limited period of time.

2.24 Finally, analysis of market power involving patented products may differ from the analysis involving copyrighted products. According to the traditional wisdom, copyright protection gives exclusivity to an expression of the idea and not the idea itself or a method of operation. Therefore, there is a potentially less

---

[35] Areeda *et al*, n 22 above, 121.

[36] According to Posner, it is enough that the product or the service is a good substitute. Posner limits poor substitutes (substitutes requiring a substantial price increase to become attractive substitutes) from the relevant market. See Posner, n 23 above, 127.

[37] The same remark applies also to copyrighted products. A small number of copyright registrations relate to commercially successful products.

[38] Areeda *et al*, n 22 above, 119, stating that the uniqueness of a product is only a concern if it is connected with a demand advantage.

[39] Areeda *et al*, n 27 above, 73.

economic basis for considering copyright as a legal entry barrier. However, in the network economy this should not be taken as self-evident. It is also possible that a work has little value unless it is copied 'bit-by-bit'.[40]

The above analysis in respect of market power doctrine was intended to illustrate one side of the theory emphasizing the supremacy of anti-trust laws.[41]   **2.25**

Market-based analysis re-examined: ability to raise costs

The outcome of traditional market-based market power analysis is clear. It shows that patents and copyright give market power to the product or to the related service only in a relatively small number of cases. This outcome would not be subject to any fundamental criticism if patent and copyright laws only provided protection against literal copying. The cost of inventing around or finding a new satisfactory form of expression would not be too high for competitors. However, patent and copyright laws recognize protection also against non-literal copying.   **2.26**

The doctrine of equivalents protects the patent owner against competing products that do substantially the same work in substantially the same way to accomplish substantially the same result, even though those products differ in name, form or shape.[42] This means that insubstantial differences are not enough in order to avoid infringement. Since avoiding infringement requires that the competing product substantially differ from the patented product,[43] inventing around the product may be very costly. Similarly, the protection of copyright has been extended to non-literal elements of the copyrighted work, eg non-code elements of computer software.[44]   **2.27**

---

[40] L Lessig, *Code and Other Laws of Cyberspace* (New York, 1999) ('the code of our time can be written such that people who own intellectual property rights have the power . . . to close off, to stop, to own an idea, and to make criminal . . . any use of that idea beyond the owner's permission').

[41] In Europe, the presumption of market power never had the same implications as in the US law. Rather, quite early the distinction was made between legal monopolies and actual monopolies. See as an example S D Anderman, *EC Competition Law and Intellectual Property Rights* (Oxford 1998); the *Finnish Committee Report* KM 1952:33, 4 (patent may sometimes contribute to the creation of actual monopoly position but a patent as such is not a cartel or monopoly); see also *Sirena v Eda* [1971] CMLR 260, para 16; *Deutsche Grammophon* [1971] CMLR 631 (the mere exercise of exclusive rights does not mean the rights holder occupies a dominant position but one must identify that she has a power to impede effective competition on a considerable part of the relevant market; if artists are tied through exclusive contracts, their popularity and the possibilities of other manufacturers to obtain comparable services should be taken into account); *EMI v CBS*, [1976] 2 CMLR 235 (market dominance did not exist while several undertakings had comparable economic strength). See discussion and analysis in I Govaere, *The Use and Abuse of Intellectual Property Rights in EC Law* (London, 1996) 245; M Meinhardt, *Die Beschränkung nationaler Immaterialgüterrechte durch Art. 86 EG-Vertrag* (Bern 1998), 10–11; Anderman, n 40 above, 151.

[42] *Graver Tank & Mfr. Co v Linde Air Products Co*, 70 S Ct 854 (1950).

[43] *Warner Jenkinson Co v Hilton Davis Chemical Co*, 520 US 17 (1997).

[44] *Whelan*, 797 F 2d 122; *Altai*, 982 F 2d 693; *Gates Rubber Co v Bando Chemical Industries, Ltd*, 9 F 3d 823 (10th Cir 1993). However, the most recent development has rejected copyright protection for certain abstract elements of computer software, see *Apple Computer, Inc v Microsoft Corp*, 35 F

2.28   This development may cause the costs of competitors in producing substitute products to increase substantially. Even though the patent owner or the copyright owner may not be able to raise its price or limit its output, the increasing costs of producing substitute products may force competitors to raise their prices and cause them to limit their output.[45]

2.29   There is some evidence that entry costs may show whether firms are actively innovating in a particular industry.[46] The ability to raise entry costs and increase the risks for fringe firms may affect both the fringe firms' and the leading firms' willingness to innovate.[47] Consequently, high entry barriers caused by intellectual property rights may have an effect on the rate of new innovation in the long term.

2.30   Traditional market-based market power theory described above[48] may not be able to respond to this development.[49] It is possible that the definition of market power needs redefinition. Instead of focusing on the behaviour of the owner of a patent or copyright, the analysis could focus on the impact of patents and copyright on the competitive behaviour of competitors manufacturing substitute products or services.[50] Consequently, modern analysis teaches that market power may not be

---

3d 1435 (9th Cir 1994) (the design of a user interface) and *Lotus Development Corp v Borland Intern*, 49 F 3d 807 (1st Cir 1995), aff'd, 116 S Ct 804 (1996), reh'g denied, 116 S Ct 1062 (1996) (a menu command structure).

[45]   Because the demand for their products decreases if their prices are higher.

[46]   J B Baker, 'Fringe Firms and Incentives to Innovate' (1995) 63 Anti-trust Law Journal 622, 636–639 (explains leading firm's willingness to adopt innovative activities of fringe firms in the motor vehicle industry by four factors: (1) the cost of innovation by fringe firms as compared to that in leading firms; (2) the ability of fringe firms to expand; (3) the risks related to innovation; and (4) co-ordinative actions among leading firms).

[47]   Tom–Newberg, n 12 above, 201 (discussing, however, the lack of appropriate evidence).

[48]   Reflected in the recent case law and in the works of Areeda, Posner and Borks, and in the economic theories of Stigler.

[49]   The current theory focuses on the patent owner's or the copyright owner's power to raise prices without losing a substantial number of its customers. The essential nature of patent or copyright protection is, however, exclusionary: it gives a limited right to control the activities of competitors and cause them additional costs in the form of additional product development. Since patents and copyright do not allow without more their owner to change its competitive behaviour in the market, current anti-trust theory only covers the competition impacts of patents and copyright indirectly.

[50]   See T G Krattenmaker and S C Salop, 'Anti-competitive Exclusion. Raising Rivals' Costs to Achieve Power over Price' (1986) 96 Yale Law Journal, 209, 223–224; W E Cohen, 'Competition and Foreclosure in the Context of Installed Base and Compatibility Effects' (1996) 64 Anti-trust Law Journal, 535, 560; B Scheffner, 'Alcatel USA, Inc v DGI Technologies, Inc' (2000) 15 Berkley Technology Law Journal, 25, 42–43 (discussing the problems of finding any abuse because a typical market definition may lead to broad relevant market); I K Gotts and H W Fogt, 'Clinton Administration Expresses More Than Intellectual Curiosity in Anti-trust Issues Raised by Intellectual Property Licensing' (1994) 22 AIPLA Quarterly Journal, 1, 16 (recognizing market power whenever one has power to exclude competitors). The other possibility is to reformulate patent and copyright doctrines, see, however, Judge Boudin's concurring opinion in *Lotus v Borland*, 49 F 3d 807, 819 (raising the concern that the Copyright Act is not well suited to take into account market realities). In Europe, see also *Eurofix Ltd v Hilti AG* [1989] CMLR 677 (a company has a dominant position whenever it has the ability to determine, or at least have appreciable influence on, the conditions under which competition will develop).

presumed from the mere existence of patent or copyright protection. Patent or copyright protection may in some cases cause the supply elasticity of the market to be lower than it would be without such protection. This requires that there are no adequate substitutes or that competitors do not have the capacity to increase their production of substitutes where there is a price increase. Generally, in order for the tying product to have market power, the demand elasticity of the tying product should also be low. This requires the tying product to be seen as attractive.

The market power derived from patent or copyright protection is further limited **2.31** by the fact that the attractiveness of the product and the patent or copyright protection are not permanent qualities of tying products. They are both transitory qualities. Every company has therefore to undertake re-investment in order to achieve or maintain these qualities.

The actual competitive impact of patents and copyright may relate to the ability **2.32** of the owner of a patent or copyright to force additional costs on his competitors and especially to the ability to affect the market of related goods and services. In at least some cases, the extension of patent and copyright protection to non-literal copying may make inventing around or the finding of alternative expressions very costly. This may force competitors to raise their prices and to limit their output. The problem of current anti-trust doctrine is that the analysis has traditionally focused only on the behaviour of the owner of a patent or copyright.

Per se rules

Other implications of this theory relate to any *'per se'* rules involving particular **2.33** uses of intellectual property rights. Firstly, a rule may be applied under which the validity and enforceability of intellectual property rights dictates whether a particular practice is lawful.[51] The best-known example of the application of this theory is the rule that a patentee may not collect royalties unless there is a valid and enforceable patent. In *Brulotte* the US Supreme Court held that it is *per se* misuse of a patent to use the bargaining leverage of the limited monopoly to extend the effectiveness of the patent beyond the patent term.[52] In Europe, a similar rule was established in *Ottung v Klee*[53] in a modified form.

---

[51] See the list of 'nine no-no's' by US DOJ, Statement on Patent Licensing, 4 Trade Reg. Rep. §13,126 (21.9.1972); these principles were first introduced by Bruce B Wilson in a speech in 1970, see for discussion and analysis Tom–Newberg, n 12 above, 178. The nine no-no's attracting the scrutiny of the enforcement agency were: (1) tying of unpatented supplies, (2) mandatory grant-backs, (3) post-sale restrictions on resale by purchasers of patented products, (4) tie-outs (restriction on customer against using competing suppliers), (5) licensee veto power over the licensor's grant of subsequent licences, (6) mandatory package licensing, (7) compulsory payment of royalties in amounts not reasonably related to sales of the patented product, (8) restrictions on sales of unpatented products made by a patented process, and (9) specifying prices licensee could charge upon resale of licensed product.

[52] *Brulotte v Thys Co* 379 US 29 (1964) (condemning the extension of royalty obligation beyond the patent term).

[53] *Kai Ottung v Klee & Weilbach A/S and Thomas Schmidt A/S* [1990] 4 CMLR 915 (the extension

2.34 The blacklisted provisions of the EU Technology Transfer Block Exemption identify in practice the current '*per se*' rules.[54]

2.35 Another example is the exhaustion doctrine. The exhaustion doctrine provides that the purchaser of a licensed item is free from any restrictions imposed by the intellectual property owner to use and further distribute it.[55] In Europe an early pan-European illustration of such rule was in *Consten/Grundig*[56] in which the European Court of Justice still discussed at length various justifications of territorial exhaustion under the 'rule-of-reason' applicable to Article 36 of the EC Treaty.[57] The doctrine has been followed in the subsequent case law as a *de facto* '*per se*' rule.[58]

2.36 An artificial distinction between tangible copies and intangible licences is frequently made[59] to explain the scope of the exhaustion doctrine. Another view of the exhaustion doctrine would be to identify it as a doctrine aimed at limiting the effects of intellectual property rights in the secondary market for products and services that make only indirect use of such rights. The holder's right would not extend to such indirect use. As analysed in more detail below, so far such interpretation has not gained popularity. Rather, the scope of exhaustion has in general been decreasing.

2.37 The supremacy of anti-trust laws was a prevailing theory in the US generally between the years 1912 and 1975.[60] Some of the cases decided by the US

---

of royalty payments beyond the patent term was not violating Art 85(1) since the licensee could terminate the licence); see, however, Commission Regulation (EC) No 240/96 (OJ 1996 L31/2) on the application of Art 85(3) of the Treaty to certain categories of technology transfer agreements Art 2(1)(7)(b) (licence terms requiring payments going beyond the duration of licensed patents does not normally restrict competition if such terms are to facilitate payment).

[54] Commission Regulation (EC) No 240/96 [1996] OJ L31/2 on the application of Art 85(3) of the Treaty to certain categories of technology transfer agreements, Art 3 (listing (1) restrictions on price, (2) restrictions on the right to compete with the licensor, (3) obligation not to serve customers from other territories, (4) division of customers between entities that were already competing, (5) restrictions on production quantities, (6) grant-back of title to improvements, (7) exclusivity periods beyond time limits (five or ten years) defined in the regulation).

[55] In the US this principle was first established by the Supreme Court in *Adams v Burke*, 84 US (17 Wall) 453 (1873) and restated in *US v Univis Lens Co*, 316 US 241 (1942).

[56] *Etablissements Consten SA and Grundig-Verkaufs-Gmbh v EEC Commission* [1966] CMLR 418 (case involving the distributor's right to stop parallel imports from another EU member state by the virtue of national trade mark).

[57] Art 30 of the Treaty of European Union. See *Dansk Supermarked v Imerco* [1981] 3 CMLR 590.

[58] The rights are generally exhausted only within the Community. If the products have been marketed first outside the Community, different rules may apply. See *Polydor v Harlequin Record Shops* [1982] 1 CMLR 677; *Silhouette International v Hartlauer*, C-335/96 [1997] ECR I-4799.

[59] W Fikentscher, 'Urhebervertragsrecht und Kartellrecht', in *Urhebervertragsrecht, Festgabe für Gerhard Schricker* (Beier, Götting, Lehmann and Moufand, eds) (München, 1995), 158 (tangible copies are subject to exhaustion, not intangible licences).

[60] Tom–Newberg, n 12 above, 170–171 (identifying *Standard Sanity Mfg Co v United States*, 226 US 20 (1912) as the starting point for this era of anti-trust/intellectual property interaction).

Supreme Court during this period still have value as precedents even internationally. In particular, the presumption of market power from the mere existence of copyright or patent protection is subject to ongoing criticism and discussion. In Europe the principal system of at least superficially avoiding 'per se' treatment had a somewhat different formulation but the outcome has been to a large extent similar.

Evaluation

Prime proponents of 'strong' intellectual property rights have criticized the theory **2.38** heavily. The greatest criticism dates back to the days of formal anti-trust analysis. If anti-trust laws are formal and based on doctrines alone,[61] the formal approach granting no privilege to the holders of intellectual property rights may lead to extreme conclusions.[62] This would take away any reasonable remedy to encourage new innovation and creative work. Therefore, it is not a surprise that some leading scholars have been hesitant even to explore the possibility of reducing the privilege of intellectual property rights: the mere idea was not viable until anti-trust analysis came up with new market-based approaches to evaluate market dominance.[63]

In the more recent discussions, the idea of this theory as being formal and unacceptable has been restated. However, many of the initial concerns are no longer present because of the introduction of economic analysis to anti-trust and competition law scrutiny.[64] There still remains the key issue of whether patent or copyright policy is or should be relevant when implementing anti-trust laws. The US DOJ refers in its *IP Guidelines* to 'per se' rules by stating that such rules will be

---

[61] See R H Bork, *The Anti-trust Paradox* (Chicago, 1978 (rev edn 1993)), 137 (criticizing theories according to which there exist business practices that are automatically and inherently deemed exclusionary, improper and anti-competitive).

[62] Eg if the existence of market power or dominant position is presumed from the mere existence of intellectual property rights, the application of anti-trust laws without any privileges could lead to the finding of illegal tie-in any time there is a sale of two separate products (one of which is protected by a patent) as a package. See *United States v Loew's, Inc*, 371 US 38 (1960); W S Bowman, *Patent and Anti-trust Law. A Legal and Economic Appraisal* (Chicago, 1973), 6 (arguing that if perfect competition is emphasized as an ideal that may involve the danger of underplaying the importance of productive efficiencies arising from innovation and dissemination of knowledge); C Sandgren, *Patentlicenser. Studier i licensavtal angående patent, patentansötningar och know-how med särskild hänsyn till amerikansk och tysk rätt* (Stockholm 1974), 144 (the description of a patent as a monopoly does not serve as a proper starting point for analysis).

[63] L Kaplow, 'The Patent Anti-trust Intersection: A Reappraisal' (1984) 97 Harvard Law Review 1815, 1818 n 10 where the author explains that his idea is not to be rigorous in proposing the supremacy of anti-trust laws but merely to illustrate the theory.

[64] Eg (1995) *Intellectual Property Guidelines* relying mainly on 'rule-of-reason' analysis of actual circumstances. See also *United States v Microsoft Corp*, 253 F 3d 34, 84 (DC Cir 2001) ('per se' analysis is inappropriate when evaluating the legality of tying arrangements involving platform software products).

applied whenever 'there is no efficiency-enhancing integration of economic activity and if the type of restraint is one that has been accorded *per se* treatment'.

2.39 The legal presumptions and '*per se*' rules do not necessarily reflect lack of understanding of economic principles. They may also reflect the rejection of efficiency as the primary principle for solving the interaction between intellectual property laws and competition. Sometimes, they may reflect the ideas of general fairness and equity, or integration of the common market, as in Europe.[65] This may be illustrated by simple examples involving external effects of intellectual property rights.

> If A buys a car, should a patentee be entitled to prohibit A from selling the car to B? The most obvious answer is no because A may have chosen his car in reliance on the fact that it had a good resale value. The access of A to the market of used cars is a positive feedback effect, which may increase the value of the new car. If the patentee had the right to limit the resale of the product, he would effectively have the right to place conditions on such sale by a fee reflecting the value of this positive feedback. Even if A took such fee into account by the time of his purchase decision, such royalty would potentially harm both the dealer of the new car and the dealer of old cars. This is because the transaction costs for A (and consequently B) would increase, thereby limiting the transaction volume.

2.40 Legal presumptions and '*per se*' rules may be effective tools in balancing the control between different external effects by limiting the right of intellectual property owners to control their customers', licensees' and distributors' ability to benefit from external effects.

2.41 The criticism of the superiority of anti-trust laws may be well founded if the anti-trust laws are used to intervene against activities protecting the rights holder against imitations. It is less convincing if rights holders enforce their rights against parties that do not compete with them through imitations.

2.42 Consequently, the main lessons of this theory on the present issue are the following:

(1) New innovations are already rewarded on the market through earlier access to networks, etc. and copyrighted works are rewarded whenever a new copy is made and distributed on the market: therefore any additional rewards through intellectual property laws should be carefully balanced.

(2) Legal presumptions and '*per se*' rules may lead to overbroad generalizations and their use should be carefully limited to specific circumstances.

(3) Legal presumptions may still sometimes be effective in solving major issues about distribution of wealth or external effects.

---

[65] See for instance *GVL v Commission* [1983] 3 CMLR 645 (refusal to deal based on nationality a '*per se*' abuse of dominant position).

Supremacy of intellectual property laws

Introduction

If an entity wishes to use its intellectual property rights as a means of gaining **2.43** business benefits, it is popular to take the position that anti-trust laws should not restrict the entity from doing so.

'Strong' intellectual property is a popular concept that has a legal connotation but **2.44** yet is controversial enough to support a range of arguments and interpretations. It is commonly claimed that strong intellectual property rights are necessary in order to encourage innovation and creativity. The concept of 'strong' intellectual property rights is used to support lobbying activities and legal concepts of various kinds.

The concept of 'strong' exclusive rights has been used to support the copyright **2.45** owner's right to control distribution of digital content, to extend exclusive rights to interim technical copies in digital networks, to support *sui generis* protection of databases and to support arguments opposing any fair use or private copying of copyrighted content.

Equally, patent owners have promoted the need for 'strong' intellectual property **2.46** rights to support the validity of granted patents, the extension of life of patents and the extensive interpretation of the scope of patents. Further, copyright, patent and trade mark owners frequently use the 'strong' argument when opposing parallel imports and advocating the right to divide geographic markets and implement price discrimination between different jurisdictions.[66]

The main justification for this theory is that such immunity from anti-trust laws **2.47** would encourage innovation and creativity, and thus increase welfare. It may be argued that intellectual property laws are a specific 'zone' of immunity that lawmakers intended to be exempted from any anti-trust laws.[67] Therefore, the independency of intellectual property rights from anti-trust scrutiny is always supported by the proponents of 'strong' intellectual property rights.

---

[66] See P J Nordell, *Rätten till det visuella* (Stockholm, 1997), 513 for various meanings given to 'strong' copyright. J Farrell, 'Standardization and Intellectual Property' (1989) 30 Jurimetrics Journal 35, 45 (using the term to describe protection with longer-lived protection, broader protection and fewer anti-trust or other restrictions).

[67] See K Rissanen, *Kilpailu ja tavaramerkit. Kilpailunrajoituslain soveltaminen tavaramerkin yksilöimiin järjestelyihin* (Vammala 1978), 234–249 for a good overview of the Scandinavian view supporting this argument (with an English summary at 355–356). See also Finnish Committee Report KM 1952:33, 4 (lawmakers have already taken into account the possible misuse or abuse of patent rights in the Patent Act); ibid, 27 (the use of exclusive rights does not normally violate any anti-trust laws); U Bernitz and V Tiili, *Suomalainen ja kansainvälinen markkinaoikeus* (Porvoo, 1974), 188–189 (when applying anti-trust laws, one should usually accept such impacts or effects that are natural consequences of the use of exclusive rights); P Blok, *Patentrettens konsumptionsprincip-patentmonopol og Fri konkurrence i national ref og Faellesmarkedsret* (Copenhagen, 1974), 62. In economic theory, these are best categorized as pecuniary externalities that have a built-in effect on the activities of other companies.

One of the early formulations of this principle was by Justice Holmes of the US Supreme Court. The case involved a patentee who was selling a patented film projector on the condition that it was to be used to exhibit only particular films.[68] Since the patentee could have excluded any others from using the patented machine and kept the machine only for himself, he should also, according to Justice Holmes, have been allowed to place conditions on the use of the machine if he did let others use it.[69]

Areeda has criticized this opinion since the patentee could not himself have operated all the theatres using its 40,000 projectors.[70] The invention certainly had value when used in a single projector that, according to the majority, the patentee was entitled to share. However, Justice Holmes also seemed to suggest that the patentee also had the right to control whether the user was entitled to benefit from any value attributable to the network of interoperable projectors. Such value was likely to exist since a large community of interoperable projectors was an attractive customer group for any film producer. Any user of the projector would potentially have had access to a larger selection of films with potentially lower prices. If the patentee were not able to operate all the projectors herself, the value of the network would have been less.

Internalization of balancing factors and 'per se' immunity

2.48   In principle, a theory emphasizing immunity of the rights holder from anti-trust laws is clearly implemented in anti-trust law analysis. It provides another *'per se'* rule. After defining the relevant market, using a market-based approach instead of any legal presumptions, it should be asked whether the existence of intellectual property rights justifies the particular activity. Such justification is presumed to exist if the practice is not based on any deceitful practices and increases the reward derived by the rights holder.

2.49   The theory has also had a long-lasting impact on national laws around the world. It was the prevailing view in US anti-trust laws in the 1890–1912 period,[71] and as discussed below, increasingly again has become part of property theory since the 1980s. In Europe the theory was generally predominant even before the effective intervention of European Union anti-trust laws in national intellectual property regimes.

---

[68] *Motion Picture Patents Co. v Universal Film Mfg Co*, 243 US 502 (1917).

[69] Justice Markey agreed with this argument by stating that 'There is an easy test to decide whether a license is a good license or a bad license—very simple. If the licensee is no more restricted after the license than he was before, it's a good license. If, after the license, the licensee is *more* restricted than he was before, it's a bad license.' H T Markey, 'Special Problems in Patent Cases' (1975) 57 Journal of the Patent Office Society, 675, 681–682. This test was used in Europe in Commission 1962 Patent Notice, C Bellamy and G Child, *European Community Law of Competition* (P M Roth ed) (5th edn, London 2001), 646 (by granting a licence, licensee opens a door that would otherwise be closed); Blok, n 66 above, 43–44; V Korah, *Technology Transfer Agreements and the EC Competition Rules* (Oxford 1996), 14 (discussing ancillary restraints that should be approved because without such restraints pro-competitive technology transfer would not take place).

[70] Areeda–Hovenkamp–Salow, n 27 above, § 1701b, 23.

[71] Tom–Newberg, n 12 above, 168–169.

The most widely spread and established outcome of this theory is the argument **2.50** that the decision to grant licences to utilize intellectual property rights is always at the owner's discretion.[72] The rights holder should not be forced to grant licences as intellectual property laws already contain time limits for protection.

In the United States the theory has been increasingly used in some recent cases. **2.51** In *In re Independent Service Organizations Anti-trust Litigation* the appeals court held that a patent owner who brings a suit to exclude others is exempt from anti-trust laws, even though such suit may have an anti-competitive effect, unless the patent was obtained through knowing and wilful fraud, or the suit is a mere sham to interfere with the business relations of a competitor.[73]

The key justification for the formal approach emphasizing the independency of **2.52** intellectual property laws from anti-trust scrutiny is the existence of built-in balancing factors in the intellectual property laws.[74] This is sometimes identified

[72] In the US see the Patents Act, § 271 (a), *Continental Paper Bag Co v Eastern Paper Bag Co*, 210 US 405, 429 (1908); *Fox Film Corp v Doyal*, 286 US 123, 127 (1932) (copyright owner 'may refrain from vending or licensing and content himself with simply exercising the right to exclude others from using his property'); *Bement & Sons v National Harrow Co*, 186 US 70 (1902) (patent pool practice exempted even though price-fixing was involved, the court stating that 'the general rule is absolute freedom in the use or sale of rights under the patent laws of the United States'); *Henry v A.B. Dick Co*, 224 US 1 (1912); *Data General Corp v Grumman Systems Support Corp*, 36 F 3d 1147, 1186–87 (1st Cir 1994) (holding that the limited copyright monopoly is based on Congress's empirical assumption that the right to exclude others promotes consumer welfare and 'we cannot require antitrust defendants to prove and reprove the merits of this legislative assumption in every case where a refusal to license comes under attack'); Areeda–Hovenkamp, n 12 above, § 705c; F K Beier, 'Exclusive Rights, Statutory Licenses and Compulsory Licenses in Patent and Utility Model Law' (1999) 30 IIC 563, 272–274. See also the Patent Misuse Reform Act of 1988 (no misuse may be found by the reason of refusing to license or use any rights to the patent) 35 USC § 271(d) (1988).

[73] 203 F 3d 1322 (Fed Cir 2000) (holding that Xerox had no obligation to sell or license its patented parts to independent service organizations): the court differentiated the case from *Eastman Kodak Co v Image Technical Services*, 504 US 451 (1992) in that Xerox was not engaging in tying. See also *Glass Equipment Development Inc v Besten Inc*, 174 F 3d 1337, 1343 (Fed Cir 2000); *Nobelpharma AB v Implant Innovations Inc*, 141 F 3d 1059, 1068 (Fed Cir 1998); for critics of this view, see R Pitofsky, 'Challenges of the New Economy: Issues at the Intersection of Anti-trust and Intellectual Property', speech at the American Anti-trust Conference on an Agenda for Anti-trust in the 21st Century (2000), D (Has the anti-trust–IP balance changed?).

[74] R A Posner, *Economic Analysis of Law* (New York, 1998) 43–44, 46–48 (discussing home-copying of movie broadcastings in light of the interests of the advertisers who have paid for its broadcasting and wish as many people as possible to see their advertisements), similar argument can be made to the favour of radio broadcastings in places where anyone has access to; T F Cotter, 'Pragmatism, Economics and the Droit Moral' (1997) 76 North Carolina Law Review, 1, 214, 250 (anti-trust circumvention may upset the delicate balance between incentive and access as codified in the intellectual property laws); P S Menell, 'Tailoring the Legal Protection of Computer Software' (1987) 39 Stanford Law Review, 1329, 1371 (suggesting that express provisions allowing reverse engineering of computer software in order to achieve interoperability should be enacted); M O'Rourke, 'Striking a Delicate Balance: Intellectual Property, Anti-trust, Contract and Standardisation in the Computer Industry' (1998) 12 Harvard Journal of Law and Technology, 1, 40–41 (suggesting that balance should be internalized into statutes); J Schovsbo, 'As If Made for Each Other—Intellectual Property Rights and Protection of Comparable Products' (1998) 29 IIC 510, 931 (suggesting that the balance could be integrated into statutes); J Schovsbo, *Graensefldesporsmål* (1996), *mellem immaterialretten og konkurrenceretten* (Copenhagen, 1996), 274–276 (discussing different methods of including the balance into

as *internalization* of anti-trust laws and public interests into intellectual property laws. The concept is simple. The utilization of intellectual property rights should not be interfered with, since balancing factors have already been built into the intellectual property laws.

The balancing factors have been used to extend fair use to home taping ('time-shifting') of copyrighted movies;[75] to allow competitors to build interoperable products;[76] to allow a competitor to use a similar menu structure in a computer program;[77] to allow a company to combine telephone directories into a compilation;[78] to allow reverse-engineering;[79] and to allow the manufacturing of compatible spare parts.[80]

Evaluation

2.53   There are a few points in the alleged immunity of the rights holder from anti-trust laws that are frequently criticized. Firstly, it has been noted that such formal view could obviously lead to an overbroad protection of intellectual property rights that are not valuable enough to preserve that.[81] Secondly, in practice legislators

intellectual property laws); E Sherwin, 'Two- and Three-Dimensional Property Rights' (1997) 27 Arizona State Law Journal, 1075, 1095–1096 (property laws do not traditionally define the lawful uses of property); I Rahnasto, 'Scope of IP Protection—Application of Abstraction Theory', in *Ånd og rett* (Festskrift til Birger Stuevold Lassen) (Oslo, 1997), 825 (suggesting that the scope of protection could be adjusted to balance various interests); G Davies, 'Copyright and the Public Interest' (1994) IIC Studies Vol 14, 157 (the public interest has already been balanced in copyright laws); O Kolstad, *Fra Konkurrensepolitikk till Konkurrancerett* (Oslo, 1998), 440; in Sweden Reg Prop 1981/82:165, 192; A Kur, 'The "Presentation Right"—Time to Create a New Limitation in Copyright Law?' (2000) 31 IIC 308, 14–18 (suggesting that copyright laws should be amended to contain 'presentation right' in accordance with the decision of the European Court of Justice in *Parfums Christian Dior SA v Evora BV*, C-337/95, [1997] ECR I-6013); V Korah, 'Patents and Anti-trust', in *Strategic Issues of Industrial Property Management* (Cottier, Widmer and Schindler eds) (Oxford, 1999), 46, 84 (suggesting that competition authorities could comment on legislative initiatives).

[75] *Sony Corp v Universal City Studios, Inc*, 464 US 417, 429 (1984) ('the monopoly privileges that Congress may authorize are neither unlimited nor primarily designed to provide a special private benefit').

[76] *Atari Games Corp v Nintendo of America, Inc*, 897 F 2d 1572 (Fed Cir 1990).

[77] *Lotus Development Corp v Borland Intern*, 49 F 3d 807 (1st Cir 1995), aff'd, 116 S Ct 804 (1996), reh'g denied, 116 S Ct 1062 (1996).

[78] *Feist Publications, Inc v Rural Telephone Service Company, Inc*, 111 S Ct 1282 (1991).

[79] The Council Directive for the Legal Protection of Computer Programs ([14 May 1991 91/259/EEC] OJ L 122/42), Art 6.

[80] Directive 98/71/EC ([1998] OJ L289) of the European Parliament and of the Council on the legal protection of designs.

[81] R P Merges, 'The Economic Impact of Intellectual Property Rights: An Overview and Guide' (1995) 19 Journal of Cultural Economics, 103, 1818, n 11. S Breyer, 'The Uneasy Case for Copyright: A Study of Copyright in Books, Photocopies and Computer Programs' (1970) 84 Harvard Law Review 281, 285–286 (indicating that if authors must get a particular value for their creative work that value could be paid even without copyright protection; reminding also that it is quite common and generally fair that workers do not always get paid in accordance with the social value of their work). *United States v Microsoft Corp*, 253 F 3d 34, 64 (DC Cir 2001) (the Appeals Court rejecting Microsoft's argument that the licence restrictions imposed by Microsoft are legally justified because Microsoft is simply exercising its rights as the holder of valid copyrights because, according to the Appeals Court, the argument is no more correct than the proposition that the use of a baseball bat cannot give rise to tort liability).

do not continually evaluate implementation of intellectual property laws and make amendments to them. This may be for various reasons, but one of the most significant is certainly the complicated nature of intellectual property rights and the slowness of political decision-making.[82]

Thirdly, any balancing factors in intellectual property laws do not necessarily **2.54** provide the same flexibility and adaptability to specific circumstances as do the application of anti-trust or competition law principles.[83] Fourthly, there is an ongoing debate on whether intellectual property legislation should be used to provide balance in regard to complicated issues of business involving law and economics.[84]

Fifthly, and particularly in the communication industry, new digital techniques **2.55** may *de facto* dictate the scope of limitations.[85] Finally, some commentators rely on the formal distinction in regard to whether the international conventions authorize intervention or not.[86]

In its most extreme application, this theory would allow owners of intellectual **2.56** property rights to maximize their revenues not only through the sale of the products

---

[82] P Goldstein, *International Copyright—Principles, Law and Practice* (Oxford 2001), 8 (while the ideal copyright legislator, before voting to extend protection to new subject matters, would require a showing that the extension is needed as an incentive to continued investment, such extension is regularly granted without any such empirical showing). Surprisingly, some legislators have a great belief in their ability to evaluate and adjust the scope of intellectual property rights, see European Parliament and Council Directive on Certain Legal Aspects of Electronic Commerce in the Internal Market ('E-commerce Directive'), Art 24 and Directive 2001/29/EC of the European Parliament and of the Council of 22 May 2001 on the harmonization of certain aspects of copyright and related rights in the information society, [2001] OJ L 167/10 (the 'EU Copyright Directive'), Art 12 (examination procedure); Art 5(2) (exhaustive list of limitations).

[83] M A Lemley, 'The Economics of Improvement in Intellectual Property Law' (1997) 75 Texas Law Review, 989, 1068 (discussing the treatment of improvements in patent and copyright laws).

[84] D Nimmer *et al*, 'The Metamorphosis of Contract into Expand' (1999) 87 California Law Review, 19, 76 (favouring the inclusion of balancing factors); J C Gingsburg, 'Authors and Users in Copyright' (1997) 45 Journal of the Copyright Society in the USA, 1, 15 (opposing any rights of the users and arguing that any exemptions, such as fair use, be only a consequence of the high transaction costs to prevent such use). See also Ginsburg op cit, 20 (promoting the idea that copyright laws are solely to promote authorship by ensuring authors' financial returns and reasonable control over their works); W J Gordon, 'Fair Use as Market Failure: A Structural and Economic Analysis of the *Betamax* Case and its Predecessors' (1982) 82 Columbia Law Review, 1600, 1610 (suggesting monetary incentives as primary goals); R E Meiners and R J Staaf 'Patents, Copyrights, and Trademarks: Property or Monopoly?' (1990) 13 Harvard Journal of Law & Public Policy, 940 (discussing suggestions that focus on internal efficiencies of intellectual property laws as if such laws were within an 'institutional vacuum'); A Quaedvlieg, 'Copyright's Orbit Round Private, Commercial and Economic Law—The Copyright System and the Place of the User' (1998) 29 IIC, 420, 432 (emphasizing that exceptions to copyright reflect important balancing of values); N Bruun, 'The Role of the Patent System in the Protection of Intellectual Property' (1992) NIR 205, 206 (illustrating some of the issues in the field of biotechnology). WTO/TRIPS Art 13 limits the scope of any balancing factors in copyright laws.

[85] L Lessig, *Code and Other Laws of Cyberspace* (1999, New York) 135 (technical architecture of software code may be used to change any balance established into copyright laws).

[86] D Eklöf, 'Konkurrensbegränsningsrätt och immaterialrättlig konventionsregler ing' (1998) NIR 391, 394 (Berne Convention allows intervention in the case of abusive uses of copyright).

or through licensing to manufacturers of licensed products. It would potentially allow the rights holder to maximize its revenues through any effects its licensees, distributors or users of products would otherwise experience. Even in the more modest applications, this theory is frequently used to support the underlying argument that the rights holder is entitled in some way to control and benefit if the distributor or user gains external benefits.

2.57 The key to the criticism of independency of intellectual property laws is the fact that substantive intellectual property laws and their implementation are different in various parts of the world. Even if WIPO or WTO harmonization efforts were successful, national effects on local competition may be different.

A particular country may have a substantial home-grown industry providing media content, software products or particular communications equipment or alternatively it may primarily be a target for the distribution of content, software or equipment created and manufactured outside the country.

2.58 Some of the differences and trends can best be illustrated with the following table:

BALANCING FACTOR	COPYRIGHT	PATENTS
Term	70–120 years	20 years
Protected subject matter	Original creation, excluding the mere ideas and other excluded elements	Invention which is novel, non-obvious and useful/ technical
Protection of third parties	*US*: Fair use Copyright misuse	Prior use US: Patent misuse
	Europe: Private copying Exhaustive list of limitations	(Particular countries: compulsory licences)
Legal presumptions		US: Patents are presumed to be valid
Infringement	Literal infringement	Literal infringement
	Various methods to define other than literal infringement	Infringement through the doctrine of equivalents
Current trends[87]	*Sui generis* protection for databases without any	Expansion of the protected subject matter to software

---

[87] It is to be noted that none of these trends are effectively designed to limit the scope of protection but rather to expand and enforce it.

BALANCING FACTOR	COPYRIGHT	PATENTS
	requirement of creative input	programs and business methods ongoing
	Definition of the application of copyright laws into digital use in different forms	The creation of legal presumptions favouring the patent
	Global harmonization ongoing	Creation of a system of utility models or 'petty patents'
	The concept of exhaustion under discussion	The concept of exhaustion under discussion
		Global harmonization

It is also relevant to note that any limitations in intellectual property laws tend to be general in nature, based on the required outcome generally in the average case. This does not mean that the outcome in a particular case would be the one desired or intended by legislators. **2.59**

If a reward to the creator is intended to be x+10, it does not mean that this would be the outcome in any single case because of difficulties in measuring the specific reward. This is relevant even if over all decisions the average outcome would be close to the desired outcome.[88]

Anti-trust scrutiny and intellectual property analysis have, in recent years and to a certain extent, been used as alternative approaches to the same problem. This indicates a continuous support for both approaches in practical decision-making. **2.60**

In *Feist Publications v Rural*[89] the US Supreme Court held that the alphabetical listings of telephone subscribers were not protected by copyright because the mere alphabetical listing did not involve even the minimum amount of creativity.

In *Magill*[90] the European Court of Justice held that the refusal to grant a licence for a weekly television programme listing protected by copyright in the UK and Ireland to a producer of weekly TV guides was abuse of dominant position. According to the ECJ, by refusing to license the TV companies were keeping the market for weekly TV guides for themselves only.

---

[88] Kaplow, n 62 above, 1820.

[89] *Feist Publications, Inc v Rural Telephone Service Company, Inc*, 111 S Ct 1282 (1991).

[90] *Radio Telefís Éireann (RTÉ) and Independent Television Publications Ltd (ITP) v Commission* ('*Magill*') [1995] 4 CMLR 718. See, however, *Renault SA v Maxicar SpA*, 11 May 2000, C-38/98 (there is no public policy within the European Union preventing the existence of national intellectual property rights).

Both cases illustrate points that are increasingly typical for converging industries: (1) there is an increasing trend to combine elements originally developed by various parties, and (2) companies try to leverage their intellectual property positions to gain business benefits in related markets.

2.61 Furthermore, intellectual property laws have generally proved to be ineffective in solving leveraging issues. They are the primary source for defining whether it is possible to use intellectual property as leverage but intellectual property laws give little if any guidance as to how this leverage may be, in practice, implemented. The same is typical for most property laws: they do not define exhaustively all the possible uses of property. It is necessary to try to solve the balance within the respective intellectual property rights themselves, because issues such as breadth and length of protection cannot be effectively solved by other means.[91] However, it is important to note that internal balancing factors cannot be the only method for creating balance in individual cases.

Theory based on the scope of exclusive rights

Introduction

2.62 The formal uses of anti-trust and intellectual property laws have had impacts on various jurisdictions. In the early days of anti-trust and competition law enforcement it became clear that the immunity of the rights holder and '*per se*' anti-trust enforcement rules needed to be combined in some way. Early attempts to combine the goals of intellectual property laws with those of anti-trust laws involved examining the definition of the scope of exclusive rights.

2.63 Typical analysis of the scope of exclusive rights starts with the question whether the particular activity is within the rights granted by intellectual property laws,[92] or whether it is attributable to intellectual property rights.[93] It may also be important whether the activity is enhancing the reward provided by intellectual property laws or not.[94] In European Union case law a slightly different approach in distinguishing between the right and the exercise of the right has been used.[95]

---

[91] B Domeij, *Läkemedelspatent* (Stockholm 1998), 39 (the criteria of patentability cannot be solved through private transactions).

[92] *Motion Picture Patents Co v Universal Film Manufacturing Co*, 243 US 502 (1917); *United States v Masonite Corp*, 316 US 265, 280 (1942) ('Since patents are privileges restrictive of a free economy, the rights which Congress has attached to them must be strictly construed . . .').

[93] *Zenith Radio Corp v Hazeltine Research, Inc*, 395 US 100 (1969).

[94] *United States v General Electric Co*, 272 US 476 (1926).

[95] *Consten/ Grundig* [1966] CMLR 418, 476 (without touching the grant of intellectual property rights, their exercise may be limited to the extent necessary for the attainment of the prohibition derived from Art 85(1)). This distinction in Europe was necessary in order for the ECJ to find jurisdiction since its jurisdiction would not extend to matters of property rights. The same justification has also broadly been discussed in other European property laws, especially as a justification for environmental policy makers to intervene where there have been environmentally harmful uses of private property rights.

In order to 'determine whether or not any patent practice is or is not in violation of the anti-monopoly laws we must determine the nature and scope of the patent monopoly secured to the patentee'.[96]

Analysis which starts with the scope of protection reflects general property theo-   **2.64**
ries used to justify limited government intervention into private property rights. These 'analytical' property theories became increasingly popular in various parts of the world after the Second World War. Such theories generally make a distinction between the ownership and the use of the property. The right of ownership has enhanced juridical protection but it does not limit the rights of the government to impose restrictions on the use of the property.

US application: misuse doctrine

The earliest application of theories emphasizing the scope of protection in the   **2.65**
intellectual property field were generally found in early US patent cases involving anti-trust arguments and in compulsory licensing provisions enacted in some countries. In the US the cases involving issues 'inherent to intellectual property rights' were later developed into the intellectual property misuse doctrine. In Europe a misuse doctrine has been a part of the traditional legal framework. However, the application of the doctrine in intellectual property rights remains as part of the anti-trust law framework, and to some extent the compulsory licensing provisions.[97]

In *Motion Picture Patents* the US Supreme Court held that the patentee's restric-   **2.66**
tion to play only particular films with the patented projector was illegal restraint of trade since the film 'is obviously not any part of the invention of the patent in suit'. The court refused to enforce the use restriction because to enforce such

---

[96] O R Barnett, *Patent Property and the Anti-Monopoly Laws* (Indianapolis 1943), 51 ('Having the clear understanding of the metes and bounds of the patent monopoly we can then determine to what extent patent property may be used in restraining trade'); M Koktvedgaard, *Konkurrencepraegede immetrialretspositioner* (Copenhagen, 1965) 39 (making distinction between normal use and particular uses); M A Lemley, 'The Economic Irrationality of the Patent Misuse Doctrine' (1990) 78 California Law Review 1599 (criticizing the doctrine because the remedy is not proportionate to the abuse).

[97] Knoph (describing international discussion in 1928 the conclusion of which was that it was not necessary to include provisions covering the misuse or '*abus de droit*' doctrines in the international copyright treaties since such doctrine was applicable universally even without express statutes); B Godenhielm, 'Om patenträtten in konkurrensrättslight hänseede', in *Uppsaster i immaterialrätt* (Lund, 1983), 25, 34 (suggesting that the general concept of 'misuse of rights' exists in the legal systems of most countries but that at least in early Scandinavian practice the exercise of that concept in intellectual property cases was considered to require amendments in the text of the statutes); see, however, A Heinemann, 'Anti-trust Laws of Intellectual Property in the TRIPs Agreement of the World Trade Organisation', in *From GATT to TRIPS* (Beier and Schricker, eds) (1996) IIC Studies Vol 18, 239, 243 (the term 'abuse' in TRIPS, Art 8(2) suggests that a broader concept of 'abuse' than the one used under Art 82 of the Treaty of the European Union may be necessary). See also KKO 1992:145 (the Finnish Supreme Court recognizing the doctrine in respect of 'first demand' guarantees).

restriction would create 'a monopoly in the manufacture and use of moving picture films, wholly outside of the patent in suit and of the patent law as we have interpreted it'.[98] Based on essentially the same grounds the courts have refused to find any contributory infringement on the supply of products even though the patentee may have had a combination patent.[99] Consequently, a considerable amount of effort has been made to define the 'inherent' scope of the intellectual property grant.[100]

2.67 In *Morton Salt* the US Supreme Court held the patent unenforceable against the manufacturer of an allegedly infringing machine since the patentee was selling the patented machine only on the condition that any purchaser buy the required salt from the patentee. The Court held that '. . . the public policy which includes inventions within the granted monopoly excludes from all that is not embraced in the invention'.[101]

2.68 The same doctrine has been applied also against enforcement of copyright. The copyright misuse doctrine was first introduced by a federal district court in *M. Witmark & Sons v Jensen*.[102] The doctrine was revitalized after *Lasercomb America, Inc. v Reynolds*.[103] In *Lasercomb* the federal appeals court held that

---

[98] *Motion Picture Patents Co v Universal Film Mfg Co*, 243 US 502, 518–519 (1917).

[99] *Carpice Corp v American Patents Dev Corp*, 283 US 27 (1931); *Leitch Mfg Co v Barber Co*, 302 US 458 (1938).

[100] *United States v Line Material Co*, 333 US 287, 309–310 (1948); *Ethyl Gasoline Corp v United States*, 309 US 436, 452 (1940); *United States v Univis Lens Co*, 316 US 241 (1942).

[101] *Morton Salt Co v GS Suppiger Co*, 314 US 488, 492 (1942). See also *Mercoid Corp v Minneapolis-Honeywell Regulator Co*, 320 US 680 (1944); *Mercoid Corp v Mid-Continent Investment Co*, 320 US 661 (1944); *International Salt Co v United States*, 332 US 392 (1947) (anti-trust violation); *United States v Line Material Co*, 333 US 287, 308 (1948) ('the possession of a valid patent does not give the patentee any exemption from the provisions of the Sherman Act beyond the limits of the patent monopoly'). In the more recent case law the same principle has been restated, *Atari Games Corp v Nintendo of America, Inc*, 897 F 2d 1572, 1576–77 (Fed Cir 1990) ('patent owners may incur antitrust liability for enforcement of a patent known to be obtained through fraud or known to be invalid, where license of a patent compels the purchase of unpatented goods, or where there is an overall scheme to use the patent to violate antitrust laws').

[102] *M Witmark & Sons v Jensen*, 80 F Supp 843 (D Minn 1948) (the performing rights society's claim of royalties from movie theatres showing movies for which a copyright licence was already paid constituted copyright misuse).

[103] *Lasercomb America, Inc v Reynolds*, 911 F Supp 970 (4th Cir 1990) (licence terms restricting licensee's right to aid others to develop competing software constituted a copyright misuse on which a competitor could rely even though it was not the party to the licence). See also other cases accepting the defence of copyright misuse, *Atari Games Corp v Nintendo of America, Inc*, 975 F 3d 832 (Fed Cir 1992); *Practice Management Info Corp v AMA*, 121 F 3d 516 (9th Cir 1997); *PRC Realty Sys, Inc v Nat'l Assoc of Realtors*, 972 F 2d 341 (4th Cir 1992); *Alcatel USA, Inc v DGI Technologies, Inc*, 166 F 3d 772 (5th Cir 1999); *Triad System Corporation v Southeastern Express Company*, 64 F 3d 1330 (9th Cir 1995) (rejecting misuse defence for copying in order to enable maintenance of operating system). See also B Sheffner, 'Alcatel USA, Inc v UGI Technologies' (2000) 15 Berkley Technology Law Journal 25, 31; R T Nimmer and M Santhan, 'The Concept of Misuse in Copyright and Trademark Law: Searching for a Concept of Restraint' (1998) 524 PLI/Pat 397; R Hannah, 'Misusing Anti-trust: The Search for Functional Copyright Misuse' (1994) 465 Stanford Law Review 401; R S Katz and A J Safer, 'Copyright Misuse: Inconsistent Cases from the 1990s and Simple

Lasercomb could not enforce its copyright in computer software against a software developer who had made unauthorized copies of Lasercomb's software to develop its own non-infringing software. If Lasercomb had prevailed in the enforcement action, it would have extended the copyright protection beyond that granted by the Copyright Act by foreclosing competition that did not infringe its copyright. The doctrine has been used at least in the following circumstances:[104] (1) when effects of a practice are *de facto* extending the rights granted by copyright laws; (2) when there are limitations of the right to develop or support the development of competing products; or (3) when there are provisions requiring exclusion of competitors' products.

European application: existence and exercise

In Europe the European Court of Justice established in its early case law a rather **2.69** different approach, that essentially has a largely similar outcome. Whereas the US and traditional German views generally considered that the core of the exclusive right was beyond anti-trust intervention, the ECJ relied after *Consten/Grundig*[105] on the distinction between the existence and the exercise of intellectual property rights. The concept of exercise may also justify intervention in the exclusive right as such even where such exercise would be 'within the scope of intellectual property rights'. In practice, after some early interventions mostly relating to the arbitrary divisions of the common market and the application of Article 36 of the EC Treaty, the core of the exclusive right has remained beyond the normal intervention.[106]

Formula for the 21st Century' (2000) 17 No 4 Computer Law 3; A X Fellmeth, 'Copyright Misuse and the Limits of the Intellectual Property Monopoly' (1998) 6 Journal of Intellectual Property Law 1, 34 (courts are divided on the issue whether anti-trust violation is a precondition for misuse); J A D White, 'Misuse or Fair Use: That is the Software Copyright Question' (1997) 12 Berkeley Technology Law Journal 251; P Goldstein, *International Copyright-Principles, Law and Practice* (Oxford , 2001), 320 (the misuse defence has been strongest where the justification for copyright is weakest).

[104] W E Thomson and M Y Chu, 'Overstepping the Bounds: Copyright Misuse' (1998) 15 No 11 Computer Law 1, 4.

[105] *Consten/Grundig* [1966] CMLR 418; see also already in Scandinavia in NU 1963:91 (the anti-trust laws should be used only against the negative effects of patents but they should not be used to nullify such rights).

[106] The distinction between existence/exercise has consequently been used in *Parke Davis v Centrafarm* [1968] CMLR 47 (exercise as such does not constitute any violation); *Sirena v Eda* [1971] CMLR 260 (rights holder may not exercise its rights to prevent imports from other member states), *Deutsche Grammophon v Metro* [1971] CMLR 631; *Centrafarm v Sterling Drug* [1974] 2 CMLR 480 (the patent right may not be exercised to prohibit the sale of patented goods in a member state if those goods have been marketed in another member state with consent); *Centrafarm v Winthrop* [1974] CMLR 480 (the same rule even if the prices of pharmaceuticals were different as a consequence of state action); *Musik-Vertried Membran GmbH and K-Tel International v Gema* [1981] 2 CMLR 44. The most extreme application of existence/exercise doctrine was probably in *Van Zuylen Freres v HAG AG ('HAG I')* [1974] CMLR 127 (one cannot rely on the exclusive right to prohibit the marketing of goods legally produced in another member state under an identical trade mark having

Evaluation

2.70   Theories based on the 'scope' of intellectual property rights have been criticized as not providing any guidance to actual decision-makers. They do not give any answer as to which activities are 'inherent to intellectual property rights' and which are not. Instead, the 'scope' theories call for the court to make its own judgment.[107] In the absence of any other criteria, the courts traditionally apply anti-trust principles.

2.71   The 'scope' theory may also effectively be used to support various overbroad generalizations. For instance, the theory was the core of the distinction between lawful and unlawful practices identified on the US Justice Department's list of nine banned practices in the 1970s.[108] The same theory has also been used to support the sovereignty of the rights holder, within the scope of the rights, to use broad discretion.[109]

2.72   In Scandinavia, the 'scope' theory has had its own application. Several Scandinavian scholars, especially in the 1970s and 1980s, supported the view that arbitrary distinctions, between the right and the use of right, unnecessarily limit the use of the exclusive right. Rather, the rights holder should always be authorized to benefit from the normal, reasonable and rational use of intellectual property rights. Any intervention should only be justified after enhanced legal scrutiny.[110] In practice, this would involve a general rebuttable presumption that the activities of the rights holder are justified. This view is supported also by the common legislative history of the Scandinavian current patent laws.[111]

the same origin but owned by a separate independent company); see after that especially *SA CNL-Sucal NV v HAG GF AG ('HAG II')* [1990] 3 CMLR 571 (effectively overruling *HAG I*); *Pharmon BV v Hoecst AG* [1985] 3 CMLR 775 (no exhaustion by compulsory licensing), also *Terrapin v Terranova* [1976] 2 CMLR 482 (the free movement of goods may not undermine trade mark protection but legitimate use must be ensured); *Hoffman-La Roche v Centrafarm* [1979] 3 CMLR 217; *Centrafarm BV v American Home Products Corp* [1979] 1 CMLR 326.

[107]   Kaplow, n 62 above, 1849; Bowman, n 61 above, 8–9 (discussing the problem of distinguishing lawful output restrictions from unlawful restrictions merely on the basis of the patent grant); W F Baxter, 'Legal Restrictions on Exploitation of the Patent Monopoly: An Economic Analysis' (1966) 76 Yale Law Journal, 267, 277 ('A promise by the licensee to murder the patentee's mother-in-law is as much "within the patent monopoly" as is the sum $50.00; and it is not the patent laws which tell us that the former agreement is unenforceable and subjects the parties to criminal sanctions'); I Govaere, *The Use and Abuse of Intellectual Property Rights in E.C. Law* (London 1996) 66–67. In respect of older discussion see Barnett, n 104 above, 59–65, 262 (emphasizing the facts whether competitors were 'wrongfully' excluded and whether the contract would restrain something that was not restrained by the mere existence of the patent or copyright).

[108]   See n 67 above.

[109]   *Bement*, 186 US at 91 (absolute freedom in the use or sale of rights); Barnett, n 104 above, 55 (within his domain, the patentee is 'czar'); *In re Independent Service Organizations Antitrust Litigation*, 1322 F 3d 1322, 1327 (Fed Cir 2000) (holding the refusal to sell or license patented property to independent service organizations lawful).

[110]   Rissanen, n 66 above, 253; U Bernitz, *Svensk Marknadsrätt* (Stockholm 1991), 73; Blok, n 66 above, 43.

[111]   NU 1963:6, 91 (the anti-trust enforcement may be directed only against the harmful effects

The Swedish *Dubbman*[112] case further illustrates this Scandinavian critical view. In *Dubbman*, several Swedish companies agreed on patent licensing and cross-licensing arrangements. In line with German and US precedents, the court held that the exclusive right of the patentee entitles the patentee to define the terms of the licence, except that such right does not allow the patentee to define the resale price of the licensee or divide market shares among the licensees. The dissent of four justices would have authorized any activity subject to an evaluation of the situation as compared to the situation in which the patentee had not granted any licences at all.[113]

The Scandinavian view is different from the popular American criticisms that **2.73** emphasize the specific immunity of intellectual property rights. Rather, intellectual property laws just provide rights that the patentee or the author should be entitled to utilize in the same manner that people are entitled to utilize their other legal rights. The intellectual property laws protect authors and inventors against imitation. Anti-trust laws should not redistribute the wealth created by innovation or creativeness but they may intervene where the lawful use of intellectual property rights may have potentially harmful consequences for the public in general.[114]

The term 'use' is a common source of confusion. If it is not possible to intervene **2.74** in regard to the 'ownership' right as such but only in the way such ownership right is used, a distinction between 'ownership' and 'use' or 'existence' and 'exercise' needs to be defined. In terms of conventional property, that distinction is quite certain. In respect of intellectual property rights, one easily made mistake is comparing the right to use the invention or work instead of the right to use the rights granted in the patent or copyright laws. However, the use of the invention or the work is not 'use' in intellectual property terms.

It may be argued that 'the right to exclude others from free use of an invention protected by a valid patent differs from the right to exclude others from free use of the owner's motor vehicle, crops or other items of personal property'.[115] In the same way, it could be disputed whether a patentee is able to block others from making use of a particular system if it is

---

caused by the exercise of the patent rights but not in a manner that would nullify the patent rights as such). This is generally interpreted as favouring patentees against anti-trust enforcement agencies but still allowing broad flexibility in respect of remedies in case of harmful externalities.

[112] *Marknadsdomstolet 1972:7 (Dubbman)*. The case was decided and based before Sweden joined the European Union. The current law and practice is largely in line with general European Union case law.

[113] The dissent gained broad support and led to the limited interpretation of the majority opinion. Compare with Justice Markey's good and bad licences, or Justice Holmes' dissent in *Motion Picture Patents Co v Universal Film Mfg Co*, 243 US 502 (1917). See also *EMI Records v CBS* [1976] 2 CMLR 235 (an agreement (in this case expired agreement) does not restrict competition if its effects do not exceed those of the national trade mark).

[114] Rissanen, n 66 above, 254–255; Bruun, n 92 above, 50.

[115] Justice Markey in the US case *Panduit Corp v Stahlin Bros Fibre Works, Inc*, 575 F 2d 1152, 1158 n 5 (6th Cir 1978).

not generally acceptable to park one's car in such a way that it blocks others from entering a public parking area.[116]

2.75 The practical consequence has been that the rights holder is allowed to benefit from the exclusivity granted by copyright or patent laws but not to engage in any activities going beyond that. In practice the rights holder has been entitled to exclude others from reproducing, distributing, modifying and publicly performing any works protected by copyright. A patentee has been entitled to exclude anyone from manufacturing, selling, offering to sell and importing goods or using methods covered by a patent. However, any other activity not directly covered by the rights granted by the intellectual property laws has been characterized as potentially limiting competition.

2.76 Despite this criticism, this theory has served to create a relatively stable environment.[117] The use of the 'scope' theory has established some almost universal rules. Consequently, it has become clear in various jurisdictions that it is not possible to leverage an intellectual property position in certain ways. A patentee may not require the licensee to purchase all necessary raw materials or spare parts from a patentee.[118] The existence of a patent or copyright does not authorize the rights holder to engage in illegal price maintenance.[119] In addition, a patentee or copyright holder may not deny the purchaser of goods the right to sell such goods further since the exclusive right has been exhausted by the first lawful sale of the goods.

2.77 One of the interesting developments has been that the proponents of 'strong' intellectual property rights are increasingly challenging these legal presumptions. The legal presumptions are said to reduce the reward provided by intellectual property laws in an unjustified way. It is popular to claim that any interference with the activities of the rights holder should be subject to an inquiry into the particular circumstances under viable economic theories.[120] These propositions are discussed in more detail below.

2.78 There are also some other significant weaknesses in the theories behind making formal distinctions between activities within the scope of the intellectual property rights and activities beyond such scope. These theories are unable to provide sound solutions and justifications in increasingly complex and dynamic situations.

---

[116] See R R Nelson, 'Intellectual Property Protection for Cumulative Systems Technology' (1994) 94 Columbia Law Review 2674, 2676 (identifying the problems of strong protection when new technology is based on existing technology or new products combine different technologies).

[117] Tom–Newberg, n 12 above, 173.

[118] *Morton Salt Co v G S Suppiger Co*, 314 US 488 (1942).

[119] *Dr Miles Medical Co v John D Park & Sons Co*, 220 US 373 (1911).

[120] See eg D J Gifford, 'The Damaging Impact of the Eastman Kodak Precedent Upon Product Competition: Antitrust Law in Need of Correction' (1994) 72 Washington University Law Quarterly, 1535 (suggesting that limitations on right holder's right to control downstream markets may impede innovation).

These formal approaches are likely to face increasing problems in novel issues involving external effects. The main problem is the narrow approach to the question. Instead of asking whether Microsoft should be entitled to combine Windows and Internet Explorer, one could ask whether the inability (because of Microsoft's intellectual property rights) of others to integrate their browsers into Windows is a problem.

Alternatively, instead of asking whether compulsory licences would nullify the inherent rights included in the very nature of intellectual property rights, it could be argued that the refusal to grant such a licence excludes a company or a group of companies from beneficial network effects not attributable to such intellectual property rights.

Intellectual property rights as property

Introduction

Intellectual property rights were long seen as exclusions from free competition.   **2.79**
They were something artificial, created by legislators. In recent years this view of the artificiality of intellectual property rights has been shifting,[121] and intellectual property rights have been increasingly recognized as property.[122] This means that creative works, inventions and information in general are presumed to be protected by intellectual property rights. For a long time, there was a general presumption that these were protected by intellectual property rights only in particular circumstances that were clearly defined by legislators.[123]

---

[121] Merges, n 6 above, 110; Pitofsky, n 72 above; W N Cornish, *Intellectual Property: Patents, Copyrights, Trademarks and Allied Rights* (4th edn, London, 1999) 358–359 (expressing the concern that the development may lead away from the liberal view that the right is only justified to the extent it encourages authorship and initial marketing); R P Merges and G H Reynolds, 'The Proper Scope of the Copyright and Patent Power' (2000) 37 Harvard Journal on Legislation, 45, 52 (suggesting that the traditional idea that all kinds of limitations were built into intellectual property laws has in recent years lost importance).

[122] By this development, it is not meant the long tradition of treating intellectual property rights as having the attributes of personal property, ie the possibility to transfer and assign them, to license them, to use them as security in credit transactions and the application of the rules relating to the rights of creditors and later assignees.

[123] D G Baird, 'Common Law Intellectual Property and the Legacy of *International News Service v Associated Press*' (1983) 50 University of Chicago Law Review 411 ('That information once published should be free for all to use is a commonplace of intellectual property laws'). Under property theory, one's 'entitlement' can be based on a property rule or on a liability rule. The application of a property rule provides that 'no one can take private property from the holder unless the holder sells it willingly and at the price which he subjectively values the property'. See also G Calabresi and A D Melamed, 'Property Rules, Liability Rules, and Inalienability: One View of the Cathedral' (1972) 85 Harvard Law Review, 1089, 1105; R A Posner, *Economic Analysis of Law* (New York, 1998), 39 (suggesting that property rights emerge as the benefits of such rights increase their costs); *Bonito Boats v Thundercraft Boats*, 109 S Ct 971 (1989) ('free exploitation of ideas will be the rule, to which the protection of federal patent is the exception'); J M Hainsee, 'An Economic View of Innovation and Property Right Protection in the Expanded Regulatory State' (1994) 21 Pepperdine Law Review 127 (distinguishing between property and privileges granted by government); T M Kivimäki, *Tekijänoikeus* (Porvoo 1948), 27–30; T M Kivimäki, *Uudet tekijänoikeus-ja valokuvauslait* (Porvoo 1966), 6 (property theory never accepted in Finland even though copyright has some attributes of personal property); see, however, PeVL 10/1986 vp., 15/1992 vp. and 1/1995 vp. (copyright, design, patent and trade mark rights protected in a similar manner as any other property rights).

It is not new to argue that intellectual property should have the same protection as any other property but there are some conclusions made from this categorization that have not been argued before. The origin of the debate dates back to eighteenth-century English common law literary property debate. This debate emerged when printers, after their exclusive rights to print books had been largely diminished in the 1709 Statute of Anne, claimed perpetual common law literary property rights. The issue involved three main questions: (1) the acquisition of property rights, (2) the identification of property rights, and (3) the economic and cultural consequences of such rights.[124] Also in Scandinavia, a similar discussion evolved in the early twentieth century.[125]

2.80 The new intensity in property theory has emerged as a response to the long standing tensions between intellectual property rights and anti-trust laws.[126] This development appears to be one further step towards a post-industrial information society. A simple chart illustrates the development:

PHASE OF A SOCIETY	KEY INGREDIENTS IN PRODUCTION	KEY SUCCESS FACTORS
Agricultural society	Land	Access to land
Industrial society	Raw materials, machines, labour	Access to raw materials, capital, machines and cheap labour
Information society	Information	Access to information and skilled labour

Early justifications

2.81 The concept of information and intellectual property as property and the consequent conclusions are not new. They are based on argument relying on both utilitarian and natural law.[127] The US proponents of this theory, in particular, frequently rely on the natural law theory contained in the famous essay *An Essay Concerning the True Original Extent and End of Civil Government* by John

---

[124] B Shermand and L Bentley, *The Making of Modern Intellectual Property Law. The British Experience, 1760–1911* (Cambridge, 1999), 20. The spill-overs of the discussion continued into the twentieth century in terms of the proper 'objects' of intellectual property rights. In this book, that discussion is not analysed.

[125] See overview of Vinding Kruse's property theory and the subsequent discussion in S Bergström, *Uteslutande rätt att förfoga över verket* (Uppsala 1954), 22; Kivimäki, n 129 above, 5–6.

[126] Tom–Newberg, n 12 above, 172–173 ('If intellectual property is comparable to any other form of property, then there is no invisible, magic line surrounding the intellectual property kingdom, the crossing of which automatically leads to antitrust penalties').

[127] D D Chisum and M A Jacobs, *Understanding Intellectual Property Law* (New York, 1992 (rep 1999)), 1–7; Breyer, n 80 above, 284; W J Gordon, 'Fair Use as Market Failure: A Structural and Economic Analysis of the *Betamax* Case and its Predecessors' (1982) 82 Columbia Law Review 1600, 1993, 1540 (arguing that Locke has incorrectly been used to support strong intellectual property rights).

Locke, first published in 1690. In his essay, Locke advocates that property rights are created through labour: 'As much land as man tills, plants, improves, cultivates, and can use the product of, so much is his property. He by his labour does, as it were, enclose it from the common.'[128] Each man has property in his person and consequently in his labour. Therefore, each man has property rights to things into which he has added his labour. Consequently, whatever is done to improve anything generally available should become the property of the person making such improvement.

Locke's theory has had an increasing importance for the underlying justification **2.82** for expansion of property rights. This has been the trend in spite of the fact, as some commentators have pointed out, that the writings of Locke were intended as a response to the aims of the English monarchy, the House of Stuart, to expand their powers at the expense of the citizens.[129]

The property part of the natural rights theory also has most of its origin in the **2.83** common law. In continental Europe, national civil law has traditionally provided a division of intellectual property rights into moral rights and economic rights. This legacy is different from the common law doctrine, although the moral rights doctrine has produced many of the same effects in intellectual property laws.[130]

Moral rights were long considered the non-property part of intellectual property **2.84** rights.[131] In 1785 Immanuel Kant argued that the main harm caused by counterfeit copying is that an unauthorized copier may take the author's work, misrepresent it and put it into circulation to an audience to which the author never intended it to be represented.[132] This was an early formulation of the idea of utilizing intellectual property rights to control the behaviour of others—not solely the behaviour of the unauthorized copier but rather the behaviour of anybody whose behaviour the work or invention may affect. Moral rights, primarily the right to be recognized as an author or inventor, and the right of integrity, are still considered, in Europe,

---

[128] J Locke, 'An Essay Concerning the True Original Extent and End of Civil Government, in Social Contract', *Essays by Locke, Hume and Rousseau* (Oxford, 1947), 28 (Chapter V '*Of Property*', para 32).

[129] W H Hamilton, 'Property—According to Locke' (1932) 41 Yale Law Journal 864, 867; E Barker, 'Introduction to Social Contract', *Essays by Locke, Hume and Rousseau* (Oxford, 1947), xxiv; S Strömholm, *A Short History of Legal Thinking in the West* (Lund, 1985), 194–195 (discussing the appeal of the theory to English middle class of that time). See also F Machlup, 'An Economic Review of the Patent System' (1958) Study No 15, Subcommittee of the Judiciary of the US Senate, Washington, 21 (society is morally obligated to recognize this property right: appropriation of one's ideas must be condemned as stealing).

[130] See also S Strömholm, *Upphovsrättens verksbegrepp* (Stockholm, 1970), 248 (identifying the requirement of originality also as an aesthetic theory: only original works are worth protection).

[131] R Sarraute, 'Current Theories on the Moral Right of Authors and Artists under French Law' (1968) 16 American Journal of Comparative Law 465.

[132] I Kant, 'Von der Unrechtmässigkeit des Büchernachdrucks', in *VIII Kant's gesammelte Schriften*, 77, 80–81.

to be a natural right of the author or the inventor.[133] The reasoning for this is not in the rationale that for the author or inventor, recognition as such is important because it enables him to obtain further assignments as author or inventor. Rather, the author or inventor is entitled to be recognized simply because the creator deserves to be recognized. Therefore, moral rights are more closely linked to the personality of the author or creator than to his actual property.[134] In practice, since the Enlightenment period, authors in Europe have not been able to assign their own moral rights.

Utilitarian justifications

2.85 Apart from the early philosophical justifications, the categorization of intellectual property rights as property rights just as effective as any other property rights has its legal roots in the nineteenth-century positivistic legal theories and on the distinction between public and private laws.[135]

2.86 The utilitarian justification of the property theory relies on a few principles. Firstly, under a theory usually attributed to Schumpeter, any investment requires structural safeguards to protect the investment against changing circumstances and against the attack of new products and technologies. Without effective patent or copyright protection, business would create other restrictive methods to protect the investment. If the protection provided for intellectual property is too limited by anti-trust laws it may also reduce the amount of investment.[136]

Without patent or copyright protection, expenditure on inventive or creative activity will be diminished. The connection between patent or copyright protection and the expenditure in inventive or creative activity is largely recognized, but it is often debated whether additional protection would produce the same effect. This is because to some extent other forms of protection of the investment may substitute for patent or copyright protection—at a cost. Overall, patent and copyright protection is likely to increase inventive and creative activity, but it may still be below a socially optimal level.[137]

[133] In patent law, the right to be named as an inventor is the traditional moral right. In copyright, the same right to be named as an author is called the paternity right. Further moral rights under European copyright laws are the right to first disclose the work, also referred to as the divulgation right, and to a certain extent the right of integrity and the right to withdraw.

[134] Sarraute, n 138 above, 465–466.

[135] Paris Convention 1883 and Berne Convention 1886; K Aoki, 'Intellectual Property and Sovereignty: Notes Toward a Cultural Geography of Authorship' (1996) 48 Stanford Law Review 1293, 1318.

[136] J A Schumpeter, *Capitalism, Socialism and Democracy* (3rd edn, New York 1950), 88 (identifying entrepreneurial innovation as the main difference between capitalistic and socialistic societies). See for commentary, D Silverstein, 'Patents, Science and Innovation: Historical Linkages and Implications for Global Technological Competitiveness' (1991) 17 Rutgers Computer & Technology Law Journal, 261, 264–266; R M Sherwood, *Intellectual Property and Economic Development* (Boulder 1990), 71–72; F M Scherer, *Innovation and Growth. Schumpeterian Perspectives* (Cambridge Massachusetts, 1984), 198 (questioning the positive impact of market power on innovative activities).

[137] See discussion in J W Schlicher, *Patent Law: Legal and Economic Principles* (1999), 2–14; I E Novos and M Waldman, 'The Effects of Increased Copyright Protection: An Analytical Approach'

Secondly, the utilitarian theories explain the interaction between exclusive rights **2.87**
and anti-trust by static and dynamic efficiencies.[138] The anti-trust theory is traditionally interested in static circumstances, whether a patentee can charge supra-
competitive prices or whether they can reduce output. The justification for
intellectual property rights is in their dynamic efficiency that provides new social
benefits. Inventors and creators of new useful features are therefore encouraged
by a limited period of exclusivity. Generally, the fact that successful innovations
may allow the patentee to collect supra-competitive rewards is supposed not to
cause harm to the buyers.[139] Put simply, people are supposed to invent more if
they are granted property rights.

Another argument on property theory is the understanding that property rights **2.88**
may encourage authors and inventors to make effective use of their inventions
and works.[140] Since intellectual property rights are presumed to be an efficient
way of encouraging innovation and creativity, and also make necessary docu-
mentation and dissemination of innovations and works,[141] property rights have
been considered to be an appropriate mechanism to encourage those activities. It
is presumed that without property rights, the resources would be allocated to
activities other than inventive or creative activities.[142]

New popularity of 'property' theory

It has become popular to rely on 'property' theory after a number of US companies **2.89**

(1984) 92 Journal of Political Economy, 236, 245 (increased copyright protection will decrease the
social harms from under-utilization); see R Towse, 'Copyright as an Economic Incentive' (1999) 17
Copyright Reporter, 15, 24 (concluding that the empirical evidence is inadequate to clearly support
this conclusion).

[138] For a good overview, see O Kolstad, *Fra konkurrenspolitikk till konkurrancerett* (Oslo 1998),
372 (separating competition in the markets of existing products, new technologies and future
complete products).

[139] See for discussion T M Jorde and D J Teece, 'Rule of Reason Analysis of Horizontal
Arrangements: Agreements Designed to Advance Innovation and Commercialise Technology' (1993)
61 Anti-trust Law Journal, 599; W J Baumol and J A Ordover, 'Anti-trust: Source of Dynamic and
Static Inefficiencies', in Jorde and Teece eds, *Anti-trust, Innovation and Competitiveness* (New York
1992) 82, 85; J A Ordover and R D Willig, 'Antitrust for High-Technology Industries: Assessing
Research Joint Ventures and Mergers' (1985) 28 Journal of Law and Economics, 311–334 and
Areeda-Elhauge-Hovenkamp, n 28 above, § 1780a; Posner, n 23 above, 36.

[140] S Breyer, 'The Uneasy Case for Copyright: A Study of Copyright in Books, Photocopies, and
Computer Programs' (1970) 84 Harvard Law Review, 281, 289; R U Cooter, *Law and Economics*
(Glenview, 1988), 112–16; M Lehmann, 'The Theory of Property Rights and the Protection of
Intellectual and Industrial Property' (1985) 16 IIC No 5, 525, 538.

[141] The patent system encourages companies to organize the innovative activities of their workers
and to establish systems for identifying and recording new innovations.

[142] Scherer found in his study that the innovative activities of AT&T and IBM after they were forced
by the government in the early 1960s to grant compulsory licences were in relative terms lower than
before they had to grant such licences. Scherer, n 143 above, 207; W Nordhaus (1969), 86–90; P S
Menell, 'The Challenges of Reforming Intellectual Property Protection for Computer Software'
(1994) 94 Columbia Law Review, 2644, 2645 (suggesting that the economic models are often based
on overly simplified models of only one innovation or work).

adopted the argument with the support of the US government.[143] Since the 1980s, there has been considerable evidence of the increasing influence of the 'property' theory. The US government and US Congress have taken strong initiatives to support this development primarily in the WTO,[144] WIPO[145] and in bilateral negotiations. In US domestic markets, the protection of a rights holder has been made stronger in response to concerns over declining research and development and increasing international competition.[146] Since the early 1980s, principles affecting the validity and scope of intellectual property rights have been modified to make the enforceability of intellectual property rights easier.[147]

The underlying idea of this development is two-fold. Firstly, if information is a central success factor, it should obviously be asked whether information should be privately owned in order for it to be effectively created, managed and used. In this respect, the ideas of John Locke emphasizing the natural right of every individual to the fruits of his labour have provided basic justification.[148]

---

[143] See L C Thurow, 'Needed: A New System of Intellectual Property Rights' (1997) Harvard Business Review, 95, 96: 'Raw materials can be bought and moved, . . . Capital is a commodity that can be borrowed . . . Unique pieces of equipment that cannot be obtained by—or are too expensive for—one's competitors simply don't exist . . . If their (knowledge-based industries) intellectual property can be copied easily, they will not be able to generate either wealth to their owners or high wages for their employees.'

[144] The US was a driving force in WTO/TRIPS negotiations. Especially Art 13 effectively limits the adjustment of copyright laws to new economic or technological circumstances. Art 13 provides that 'members shall confine limitations or exceptions to exclusive rights to certain special cases which do not conflict with a normal exploitation of the work and do not unreasonably prejudice the legitimate interests of the rights holder'. See, however, also Art 8 that allows intervention where there has been abuse of intellectual property rights. For commentary on Art 8, see Andreas Heinemann, 'Anti-trust Laws of Intellectual Property in the TRIPs Agreement of the World Trade Organisation', in *From GATT to TRIPs* (Beier and Schricker eds) (1996) IIC Studies Vol 18, 241 (suggesting that 'abuse' does not necessarily require dominant position); P Samuelson, 'Challenges for the World Intellectual Property Organisation and the Trade-related Aspects of Intellectual Property Rights Council in Regulating Intellectual Property Rights in the Information Age' [1999] EIPR 578, 591 (expressing concerns that 'the true mission of TRIPS is not to raise levels of intellectual property protection to ever higher and higher planes, . . . but to encourage countries to adopt intellectual property policies that promote their national interests in the way that will promote free trade and sustainable innovation').

[145] See P Samuelson, 'The US Digital Agenda at WIPO' (1997) 37 Virginia Journal of International Law, 369, 380.

[146] R P Merges, 'Commercial Success and Patent Standards: Economic Perspectives on Innovation' (1988) 76 California Law Review, 805, 805–806.

[147] These measures include the creation of the Court of Appeals of Federal Circuit, see M J Adelman, 'The New World of Patents Created by the Courts of Appeals for the Federal Circuit' (1987) 20 University of Michigan J L, 979; the adoption of a presumption of validity for patents and a number of decisions by the US Supreme Court, such as redefinition of Doctrine of Equivalence for patents by the US Supreme Court in *Warner Jenkinson Co v Hilton Davis Chemical Co*, 520 US 17 (1997) (redefining doctrine of equivalence); *Ruckelhaus v Monsanto*, 467 US 986 (1984) (research data submitted to a federal agency could be considered 'property'); *Carpenter v United States*, 108 S Ct 316 (1987) (reporter's knowledge of publication schedule of his newspaper considered as property which can be misappropriated if it is used to buy securities for one's own gain); see, however, *Festo Corp v Shoketsu Kogyo*, 187 F 3d 1381 (Fed Cir 2000) (limiting the doctrine of equivalents by holding that an amendment to a disputed element is a bar to the application of the doctrine).

[148] The US Supreme Court in *International News Services v Associated Press* when accepting the

Secondly, from the point of view of post-industrial societies such as North America or Western Europe, the access to the best land, the richest natural resources or the cheapest labour are not likely to be their primary competitive edges in global competition. Therefore, it is logical to establish property rights for information which these societies have a strong tradition of creating and disseminating.[149]

The categorization of intellectual property as property is a traditional formal **2.90** approach. As such it has long been recognized that intellectual property laws grant the author or the inventor a limited property right to exclude others. The new trend is to use theories established in the field of other property rights to support interpretation of intellectual property rights. Furthermore, the property theory is increasingly advocated so as to limit the powers of lawmakers to come up with new limitations on intellectual property laws. Since private property is in many countries protected from government intervention, the same theory is applied in increasing frequency to intellectual property rights.

Conclusions made from categorization

The categorization of intellectual property rights as property is used to support **2.91** several different conclusions and interpretations. The most balanced conclusion is that any economic activity related to intellectual property rights should be judged by the same principles found in intellectual property and other cases.[150] Policy involving licensing should not be distinguished from policy involving leasing of any other asset. According to this conclusion, neither intellectual property laws nor anti-trust laws should be held as supreme since there is no need to emphasize the supremacy of either. Apart from this pragmatic view, property theory is increasingly used to support a number of arguments.

In the copyright field, the famous *Six Ideals of Copyright Law* by Chaffee have **2.92** gained international significance.[151] The problem with these ideals is that they do not discuss the external effects of copyright. The *Ideals*, first published in 1945, established the grounds for 'strong' copyright protection:

---

misappropriation claim of Associated Press stating that INS should not be allowed to copy news from the US East Coast newspapers and publish in the West Coast. See *International News Services, Inc v Associated Press*, 248 US 215, 235 (1918).

[149] Merges and Reynolds, n 127 above, 45 (property is increasingly likely to be intellectual property).

[150] Areeda-Elhauge-Hovenkamp, n 28 above, § 1780b3; *Mallinckrodt, Inc v Medipart, Inc*, 976 F 2d 700, 708 (Fed Cir 1992) ('patent owners should not be in a worse position, by virtue of patent right to exclude, than owners of the property used in trade').

[151] Z Chafee, 'Patent Pools and the Anti-trust Dilemma' (1999) 16 Yale Journal on Regulation, 359, 504–515. The author himself emphasized that the scope of protection should depend on the benefits and burdens caused by such private ownership. Id at 510. The arguments are frequently used without this general notion.

(1) Complete coverage: the protection should cover any creation.
(2) A single monopoly: the protection should cover all channels through which the work is marketed.
(3) Protection should be international: authors should benefit from the same protection globally.
(4) Protection should not go beyond the purpose of protection: the purpose is to reward authors and their families.
(5) The protection of the copyright owner should not stifle independent creation by others: authors should still have control over distribution channels for their works.
(6) The legal rules should be convenient to handle.

2.93 The first popular conclusion, based on the categorization of intellectual property rights as property rights, is the need to define the manner in which property rights can be acquired. In this respect 'property' theory is used to support the expansion of protected subject matter: property rights are acquired whenever someone creates something.[152] The existence of such rights is generally presumed. If property rights do not readily exist, there is a presumption that the creator has a 'natural' right to have such right established. The basic idea is that if the public has free access to inventions and works, this free access does not encourage inventors and authors to allocate resources to such activities. Property rights also form a sound basis for the dealings of inventors and authors with others.[153]

The issue may have practical implications in various disputes. It may be helpful when deciding whether *sui generis* protection should be provided for databases, whether interface information should be categorized as property, whether the owner of a technically necessary patent can maximize its royalty revenue, whether technical intermediary copies of a work are within the exclusive rights of the author or whether the copyright holder should be compensated for private copying or fair use of works.

In the US, the issue already was being discussed in *International News Services v Associated Press*,[154] and again more recently in *Lotus v Borland*[155] and *Feist v Rural*.[156] Consequently, the issue remained unsolved. In Europe the European Union seems to have at least initially adopted this element of the property theory in the Copyright Directive.[157]

---

[152] Chafee, n 158 above, 504.
[153] H Demsetz, 'Towards a Theory of Property Rights' (1967) 57 American Economic Review, 347 (the property right conveys the right to harm others).   [154] 248 US 215 (1918).
[155] In *Lotus v Borland*, the US Supreme Court affirmed by a 4–4 decision the previous decision of the Appeals Court in regard to the issue whether information arranged in the form of pull-down menu interfaces in a computer program should be categorized as property. *Lotus Dev Corp v Borland Int'l, Inc*, 49 F 3d 807 (1st Cir 1995), aff'd 116 S Ct 1062 (1996) (denying protection for methods of operation). See also Aoki, n 142 above, 1317–1318.
[156] In *Feist v Rural*, the US Supreme Court rejected the copyright protection for alphabetically arranged *White Pages* of a telephone directory. *Feist Publications, Inc v Rural Telephone Serv Co*, 499 US 340 (1991).
[157] Directive 2001/29/EC of the European Union and of the Council of 22 May 2001 on the harmonization of certain aspects of copyright and related rights in the information society, Art 2 (exclusive

The second popular conclusion is the need to define whether there is any kind of   **2.94**
restriction limiting the use of the property. There is increasingly a presumption
that the rights holders may use their own intellectual property without restrictions
and any use restrictions must be based on well-defined principles.[158] Part of
'property' theory is that the rights, duties and privileges accompanying the property are absolute and universal. Therefore, if this absolute right is limited, the
author or inventor should be duly compensated.[159] The supporters of this principle usually rely on the takings laws. In the US it is popular to refer to some fairly
recent Supreme Court cases involving real property, such as *Loretto*.[160] The
proponents may also rely on the distinction between static and dynamic efficiencies. Some static short-term inefficiencies may not be harmful as compared to the
dynamic long-term benefits of increased innovation or creativity.

The third popular conclusion is that if inventions and works cause anyone else   **2.95**
than the rights holder to gain benefits from such usage, the rights holder should
be compensated for such benefits.[161] This conclusion is based on the idea that any

---

reproduction right covers all temporary or permanent copies by any means and in any form). See also
F K Beier, 'Exclusive Rights, Statutory Licenses and Compulsory Licenses in Patent and Utility Mode
Law' (1999) 30 IIC, 251, 255 (reward concept is the guiding principle of exploitation of all intellec-
tual property rights).

[158] In 1912, the US Supreme Court implied that the patentee could undertake virtually any form of
licensing arrangement that tended to maximize the value of its patent. *Henry v A B Dick Co*, 224 US
1, 25 (1912). Overruled by *Motion Picture Patents* in 1917; see also R V Ayyar, 'Vaidyanatha: Interest
or Right? The Process and Politics of a Diplomatic Conference on Copyright' (1998) 1 Journal of
World Intellectual Property, 3, 1 (discussing the issue whether rights holders are one of the interest
groups in a society or are they a privileged group with absolute rights); G Karnell, 'Vidarespridning
av utgivna verksexamplar, särskilt om vidareförsäljning, uthyrning och utlåning av videogram: Skall
vi leva med nordisk rättsolikhet?' (1984) NIR 265 (reprinted in *Karnell om Upphovsrätt*, (Stockholm,
1990), 221–222 (the primary issue is whether the rights holder should have control over all uses of
work unless an important public interest otherwise dictates); *United States v Microsoft*, 253 F 3d 34,
62–63 (D C Cir 2001) (Microsoft arguing that its licence restrictions are legally justified because it is
just exercising its rights as the holder of valid copyrights).

[159] This was advocated by some commentators as a condition for providing compulsory access to
Windows operating system as an anti-trust remedy against Microsoft. See A B Lipsky and G J Sidak,
'Essential Facilities' (1999) 51 Stanford Law Review, 1247.

[160] *Loretto v Teleprompter Manhattan CATV Corp*, 458 US 419 (1982). *Loretto* involved the right
of the landowner to obtain compensation when cable television cables were installed on his property.
The US Supreme Court held that the property owner has the right to fair compensation even when the
action 'has only minimal economic impact on the owner'. The critics of the same idea usually refer
to *Ruckelshaus*, in which the US Supreme Court held that the government agency had the authority
to disclose private research data provided that the rights holder could reasonably expect the information to be disclosed. See *Ruckelhaus v Monsanto*, 467 US 986 (1984).

[161] Chafee, n 158 above, 512; J Ginsburg, 'Copyright and Intermediate Users' Rights', in *Festskrift
till Gunnar Karnell* (Stockholm, 1999), 227; S M Besen and L J Raskind, 'An Introduction to the Law
and Economics of Intellectual Property' (1991) 5 Journal of Economic Perspectives, 1, 3; Beier, n 164
above, 255–256 (suggesting this to be the 'guiding principle of intellectual property rights'); G Davies
and M E Hung, *Music and Video Private Copying* (Sweet & Maxwell, 1993), 11–15 (identifying
private or fair copying as an 'abuse' of author's right); OPM 1995:13, 15 (the opportunity for the end-
user to make more efficient use of her copy of a work tends to put pressure on increasing the compensation of the rights holder).

use of works or inventions which create benefits is royalty-free only as a consequence of a market failure. When property rights are extended to cover such an activity, the activity is 'internalized'. It is now up to the rights owner and the addressee to agree between themselves the commercial terms for such activity.[162]

2.96 This conclusion has traditionally been applied to imitation. Imitation is a side effect created by anyone making its work or invention public. By giving authors and inventors property rights, imitation became an issue between an imitator and the rights holder. The increasing trend is to extend the same principle to activities other than imitation and to those other than competitors.

2.97 A typical example of this new trend is in a radio station that saves costs if the music played during a particular show is pre-recorded in a manner that allows it to be played during the show without anyone changing disks. This practice as such does not cause the record companies to lose any revenue since the radio station is still acquiring copies of the original recordings. However, according to the property theory the rights holder should be separately compensated for such activity because it has a positive impact on the radio station's net revenue through cost savings.[163]

2.98 Consequently, under the 'property' theory, the owner of the property should have the right (1) to decide who may benefit from someone's use of the work or invention, and (2) to require compensation from anyone gaining such benefit.[164]

2.99 The application of this theory has created and will create new opportunities to obtain leverage positions. It is also likely to create the need for companies to control and oppose other companies that try to leverage their intellectual property rights. There are strong indications that this is already happening.[165]

---

[162] Demsetz, n 160 above, 350 (new private and state-owned property rights are a response to changes in technology); see also P A Samuelson and W Nordhaus, *Economics* (12th edn, New York 1985), 540 (referring to studies indicating that the benefit to innovators is three times the amount the reward collected by the inventor); G Davies, *Copyright and the Public Interest*, IIC Studies Vol 14 (Munich 1994) 167 (suggesting that time-shifting and similar other technical possibilities enhancing the end-user's opportunities to make effective private use of her copy are not within normal exploitation of works and should be separately compensated).

[163] See *Ministère Public v Tournier* [1991] 4 CMLR 248 ('SACEM') ('mechanical reproduction' rights held justified in Europe). Another similar approach is the right of the rights holder to be compensated for private (or fair) copying by end-users. The underlying ratio is that the private copying even for time-shifting purposes causes positive externalities to end-users.

[164] See L C Thurow, 'Needed: A New System of Intellectual Property Rights' (1997) Harvard Business Review, 95, 103 (suggesting that discrimination between wealthy nations and developing countries should be allowed); W Nordemann, 'A Right to Control or Merely to Payment?—Towards a Logical Copyright System' (1980) 11 IIC, 49 (explaining the basic approach of the German copyright laws not to allow any limitations of right merely because of the economic interests of the users); W C Holmes, *Intellectual Property and Anti-trust Law* (West Group, 2000) 1–4 (the patentee as the owner of the property has the fundamental right to choose how he will exploit it); Chafee, n 158 above, 505 (the author should control all channels through which his works reach the market).

[165] In certain respects, Europe has been more receptive to all elements of the theory treating intellectual property as property than the US. This may be because of the tradition of powerful and active

A fourth conclusion based on this categorization relates to the pre-emption **2.100** between contract rights and intellectual property laws. If intellectual property rights are property, the proponents argue, the owner should be able freely to control such property through the use of private agreements. The practical consequence would be the power of the rights holder to leverage terms and conditions for its licensees that go beyond the provisions of substantive laws.[166]

The rights holder would be allowed to authorize that, for example, the royalty payments be requested for sales even in countries in which the rights holder does not hold any enforceable intellectual property rights or after exclusive rights have expired. The rights holder would also be entitled to authorize that the licensee may not reverse-engineer even in those cases in which the copyright laws would allow the licensee to do so or the rights holder may protect otherwise unprotectable information by using non-negotiable contracts.[167]

Importance of private transactions

Property theory has similarities to the competitive superiority test introduced by **2.101** Bowman in 1973. The 'competitive superiority' application of the 'property' theory is also usually referred to as a theory supported by the proponents of the Chicago School of anti-trust theory.[168] The 'competitive superiority' theory has also gained support outside the US. This theory assumes that a rights holder should be allowed to engage in a restrictive practice if the reward gained from such practice is equal to or less than the invention's or work's competitive superiority over substitutes.[169]

If a buyer or a licensee is willing to accept a restriction proposed by a rights **2.102** holder, this is, according to this theory, objective evidence of the acceptability of the practice. The theory does not in general accept any leverage, exclusion or foreclosure arguments to be relevant for anti-trust or competition law analysis.[170] However, some similar consequences may be drawn from the formal limitation

---

user and consumer groups in the US. The European tradition of consumer protection has primarily been arranged through special authorities or semi-public organizations that have decided not to get involved with the discussion involving intellectual property rights.

[166] *ProCD, Inc v Zeidenberg*, 86 F 3d 1447 (7th Cir 1996) (the enforcement of shrink-wrap licences was not pre-empted by Copyright Act). See, however, Lemley 1999, 111 (application of UCC § 2b is limited by federal pre-emption, misuse and even other doctrines of public policy).

[167] See D Nimmer *et al*, 'The Metamorphosis of Contract into Expand' (1999) 87 California Law Review, 19, 76 for concerns in respect of the role of copyright laws solely in maximizing the economic return of the author and not as a balance between the rights of the user and the author; T J Brennan, 'Copyright, Property, and the Right to Deny' (1993) 68 Chicago-Kent Law Review, 675, 680 (questioning whether copyright protection goes too far). See also L Torvalds and D Diamond, *Just for Fun—Menestystarina* (Keuruu 2001), 115 (primary value of copyright for open-source projects, such as Linux, is that through copyright protection one can enforce licence terms that require royalty-free grant-back licences for any changes made to the open code).

[168] Bowman, n 61 above, R H Bork, '*The Anti-trust Paradox* (Chicago 1978 (rev edn) 1993)).

[169] Kaplow, n 12 above, 1849.   [170] Bowman, n 61 above, 54–61.

of the rights holder's conduct on the scope of the legal monopoly. Horizontal cartels are also condemned by this theory.

2.103   The 'competitive superiority' theory has been criticized because it focuses solely on the reward of the creator or the inventor. It does not take into account the potential cost or harm caused by such reward.[171] The only limitation is the level of harm the market could bear. This is generally considered an inadequate limitation. A further criticism is that competitive superiority does not have any independent meaning under this theory since competitive superiority is defined by the willingness of the market to accept such limitations. The 'competitive superiority' theory is easily demonstrated by the example at the end of the previous chapter, the obligation to pay royalties in countries where there is no valid patent and there are contractual restrictions limiting reverse engineering that go beyond the statutory limitations. The competitive superiority test seems to suggest that policy-makers should not intervene in the practices individual companies use to leverage their intellectual property portfolios.

2.104   A system based entirely on private transactions also contains the defect that it only accounts for the interests of the individual parties. Private interests do not necessarily lead to the most efficient allocation of resources from society's point of view.[172]

Evaluation

2.105   The categorization of intellectual property rights as property and the tendency to make conclusions as to the consequences of such categorization is clearly a formal approach. It can be criticized as not being able to provide practical solutions for issues that require balancing of competing interests. It has also been criticized as being too simplistic in its approach: the idea of absolute property rights was abandoned in several Western countries in the mid-twentieth century.[173]

2.106   Such a formal approach cannot provide satisfactory analytical answers except in very simple factual circumstances. Therefore, the mere categorization as property does not provide answers to questions involving externalities and leveraging of intellectual property rights. The main deficiency of this 'property' theory is that by 'internalizing' potentially marginal externalities, one may create several new externalities. Therefore, at its best the 'property' theory provides answers to rather simple issues such as the problems of imitation, and is unable to provide rational explanations for the problem of conflicting interests and rights.

---

[171] Kaplow, n 12 above, 1851.   [172] Domeij, n 99 above, 34.

[173] Aoki, n 142 above, 1320; Lessig, n 93 above, 131 (there is no property that does not have to yield at some point to the interests of the state); R H Posner, *Economic Analysis of Law* (New York 1998), 55 (recognizing this in respect of all kinds of property). Further, the references to some early philosophers may be misleading since the concept of property as a bundle of rights rather than as a physical thing is the product of the twentieth century.

Further, there is one main difference between intellectual property rights and **2.107**
other types of property. Property may typically be possessed and used by one
party at any given time.[174] Therefore, if anyone has access to tangible property,[175]
the property is likely to be overused. Consequently, the most efficient way of
making use of the property may be to allow a single private party to decide upon
such use. However, intellectual property rights are not subject to the same limitations. Several parties may effectively use the same intellectual property at the
same time. Therefore, the effective use of intellectual property does not require
the use by only a single party at a time. There is no real risk of overuse.[176]

The same argument has also been used to support the demands of stronger intel- **2.108**
lectual property rights.[177] Since the 'trespassing' of these rights is not as readily
detectable, activities to detect and stop any infringement should be more effective
and justify more anti-trust immunity. This is claimed to be necessary in order to
enhance the incentives to allocate resources to inventive and creative activities.

The 'property' theory may also be used to support the argument that any gains **2.109**
from the external effects should belong to the parties investing 'their labour' to
gain such benefits. That would mean that between the network or system and its
component parts, the system manufacturer or the network operator should be
allowed to benefit from the increased value of the network rather than the individual component supplier.[178] Any component technologies should not be
rewarded based on the value added by the network. As to the interaction between
the user and the supplier, this conclusion is no clearer. If accepted, this argument
would effectively limit the rights holder's right to maximize its revenue at the
cost of the party investing in the creation of such network benefits. However, the
practical implementation of this argument is not clear.

Even critics of the 'property' theory usually recognize that intellectual prop- **2.110**
erty rights promote creativity.[179] However, their main argument is that there
must be proper limitations to the use of such rights in order to maintain the
balance between the free flow of ideas and rewards to the authors and

---

[174] See Cornish, n 72 above, 35–36 (noting two competing views).
[175] See for discussion in respect of 'Tragedy of Common Property', M A Heller, 'The Tragedy of
the Anti-commons: Property in the Transition from Marx to Markets' (1998) 111 Harvard Law
Review, 621, 624.
[176] See eg J P Barlow, 'The Next Economy of Ideas', Wired Magazine (October 2000), 240, 241
(free access does not decrease commercial value of copyrighted works, it may even increase such
value).
[177] Tom–Newberg, n 12 above, 173 n 34.
[178] See W J Gordon, 'A Property Right in Self-Expression: Equality and Individualism in the
Natural Law of Intellectual Property' (1993) 102 Yale Law Journal, 1533, 1606–1608 (supporting
traditional privileges of the general public).
[179] See eg D G Baird, 'Common Law Intellectual Property and the Legacy of *International News
Service v Associated Press*' (1983) 50 University of Chicago Law Review, 411, 413. The fact that land
and intellectual property are not fully analogous does not mean that such analogy should not apply at
all.

inventors.[180] Furthermore, the term property is generally used in laws as a flexible description of the 'bundle' of rights the rights holder has. This bundle may be thicker or thinner but it does not have to be of any particular thickness in order to gain the status of property.[181]

Cost-benefit theories

Introduction

2.111   As the previous theories failed to define the appropriate strength of 'strong' intellectual property protection, economists have provided economic theories targeted to provide that answer. Under these theories, it is asked whether the benefit from allowing or condemning a particular practice would exceed the social costs caused by the same practice. Therefore, these theories are often characterized as *cost-benefit theories*.

The private value of the software to the developer is the difference between the revenues generated by the software and the costs incurred in its development and production. The social value should also take into account any additional costs or benefits which accrue to society but which are not captured or incurred by the producer. For example, production and use of the software might lead to various (such as environmental or network-related) costs or benefits which accrue to society but which are not taken into account by the firm. There is therefore a policy concern whether private and social costs and benefits differ.[182]

2.112   The common goal or benefit that should be achieved by the combination of intellectual property and anti-trust laws is relevance to the result of the analysis. The prevailing understanding is that the goal of both intellectual property laws and anti-trust or competition laws is to increase consumer satisfaction in an efficient manner.[183] In the prevailing theories, the most effective allocation of resources is the common goal of both regimes.

2.113   The conclusion that society should encourage the allocation of resources into innovation and creativity is rarely challenged. However, no definite conclusion has been drawn about the issue of at which stage of innovation or creativity should the resources be allocated: should the initial creativity be promoted, or the

---

[180] S D Anderman, *EC Competition Law and Intellectual Property Rights* (Oxford, 1998) 4 (interference of competition policy into incentive should be minimized).

[181] P Samuelson, 'Information as Property: Do Ruckelhaus and Carpenter Signal a Changing Direction in Intellectual Property Law' (1989) 38 Catholic University Law Review, 365, 370; compare to Koktvedgaard, n 104 above, 54–55 (concluding that by the end of the nineteenth century and before the influence of competition laws, intellectual property rights had emerged as rights independent from any concerns of competitors' rights).

[182] Machlup, n 3 above, 57–58.

[183] Bowman, n 61 above, 9; P E Areeda and H Hovenkamp, *Anti-trust Law. An Analysis of Anti-trust Principles and their Application* (1997, Vol 1, rev edn), 42; Bork, n 60 above, 110–112.

packaging of such information into products, or the dissemination of the products to the public, or the use of the products?[184] This is closely related to the other competing goals of anti-trust laws. The equitable distribution of wealth is one such goal.[185] In Europe another essential goal is the improvement of the common market.

Cost-benefit theories do not form any uniform framework. They do not rely on **2.114** any single method and they do not provide any precise analysing tools. In this book the following different cost-benefit theories are introduced and analysed:

(1) Ratio theory
(2) European proportionality test
(3) 'Life adjustment' theory
(4) 'Selection' theory
(5) 'Allocation effects' theory

Ratio theory

Traditionally, patent systems have been designed to encourage the dissemination **2.115** of inventions.[186] An alternative to the patent system would be no protection at all. However, the system with no protection would encourage inventors to keep any inventions shrouded in secrecy. The social cost of secrecy may be low or high depending on the nature of the invention.[187] Typically, such costs are presumed to be high for manufacturing processes the efficient exploitation of which requires production and therefore knowledge by a large number of companies.[188]

---

[184] Machlup, n 3 above, 74 (questioning whether it makes sense to allocate more resources to innovating enterprises at the cost of other outlets).

[185] R H Lande, 'Wealth Transfer as the Original and Primary Concern of the Anti-trust: The Efficiency Interpretation Challenged' (1982) 34 Hastings Law Journal, 67, 68 (arguing that the prevention of transfer of wealth from consumers to monopolists is the primary goal of anti-trust laws); Anderman, n 187 above, 19–21 (fairness is one of the goals of EC competition policy); P Virtanen, *Määräävän markkina-aseman kontrolloinh* (Jyväskylä, 2001), 199 (emphasizing long-term effects); W B Tye, 'Market Imperfections, Equity and Efficiency' (1992) 37 Anti-trust Bulletin, 1, 5 (arguing that practical business will not necessarily provide the most efficient result). 'Equity' means the consequences of the chosen policy for the distribution of costs and benefits (how the pie is divided). It contains standards such as 'just and reasonable' and the notion of 'fairness' associated with any responsibilities to satisfy commitments in a contractual, regulatory or legal relationship. See also P E Areeda and H Hovenkamp, *Antitrust Law. An Analysis of Antitrust Principles and Their Application* (1997) 114–16 (arguing that anti-trust and competition laws can only help to ensure the desired starting point but any redistribution of wealth is an inadequate goal). See also Bork, n 60 above, 110–112 (not accepting wealth distribution as a goal for anti-trust enforcement). The broadest unity exists in respect of wealth transfers that affect separate markets.

[186] Machlup, n 3 above, 32 (commenting that this has not been generally favoured by economists).

[187] Thurow, n 171 above, 98 (arguing that since 73% of private patents are based on knowledge generated by public sources, one needs to encourage publication in order to generate a base for the creation of next-generation knowledge).

[188] Bowman, n 61 above, 13 (arguing that dissemination of information is not the primary goal of patent systems).

2.116   In the modern interpretation, the dissemination of innovations and creative works is not necessarily seen as the primary goal of intellectual property systems. Rather, the encouragement of innovations and creative works is the goal of the system.[189] Dissemination is increasingly seen as a side effect of this system. There may also be other goals but their role in the analysis of such systems has been of decreasing importance.[190]

2.117   Consequently, this basic application of the cost-benefit theory identified here as 'ratio' theory proposes that any practice to leverage one's intellectual property rights should be approved if the ratio of benefit exceeds the ratio of costs, or alternatively, if the profit gained by the rights holder through such leverage is more than the harm caused.[191]

PROFIT OF	$>$	HARM
RIGHTS HOLDER		CAUSED

2.118   The simple reasoning behind this proposition is the following: it is in the interests of society to maximize any inventive or creative output but not if the social cost of such output exceeds its social value. The social costs are, under these theories, typically identified as losses imposed on consumers through higher prices and reduced output, as well as other costs of running the system.[192] Any practice

---

[189] Bowman, n 61 above, 13, emphasizing, though, the combined goal for anti-trust and intellectual property laws of promoting the effective use of scarce resources. See also Pitofsky, n 72 above (questioning whether this combined goal (and not just the maximization of reward) is taken into account in the case law).

[190] Such as equity, retaining consumers' choices, distribution of wealth, improving the function of the common market and continuing the growth of the economy. Bowman, n 61 above, 10–12 (questioning the primary necessity of these goals in this connection). See also *Data General v Grumman Systems Support*, 36 F 3d 1147, 1186–87 (1st Cir 1994); *In re Independent Service Organizations Anti-trust Litigation*, 203 F 3d 1322 (Fed Cir 2000).

[191] Kaplow, n 12 above, 1821–1822; Tom–Newberg, n 12 above, 211–212; Machlup, n 3 above, 42 (recognizing that many defenders of intellectual property systems emphasize only the positive effects without recognizing any social costs); S M Besen and L J Raskind, 'An Introduction to the Law and Economics of Intellectual Property,' (1991) 5 Journal of Economics Perspectives, 1, 3.

[192] See F M Scherer, *Industrial Market Structure and Economic Performance* (1980), 450–454 for discussion of typical social costs such as (1) monopoly pricing, (2) extensive patenting, (3) potential suppression of inventions, (4) blocking of useful improvements, (5) cross-licensing to fix prices, (6) potentiality of strategic and selective litigation, (7) possibility for powerful corporations to harass weak firms, (8) direct costs of the patent system (suggesting the system of utility models as a solution to avoid extensive social costs caused by insignificant patents); Machlup, n 3 above, 64 (listing costs of restrictions in the use of inventions or works, costs of transcendent restrictions upon production caused by the exclusivity and cost to potential other inventors); W M Landes and R A Posner, 'An Economic Analysis of Copyright Law' (1989) 18 Journal of Legal Studies, 325, 326 (identifying losses from limiting competitors' access and the cost of administering protection); W F Baxter, 'Legal

may have an effect on output and price. For example, the higher prices and lower output of particular goods are primary social costs under this theory. The underlying reasoning is that the use of intellectual property rights entitles the rights holder to derive monopoly profits but the loss to the society from such monopoly profits may not exceed the value of the property.

'Ratio' theory has gained universal popularity in the case law since the late 1970s, **2.119** although the same reasoning had already been used in some early commentary and case law.[193] It is increasingly used to support the argument that lawmakers have established a balance between benefits and costs by defining the copyright or patent term that is appropriate to reward the innovative or creative activity. Within the limits of this fixed term and the rights granted, the rights holder should be able to maximize his profits without any restrictions. The underlying principle is based on the idea that this would lead to the most efficient use of intellectual property rights and to the greatest social benefits to society.[194]

The weakness of this theory is that it does not provide any information about **2.120** what the specific threshold between the reward and the cost or harm should be.[195] The application of this theory suggests that any practice that brings more benefits than costs should be approved. Such application does not necessarily lead to a correct result, since it would be appropriate to optimize the protection on the level where the difference between profit and cost is the highest. However, the test is difficult to apply because different regimes of protection may lead to different goods being available to consumers.

The 'ratio' theory does not suggest which practices to authorize and which to **2.121** prohibit. The principles of equal and equitable treatment may require that a particular practice be prohibited if the harm to the rights holder from a particular intervention is lower than the cost to the society from allowing a certain practice. For example, according to this theory, it has been argued that a royalty rate is fair and reasonable if there are patent licensees who are willing to take a licence. In this application of the theory, the harm caused to competitors by the inability to utilize a patent may be seen as equal to the value of the patent or copyright. If the harm caused to competitors by the inability to utilize a patent is more than the royalty rate a patentee is asking, a sensible licensee would take a licence. At some point, the requested royalty rate may become excessive and cause costs to the society at large (consumers) in a form of reduced output. If the cost of reduced

Restrictions on Exploitation of the Patent Monopoly: An Economic Analysis' (1966) 76 Yale Law Journal, 267, 271 (listing (1) social value of alternative investment targets such as medical care and education, (2) administrative costs of system, (3) greater amount of discarded equipment and displaced labour caused by new innovation, and (4) monopoly losses); J W Schlicher, *Patent Law: Legal and Economic Principles* (1999) 2–33.

[193] *Standard Oil Co v United States*, 221 US 1, 58 (1911); *United States v Aluminium Co of America*, 148 F 2d 416, 428–429 (2d Cir 1945).

[194] Bowman, n 61 above, 64 (arguing this to be efficient both privately and socially).

[195] Kaplow, n 12 above, 127.

output is exceeding the additional revenue available to the patentee, there may be a public interest to intervene into the royalty rates requested by the patentee.

2.122   Furthermore, the theory does not suggest what is the right reward to be provided for the creator. It merely suggests that the reward should be high enough to encourage innovation and creativity, but there is no upper limit. As a consequence, when applied together with the property theory, there is not necessarily any upper limit even though the absolute cost for society may increase substantially. It could also be argued that it would make sense to limit the benefit gained from the intellectual property rights if the harm to the inventor or the creator is potentially less than the benefit to consumers. This argument has sometimes been raised in connection with issues involving compatibility of products.

2.123   Finally, the theory does not suggest any international implications. It does not suggest whether the harm should be for the global economy or for just the local economy. Furthermore, it does not suggest whether it makes any difference whether the profit is gained from another country.

European proportionality test

2.124   In Europe, the European Court of Justice has recognized a similar theory. The theory is normally identified as a *justification test* or *proportionality test*. The test was first introduced in *Deutsche Grammophon Gesellschaft*.[196] The ECJ held that the exercise of national rights provided by national copyright laws might violate anti-trust laws. The ECJ established that any restrictions on the freedom of trade must be justified by the protection of rights that form the specific subject matter of this property.[197] Consequently, the intervention of anti-trust laws is justified if the effects of the exercise of rights are not justified. The principle was continued in subsequent case law. However, the definition of 'specific subject matter' or the essential function of intellectual property rights has created constant problems and been subject to much criticism.[198]

2.125   A popular concept is to argue that the specific subject matter of copyright or patents is to provide rewards to inventors and authors. Therefore, the rights holder should be entitled to decide the form and amount of reward that is derived from the protection.[199] The criticism of this argument is that, while authors and

---

[196] *Deutsche Grammophon Gesellschaft mbH v Metro-SB-Grossmärkte GmbH & Co KG* [1971] CMLR 631. See also *HAG I* [1974] 2 CMLR 127; *Centrafarm v Sterling Drug* [1974] 2 CMLR 480; *Terrapin v Terranova* [1976] 2 CMLR 482; *Hoffman-La Roche v Centrafarm* [1979] 3 CMLR 217; *Musik-Vertried Membran GmbH and K-Tel International v Gema* [1981] 2 CMLR 44; *EMI Electrola GmbH v Patricia Im- und Export* [1989] 2 CMLR 413.
[197] *Deutsche Grammophon* [1971] CMLR 631, 657 [11].
[198] See I Govaere, *The Use and Abuse of Intellectual Property Rights in EC Law* (London, 1996), 76 (arguing in favour of the clear rule that national intellectual property laws are not *per se* exempt from competition laws).
[199] See Davies, n 73 above, 141; Chafee, n 158 above, 505.

inventors have justified interests to be rewarded, the reward as the 'subject matter of protection' undermines the fact that the interest of rewarding inventors and authors may compete with other important interests.

In Europe the interest of creating the common market has had high priority. Consequently, an argument that the form and amount of reward in Finland, Germany and the UK should in each country be at the discretion of the rights holder has been balanced with the interest of creating the common market and the free movement of goods. The European Court of Justice has rejected such argument in respect of intra-Community exercise of national intellectual property rights.[200]

The ECJ discussed the issue of specific subject matter in *Centrafarm v Sterling* **2.126** *Drug*.[201] The court held that the reward to the rights holder is the goal of such protection but that the law provides two means to achieve this goal. These means are the specific subject matter of the protection. Firstly, the law provides to the rights holder the exclusive right, in the case of patent laws, to manufacture industrial products. Secondly, the law provides the rights holder the right initially to distribute such product, either directly or by the grant of licences to third parties. The exclusive right means that the rights holders may oppose infringing activities in order to protect their rights.[202]

In *Terrapin v Terranova*,[203] the analysis was developed further. The court held **2.127** that the balance between the free movement of goods and the exclusive rights of a trade mark owner is in favour of the exclusive right of the trade mark owner if (1) there are no agreements restricting competition, (2) there are no legal or economic ties between the undertakings and (3) the respective legal rights of the

---

[200] In *HAG I* [1974] 2 CMLR 127, the ECJ compared two competing interests, the interests of free movement of goods and the interest of consumers to obtain information about the correct origin of the goods. The ECJ held that such information may be ensured by means other than those that would affect the free movement of goods. See also *Centrafarm v Winthrop* [1974] CMLR 480 (competing interests of free movement of goods and the exclusive right in case of controlled prices of pharmaceuticals in one member state solved in favour of free movement of goods). In addition to free movement of goods and competition, the same balance of justifications may also be made at least against consumer interests, effectiveness of fiscal supervision, the protection of public health and the fairness of commercial transactions. See *Rewe v Bundesmonopolverwaltung für Branntwein ('Cassis Dijon')* [1979] 3 CMLR 494; *GB-Inno-BM v Confédération du Commerce Luxembourgeois*, C-362/88. See also C-349/95 *Loendersloot v Ballantine* [1997] ECR I-6227 (combating counterfeits may provide justification against repackaging); see also O A Rognstad, *Spredning av verksexemplar* (Oslo 1999), 179–199 (identifying other balancing factors such as private interests, public interest of competition, need of clearly identifiable rights, integration of common markets, international trade and simplification of legal system).

[201] *Centrafarm v Sterling Drug* [1974] CMLR 480; see also *Merck & Co Inc v Stephar BV* [1981] 3 CMLR 463; *Generics v Smith, Kline & French Laboratories* C-316/95 [1997] ECR I-3929 (national rule to allow patentee to oppose production of samples justified).

[202] The court went further to compare the interest of the rights holder to protect the 'specific subject matter' of protection and the interest of free movement of goods and held that an obstacle to free movement of goods is justified if the products have not been manufactured or marketed with the consent of the rights holder.

[203] *Terrapin v Terranova* [1976] 2 CMLR 482.

two competing trade mark owners have arisen independently of each other. Consequently, the rights of trade mark owners to enforce their exclusive rights against imitators were given priority and such rights cannot be 'undermined'.[204]

2.128   In *Hoffman-La Roche v Centrafarm*,[205] the ECJ followed the reasoning established in *Centrafarm v Sterling Drug* and established a similar analysis in respect of trade marks.[206] The court went further in the analysis and held that the use of an exclusive right against the defendant would prevail in the balance against the free movement of goods only if such exercise was within the essential functions of the exclusive right. For trade marks, one such essential function was the identity of the origin. The identity of the origin means that the product has been manufactured by the rights owner or with her consent, and no one has, without the consent of the rights owner, interfered with the product itself.[207]

2.129   Finally, in *Coditel I*,[208] an essentially similar analysis was also used with respect to copyright. The court held that the right of a copyright owner and its assignees to require fees for any showing of movies is a part of the essential function of copyright in respect of such works. The court faced some problems in making the balance between the practice of assigning exclusive broadcasting rights in accordance with national geographic boundaries, and the interest of avoiding the partitioning of the European market. The court concluded that since television was largely organized on the basis of legal broadcasting monopolies, a method other than geographical application of broadcasting assignments would have been impracticable.[209]

---

[204] Similar analysis was used in *Keurkoop BV v Nancy Kean Gifts BV* [1983] 2 CMLR 47 (design protection), *CICRA and Maxicar v Renault* [1988] 4 CMLR 265; *EMI Electrola GmbH v Patricia Imund Export* [1989] 2 CMLR 413 (copyright protection in one member state had expired); *SA CNL-Sucal NV v HAG GF AG ('HAG II')* [1990] 3 CMLR 571. See in the US *Sony Corp v Universal City Studios, Inc*, 464 US 417, 429 (1984) ('the monopoly privileges that Congress may authorize are neither unlimited nor primarily designed to provide a special private benefit').

[205] *Hoffman-La Roche v Centrafarm* [1979] 3 CMLR 217.

[206] A trade mark owner has an exclusive right to put the product into circulation for the first time and therefore protect itself against competitors wishing to take advantage of the status and reputation of the trade mark by selling products illegally bearing that trade mark.

[207] The court went further to allow repackaging of pharmaceuticals by a parallel importer on specified conditions. See also *Centrafarm BV v American Home Products Corp* [1979] 1 CMLR 326 (a product marketed under one name may not be relabelled by another name); *Pfizer v Eurim Pharm GmbH* [1982] 1 CMLR 406 (repackaging of original pharmaceuticals).

[208] *Coditel v Ciné Vog Films* [1981] 2 CMLR 362 ('*Coditel I*'). Coditel had obtained a signal from a German broadcaster and resent it to its cable customers in Belgium. Ciné Vog had acquired exclusive distribution rights for Belgium and this practice harmed its opportunities to make use of the exclusive right. Coditel relied on the argument that since the signal was available from Germany, it could use it freely in Belgium.

[209] The German broadcaster obviously did not have any commercial interest in having its broadcastings seen also in Belgium since (1) its licence was limited to Germany, and (2) as a national broadcaster, it did not rely on advertising revenue which would have been affected by the number of people watching the movie. See also *Warner Bros Inc v Christiansen* [1990] 3 CMLR 684 (holding that the national right to prevent hiring of video cassettes was justified).

In *Coditel II*,[210] the issue was further analysed under Article 85 of the EC **2.130** Treaty.[211] The court held that it is for the national courts to establish whether or not the exercise of the exclusive right to exhibit cinematographic films is justified under Article 85. The court established three criteria to be used in the balancing test: (1) Does the exercise create barriers which are artificial and unjustifiable in terms of the needs of the cinematographic industry? (2) Does the practice create the possibility of charging fees which exceed a fair return on investment? (3) Does the practice have an exclusive duration which is disproportionate to those requirements? These criteria should be balanced with the issue whether, from a general point of view, such exercise is such as to prevent, restrict or distort competition within the common market.

In *Dior v Evora*,[212] the proportionality test was extended to new applications that **2.131** possibly indicate the dawning of an entirely new era in the court's practice. The principal issue was the exhaustion of trade mark rights and the right of the trade mark owner to prevent importation and resale of goods in another member state.[213] As a side issue, the court also made a decision involving the possibilities of the rights holder to rely on copyright to control the marketing activities of a parallel importer.

The European Court of Justice held that copyright may make it possible for a **2.132** rights holder to control the marketing practices of third parties even in cases where such a third party is lawfully selling products. In such cases, the interest of the copyright owner in remuneration from the commercial exploitation of copyright must be balanced with the interest in allowing the reseller to sell the products in the normal course of business. In this particular case, the rights holder was relying on its copyright on the bottles of perfumes and on their packaging. The court concluded that a holder of copyright was not entitled to oppose the habitual use of the copyright by the reseller for the purpose of bringing to the public's attention the further commercialization of goods first fielded with the consent of the rights holder.

It has been suggested that *Dior v Evora* established a new limitation to copyright, **2.133** the 'presentation right'.[214] The decision was not likely to establish any general limitations on the protection of products through more than one intellectual property right or to suggest that the reproduction right of the rights holder would be

---

[210] *Coditel v Ciné Vog Films* [1983] 1 CMLR 49 ('*Coditel II*').

[211] Art 81 of the Treaty of the European Union.

[212] *Parfums Christian Dior SA v Evora BV*, C-337/95 [1997] ECR I-6013.

[213] The court held, in accordance with the already established practice, that the trade mark may not be relied on to oppose such practice, even if the goods were not exactly of the same quality as the goods sold in that member state. See J Schovsbo, 'Markedsforing af Parallelimporterede Markevarer' (1998) UFR, 16; R Sack, 'Der Markenrechtliche Erschöpfungsgrundsatz in deutschen und eurōpaischen Recht' (1998) Wettbewerb und Recht und Praxis, 549, 575.

[214] Kur, n 73 above, 314–318 (suggesting that the limitation be 'internalized' into copyright laws).

exhausted upon the first lawful reproduction. Rather, the case established that sometimes a balancing between the limitations of different rights is appropriate.[215]

2.134   Based on the above, this book suggests that if the concept of 'specific subject matter' is used, such subject matter should be identified as 'protection against imitations'.[216] The reward as such is only an indirect consequence of the protection against imitations. Also, the imitations are the 'evils' that justify limited exclusive rights.[217] Consequently, a particular practice should only be *'per se'* justified to the extent it is primarily directed to stop imitations and also has such an effect. The exercise of an exclusive right that has harmful effects seems, at least in Europe, to be rebuttable especially if it is not directed to object to imitations but rather to maximize the reward of the rights holder.

2.135   This would be consistent with most other property rights. Any property rights have a primary effect that they create a market for such property.[218] However, the market defines the reward the owner of the property right derives. One of the primary goals of the competition and anti-trust laws is to intervene in the practices used to collect the reward and to ensure that the market for the property is functioning effectively.[219]

2.136   Some commentators have been critical of the proportionality test as used by the European Court of Justice. The primary point of criticism can be summarized by the notion that the balancing test between intellectual property rights and the free movement of goods does not need to be the same as that between intellectual property rights and the competition laws, especially Articles 81 and 82.[220]

2.137   It may be argued that even if it were possible to accept the argument that the social benefits from innovative and creative activities exceed the private benefits derived by authors and inventors, this does not justify a general exception in

---

[215] Kur, n 73 above, 313. See also in the US, *M Witmark & Sons v Jensen*, 80 F Supp 843 (D Minn 1948) (the performing rights' society's claim of royalties from movie theatres showing movies for which a copyright licence was already paid constituted copyright misuse).

[216] Cornish, n 72 above, 359–360 (extending the reward right beyond the initial marketing has the threat of bringing the eighteenth-century 'Battle of the Books' back); O-A Rognstad, *Spredning av verksexemplar* (Oslo 1999), 169 (discussing reward/imitation issue). See, however, *Warner Bros Inc v Christiansen* [1990] 3 CMLR 684 (discussing the need to reward movie producers as a justification for a separate rental right for videos). If understood as a separate market of video cassettes in which the effects of such rights are limited, even this case is in line with this approach.

[217] See Levin, *Formskydd* (1984) 63–64 (effects of imitation on Scandinavian design industry); ibid, 438 (the need to protect against imitations is the primary justification for stronger and more effective protection); Lehmann, n 127 above, 534; R Oesch, *Oikeus valokuvaan* (Jyväskylä, 1993), 4; in Sweden Reg.prop. 1981/82: 165, 187; Bruun, *The Role of Patent System in the Protection of Intellectual Property* (1992), 32–33 (rejecting the view that the reward for the inventor would be the leading principle of patent laws).

[218] W P Heller and D A Starret, 'On the Nature of Externalities' in *Theory and Measurement of Economic Externalities* (Steven, eds) (London, 1976), 9.

[219] Rissanen, n 66 above, 254; Anderman, n 40 above, 3–4.

[220] Govaere, n 205 above, 103.

allowing the rights holders to maximize their reward. It is for example similarly likely that the social benefits created by teachers, doctors and even real estate developers exceed the private benefits these groups derive. It may therefore be desirable that the production of their services be supplied in higher quantities and they be paid more in order to encourage further production. However, laws are not amended to allow them to derive their reward from markets other than the one in which they are immediately active.[221]

Consequently, other commentators have suggested that the 'specific subject **2.138** matter' should not provide 'an intervention-free zone' for intellectual property rights. Rather, the concept provides the control-point against which anti-trust treatment should be balanced.[222] These views are consistent with the above conclusion by this book's author.

Life adjustment theory

Since it may be difficult or even impossible to determine the costs and benefits **2.139** of a particular practice, it may also be concluded that an adjustment be made within intellectual property rights to the term of protection. It is also possible to use the term of protection as a measuring stick for acceptable intervention into rights holders' practices. Because life adjustment theory stresses the need to avoid the intervention of anti-trust laws, this theory has many similarities with traditional theories which emphasize the supremacy of intellectual property laws.[223]

According to the life adjustment theory, the acceptable ratio between a rights **2.140** holder's reward and the monopoly loss or social cost of the society is set primarily by the term of the protection. It is presumed that legislators set the term of the protection to reflect the acceptable ratio between the rights holder's reward and the level of monopoly losses or other social costs of the society. Whenever one decides to allow a practice that is presently forbidden, one has to define whether such a decision would have a similar effect as the extension of the protection by one year. If the ratio between the rights holder's incremental reward and the monopoly loss from allowing the presently forbidden practice is higher than the ratio between the rights holder's incremental reward and the monopoly loss from

---

[221] Breyer, n 147 above, 256–257.

[222] Heinemann 4. Teil, C.5.e) (suggesting that this would extend the use of the same analysing tools to the entire field of law); Kolstad, n 73 above, 448 (if the balance cannot be derived through balancing factors inside the respective intellectual property rights, anti-trust laws may intervene).

[223] Kaplow, n 12 above, 1829; I Ayres and P Klemperer, 'Limiting Patentees' Market Power without Reducing Innovation Incentives: The Perverse Benefits of Uncertainty and Non-injunctive Remedies' (1999) 97 Michigan Law Review, 985, 988; M Koktvedgaard, *Larebog in Immaterialrett* (Copenhagen, 1999), 10 (limited term of protection is the most important balancing factor); M Koktvedgaard and M Levin, *Lärobok i immaterialrätt* (6th edn, Helsingborg 2000), 29–30; Lehmann, n 127 above, 535.

extending the term of the protection by one year, one should not allow the practice. This is because by setting the term of protection, legislators have presumably defined the acceptable ratio between the reward of the rights holder and the acceptable level of monopoly loss. Any additional reward that exceeds the established ratio should therefore be for the legislators to define. Under this theory, the adjustment of the term of the protection is preferred as the method of providing additional rewards to the rights holders. This theory has been applied to various circumstances. One decision has been to extend the patent life by five years for pharmaceutical inventions and the term of copyright protection to seventy years.

2.141   The life adjustment theory may also be used to limit the possibilities of anti-trust authorities and courts to forbid presently allowed practices. If the decision to forbid a presently allowed practice causes the ratio between rights holders' reduced reward and the corresponding reduced monopoly loss to be lower than for the reduction of the term of protection by one year, one should not forbid the practice.

2.142   One of the key presumptions of the life adjustment theory is that the original ratio between the reward and the monopoly loss represents the optimum set by legislators. Since the legislator has set the ratio, the ratio should only be amended within certain limits. This allows any rights holders to argue that if there were any additional restrictions for them to use intellectual property rights as a leverage to obtain business benefits, such additional or novel restrictions should somehow be compensated for otherwise no such restrictions should be implemented. Such arguments are frequently used to oppose the approval of parallel imports,[224] to support levies for consumer electronics equipment in countries where the copyright laws allow some kind of fair use or private copying and to oppose any kind of compulsory licensing of intellectual property rights.

2.143   It may be impossible to obtain the necessary information to make sophisticated ratio calculations. The lack of appropriate and accurate information can easily make this life adjustment theory a superficial argument that can be readily used in any kind of lobbying activity.

Kaplow used the following example in his influential article: from society's point of view it could make sense to allow discrimination in royalty rates since the monopoly loss may be offset by the more extensive output by the industry as a whole. This argument has been used as a popular lobbying argument by the pharmaceutical industry to support international price discrimination.

The argument has a few practical deficiencies. Firstly, there is seldom any evidence that the restrictive practice of not allowing international price discrimination would *de facto*

---

[224] Since the acceptance of parallel imports would, so it is argued, take away a substantial part of the reward of the pharmaceutical and media industry. See also *OECD Report*, 19 (suggesting that the evidence is incomplete for establishing whether output is reduced because discrimination is in many jurisdictions not allowed).

reduce output in developing countries. Secondly, any discrimination necessarily affects the allocation of resources in the related markets.[225] Thirdly, if the output is reduced (because of the inability to charge low prices and the threat of price erosion in developed countries), there are usually other less harmful practices for controlling any mass parallel export from low-cost countries to developed countries, eg allowing lower prices only for amounts appropriate for personal use.

A further deficiency or source of criticism has been the risk attached to time. Any **2.144** rights holder must make the judgment whether it makes sense to maximize the revenue in the short term or in the long term, in its own production or through licensing. There is always a risk factor attached to any choice the rights holder makes. Therefore, if the ratio theory is applied, one must still decide how to value the risk factor.[226] Should the rights holders also be rewarded if, because of some new limitations, they have to assume higher risks? Should the reward be more limited if the risk is less than it otherwise would have been?[227]

In spite of these open issues, life adjustment theory provides some guidance to **2.145** the decision-maker. It should be possible to leverage the holder's intellectual property right to gain commercial benefits if the profits do not exceed the harm caused. As a practical matter, it could be imagined that the harm caused by the refusal to license the patent whenever such patent is one of many technically necessary patents for a particular communications standard could outweigh any benefit gained by the patentee.

Selection theory

Even if it is not possible to derive any satisfactory balance between the costs and **2.146** benefits of a particular practice, it would still be possible to compare different practices and choose to prohibit such practices that have the lowest ratio and allow those practices that have the highest ratio. This would mean that of a number of practices that all have the same reward for the rights holder, society would approve those practices that lead to the least harm to society.[228]

---

[225] Internationally, this involves difficult issues on relative competitiveness of nations. If some key production factors are substantially lower or higher in particular countries that potentially affects the allocation of resources between different countries in a particular industry. For a single nation, it is normally in its interests to encourage the allocation of resources into that country.

[226] See Ayres–Klemperer, n 230 above, 1017 (suggesting that an increase of uncertainty in enforcement would substantially increase the social benefits without decreasing patentee's profits). See also ibid. at 1026 (suggesting that the patentee should be allowed to agree lower royalty rates against licence term going beyond the patent life). The obvious risk with this approach is that a patentee will use its market power to collect the same annual royalty and only the term will be longer.

[227] One could argue that in respect of any standards-related patents the reward should be less than normal since the implementation of a certain patented technology as a standard reduces the risk of the patentee to a minimum. Similarly, one could argue that the harm for society is easily increasing the value of a patent whenever a patent is included in the standard, and therefore the royalty rates should be modest.

[228] Kaplow, n 12 above, 1834.

2.147   The proponents of this 'selection' theory argue that there may be circumstances in which any cost of a practice is actually the price of the transfer of economic value from other entities to the rights holder. This may happen when there is no actual limitation of output as a consequence of the practice. In such circumstances, the practice should be allowed. This author agrees with this basic proposal. However, such circumstances are generally available only if the rights holders enforce their rights solely against direct imitators in the same relevant market in which the rights holders are active. If any other external effects are present, this proposition is not entirely justified.

2.148   Furthermore, this theory has been used to argue that it should be relevant to whom the reward accrues. It makes a difference whether the reward is accrued to the parties involved in the restrictive practice or to some other parties. Therefore, it may be possible to allow a restrictive practice if a large reward or benefit resulting from such a practice is accrued to parties other than the parties involved in the practice, eg parties other than the licensor or its licensees. It is further argued that if the licensee gained additional rewards in which the licensor was not participating, such licensee's rewards should not be taken into account.[229] The problem with this approach is that it also presumes a society without any built-in risk. A typical example used is that the approach assumes that a company makes a decision to invest in development work where it knows that by investing a certain amount of money it should be guaranteed a particular reward. Yet real life is not that simple and particularly in the communications industry the convergence of media, telecommunications and data-processing industries has made the market environment too unpredictable for this kind of presumption.

2.149   This 'selection' theory has almost the same strengths and weaknesses as the initial ratio theory. The theory is inadequate when responding to the complex issue of the network economy.

2.150   If Media Company A invests in creating a musical performance which, due to technical development, can then later be distributed by a data network, should such Media Company A be entitled to an additional reward from the following parties (in addition to anyone who first makes a copy available in such a network):

(1) telecommunications operators acting as mere intermediaries; or
(2) consumers who want to play a copy of it not only with the equipment that they had when they first acquired such copy, but also on any new equipment implementing various play-back technologies; or
(3) equipment manufacturers supplying new equipment to consumers; or
(4) Internet service providers that allow the downloading of the work from their websites.

---

[229] Kaplow, n 12 above, 1836.

'Selection' theory seems to suggest that the acceptability of the use of such lever-   **2.151**
age would depend on the following questions. Firstly, it would be relevant
whether the only effect of the decision to allow Media Company A an additional
reward would mean the transfer of compensation from telecommunications operators, equipment manufacturers, end-users or Internet service providers. Under
'selection' theory, the practice should be acceptable if this is the primary outcome
of such practices. Secondly, if this decision to allow Media Company A an additional reward would mean that telecommunications operators, consumers, equipment manufacturers or Internet service providers would start to implement
protective measures and reduce or delay their output of services or products, the
practice would not be permissible.

Under 'selection' theory, this is the core of the entire leverage issue: would the   **2.152**
telecommunications operators or equipment manufacturers really reduce access
to the networks and/or reduce their output? Similarly, would a restrictive practice
by rights holders really slow down technological development of new equipment? Alternatively, if there is a difficult copyright piracy problem and some of
the technology providers decide not to co-operate with the content owners in
order to minimize that problem, would that really reduce the incentive of such
content providers to invest in the creation of the content?

The issue for policy-makers is whether this makes any difference and whether   **2.153**
they should intervene. If the size of the potential future market is big enough,
there would be no real limitation of output and the only outcome would be that
some participants would get bigger rewards than others. Should that be a concern
to policy-makers?

'Selection' theory does not provide any answers to this dilemma. However, it   **2.154**
recognizes that the connection between a reward and the incentive is complicated.[230] As a starting point, the decision to invest is based on assumptions made
at the point when such investment is made. These assumptions, again, may not be
entirely relevant in the network economy.

This 'selection' test may also be used as a simple rule to choose the practice that   **2.155**
is the least restrictive. A rights holder should be entitled to extract monopoly
income by restricting utilization of its invention or creation, provided that it
confines the restriction as narrowly and specifically as the circumstances permit.
In particular, the benefits derived by the rights holder must be in relation to the
burden imposed on licensees.[231]

---

[230] Kaplow, n 12 above, 1838–1839. D F Turner, 'The Patent System and Competitive Policy'
(1969) 44 New York University Law Review, 450, 459 ('one can rarely, if ever, calculate with any
degree of precision the ultimate commercial value that will be gained').
[231] W F Baxter, 'Legal Restrictions on Exploitation of the Patent Monopoly: An Economic
Analysis' (1996) 76 Yale Law Journal, 267, 355.

Allocation effects theory

2.156   The 'allocation effects' theory introduced by Baxter is the only mainstream cost/benefit theory that expressly discusses the use of intellectual property rights in terms of the effects they produce in the economic behaviour of parties other than the rights holder.

2.157   The value of a particular practice to the rights holder may be different than its value to the parties that are affected by such a practice. This difference in respective values makes private bargaining the most effective method for the affected parties to adjust their respective positions. However, sometimes the value derived by the rights holders from their exclusive rights may cause harm to others. It may be that the most profitable practice in using intellectual property rights is profitable only because it is injurious to third parties.[232] Such effect may, according to this theory, constitute adequate reason for intervention or interference in a particular practice.

2.158   The impact of particular practices on resource allocation is a particular concern under this 'allocation effects' theory. In general, a rights holder should not be entitled to engage in practices that affect the allocation of resources to activities that are not covered by intellectual property rights. Similarly, as the effective allocation of limited resources to innovation and creation is one of the primary underlying policy concerns of intellectual property laws, the same allocation problem should be considered when discussing the practices the rights holder may use. The rights holder should not be entitled to use its exclusive right to interfere in the market mechanism of resource allocation. In its most extreme application, the allocation of resources to non-protected activities should be neutral from intellectual property protection.[233]

2.159   The Finnish case of royalty discrimination serves as a useful example. The Finnish music copyright collecting society Teosto ry grants copyright licences for the use of music in television and radio broadcasts. The licence fee for the use of copyrighted music was in an arbitral award in 1993 established at the level of €6 per minute for the national broadcaster Oy Yleisradio Ab and €16 per minute for the commercial television station MTV3. The local commercial television broadcaster MTV Oy filed a complaint with Kilpailuvirasto, the local anti-trust enforcement agency. Kilpailuvirasto initiated an enforcement action and the case was finally decided by the Finnish Supreme Administrative Court, KHO, in 1999.[234]

2.160   The complaint of MTV Oy and the enforcement action of Kilpailuvirasto were

---

[232] Baxter, n 238 above, 277–278.
[233] Baxter, n 238 above, 353 (suggesting that royalties should not be charged from the entire product for component technologies because that affects the allocation of resources into the non-protected development of end products).
[234] *Teosto/YLE/MTV*, KHO, 9 June 1999/1540.

based on the theory that Teosto ry abused its dominant position by discriminating between different broadcasters. The core of the complaint was the issue whether different licence fees may be applied for use of copyrighted music in radio and television broadcasts. Oy Yleisradio Ab also provides extensive radio broadcasts whereas MTV3 focuses on television broadcasting. The Supreme Administrative Court found no abuse. Teosto ry filed studies that indicated such differences in licence fees were consistent with practices in most European countries. The court held that the differences were justified because the licensing principles followed intellectual property rights policy, the respective share of radio and television broadcasts differed, the absolute amount paid by MTV3 in comparison with the number of viewers was fair, and that similar amounts were paid not only internationally but also in Scandinavia. Similar cases were initiated around Europe after the decision of the European Court of Justice in *SACEM*.[235]

The Supreme Administrative Court decision appears to have seen the matter **2.161** primarily from the viewpoint of a rights holder. In patent and copyright licence agreements there is a long tradition justifying different licence fees for different types of usage, and the decision did not introduce any new principles in this respect. The decision also established that issues such as technological differences, potential commercial value of the use and the potential number of listeners or viewers may have an impact on the analysis since they affect the definition of the relevant market. The decision did not discuss the potential effects the different licence fees may have caused on allocation of resources between different markets. 'Allocation effects' theory suggests that an analysis of such effects would have been appropriate.

If music-based programming attracts more advertisers than most other types of **2.162** programming, different licence fees may encourage advertisers to allocate their advertising to radio stations at the cost of commercial television broadcasters. This author does not suggest that such an effect would necessarily have been found in this particular case. It may well be that the supply elasticity of television programming is so low that the licensing fees, as long as they are not prohibitive, have no impact on the supply of music-based programming. Rather, differences in production costs of television and radio advertising may be the more appropriate explanation for potential allocation of resources.[236] The same issue of

---

[235] *Ministère Public v Tournier* [1991] 4 CMLR 248 ('*SACEM*') (fees imposed by national collecting societies may indicate an abuse of dominant position if they are appreciably higher than in other member states). See in Sweden *STIM v TV3*, Marknadsdomstolen 1998:5 (licensee fees favouring TV stations with larger coverage area constituted an abuse of dominant position); in Finland *STT*, Kilpailuvirasto 20 June 2001, 129/61/2001 (the licensing of intellectual property rights may involve discrimination if different licence fees are claimed from the same usage on the same product market from similarly situated licensees, and the difference is not justified by cost differences or other justified reasons).

[236] However, the complaint of MTV3/MTV Oy suggests that it had a commercial interest to initiate such action.

discrimination remains in the emerging area of Internet advertising where the production costs of a website are somewhat lower than in television advertising. The general cost structure is likely to favour the allocation of advertising resources to such media. The demand elasticity for Internet advertising is also likely to be significantly higher than for other (traditional) media. The licence fees for the use of music in advertising are likely to be the critical element. This would mean that advertisers are likely to implement their music-based advertisements in other media if the licence fees were high. Should the licence fee be at the level of television or radio advertising, or at the level of music played in shopping outlets? This theory suggests that only such licence fee structures that have minimal impact on the allocation of advertising resources between different media should be approved.

2.163 'Allocation effects' theory differs from 'property' theory in that it does not allow the rights holder to demand anything that commerce will bear. Instead, it requires any restrictions to be tailored as narrowly as possible. In the above example, the theory would suggest that the licence fees should be established in such a way that they do not affect allocation of advertising resources between different media. If a particular medium is likely to attract more resources than another medium, the licence fees should not be used to change that relative attractiveness.

2.164 In other respects, 'allocation effects' theory has been subject to the same criticism, by some commentators, as 'property' theory: that it focuses only on the reward and excludes any cost or harm caused by the attempts to collect such reward.[237] Another criticism is the view that it focuses solely on the cost or loss side of the equation used in 'ratio' theory. 'Allocation effects' theory introduces a *de minimis* rule to the application of intellectual property rights. Any policy decisions and law enforcement activity should always aim at minimizing the cost or the harm caused by restrictive activities. If the rights holder were to license other parties to make use of the rights holder's proprietary interface invention, it would, under this theory, be allowed to implement patent grant-back clauses. However, they should be drafted to be as limited as possible in order to achieve the goal and avoid the situation in which the licensee could block the licensor's own future developments.

2.165 In this book's subsequent analysis, 'allocation effects' theory provides a useful framework. It establishes that (1) external effects may and should be taken into account in the analysis, and (2) new factors are to be added to the cost side of the cost-benefit analysis by establishing that the practice must be justified by the necessity of stopping imitation.

---

[237] Kaplow, n 12 above, 1853–1854.

3

EXTERNAL EFFECTS AND BALANCING THEORIES

Introduction

This chapter further explores the theories introduced previously in terms of the **3.01**
external effects they address. This discussion has an increased focus on practical
business practices and strategies. It also highlights, in a slightly different way,
some elements used in the analysis of the theories. Finally, the chapter proposes
a structural balancing theory and policy for the network economy. The outcome
of the balancing factors analysed in the previous chapters has been used to
provide the general analysing framework. The analysing framework has the
following elements as rules of thumb:[1]

(1) Restrictions in intellectual property agreements are not automatically
    approved.[2]
(2) Any restriction is not invalid merely because it is in the intellectual property
    agreement.
(3) The acceptability of restrictions in intellectual property agreements depends
    on economic circumstances.

The key elements of the balancing theories (previously discussed) for the purpose **3.02**
of further study are best illustrated by the table on page 80.

The limited scope of these theories can best be illustrated by defining the typical **3.03**
pattern these theories use in order to try to solve the problem of establishing intellectual property policy (see top of page 81).

Typically, most theories have been used to solve the problem whether the rights **3.04**
holder is entitled to, or as a policy, should be entitled to, engage in restrictive

---

[1] R C Nordhaus, *Patent-Anti-trust Law* (2nd rev edn, Chicago 1972) 102.
[2] The fact that the rights holder may refuse to enter into the agreement is not sufficient reason to
permit it to enter into an agreement on whatever conditions.

TABLE. Key elements of balancing theories.

Balancing Theory	Key Elements
Supremacy of competition laws	Any use of the exclusive right should be subject to anti-trust and competition laws
Supremacy of intellectual property laws	Any balancing factors should be implemented into intellectual property laws themselves
Scope of intellectual property rights	Only acts that are inherent to the nature of exclusive rights have privilege under anti-trust and competition laws
Intellectual property rights as property	Any creative work is presumed to be protected under intellectual property laws and the owners should have broad rights to control the use of such rights
	Intellectual property is like any other property
	Any practice accepted by the market is acceptable
Cost-benefit theories	Is the reward gained through the implementation of a restrictive practice higher than the harm caused to society?
	Is the practice justified when balanced with competing interests?
	Is the incremental reward from a practice higher than the incremental monopoly loss in extending the term of protection?
	The practice leading to the highest reward as compared to the monopoly loss should be favoured
	One must tailor any practice as narrowly as possible and in comparison with the protected interest
	The effects of any practice on the allocation of resources in related markets should be minimized

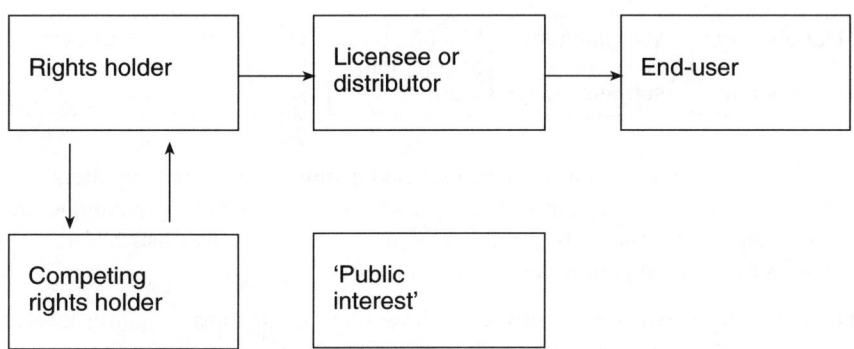

practices when selling its proprietary product to a distributor. Similarly, these theories have focused on the treatment of similar restrictions when the rights holder is granting a licence to a licensee to manufacture this proprietary product.

Furthermore, it has been of interest to explore under these theories firstly whether **3.05** particular practices have an impact on the price the end-user pays for the product. The second issue is whether the rights holder is entitled to impose similar restrictions on the end-user as applied to the licensee or the distributor. The third and final issue is whether the rights holder is engaging in anti-competitive activities through indirectly fixing the price when making cross-licensing arrangements with competing rights holders.

The use of these analysing tools has led to established criteria and rules involving **3.06** price restrictions, cross-licensing, resale price maintenance, price discrimination, royalties on unpatented products and settlements involving competing patents.

There are problems with these theories adequately dealing with two increasingly **3.07** important issues discussed in more detail below:

(1) How is it possible to take into account the possible effects of the use of intellectual property rights on related businesses of third parties?
(2) How is it possible to take into account the increasing fragmentation of rights and the problems that causes?

How to identify the correct theory which will provide appropriate tools for analy- **3.08** sis is best shown by increasing the complexity of the case information. This increasing complexity better reflects ongoing development in the emerging network economy.

Firstly, there is increasingly *interaction between different levels of the value* **3.09** *chain*. The theory of the value chain is based on the principle that each end product is an outcome of the efforts of a number of parties.

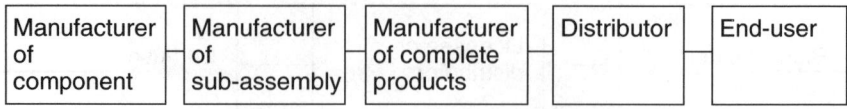

3.10 In a traditional value chain, the end-user had a supplier, or some suppliers, for a particular product or products. Those products were created by manufacturers from components and subassemblies which were sold by distributors. This reflected the general pattern used in any industry.[3]

3.11 The emerging network economy will allow more companies to gain a leverage position. At the same time an entirely new set of parameters are entering the value chain. This can best be addressed as a *network-based value chain*. Typically, such value chains are characterized by increasing fragmentation of value-producing activities.[4] The fragmentation of the value chain may be illustrated by the example, a model of value creation in the Internet economy identified in the EU study CONDRINET:[5]

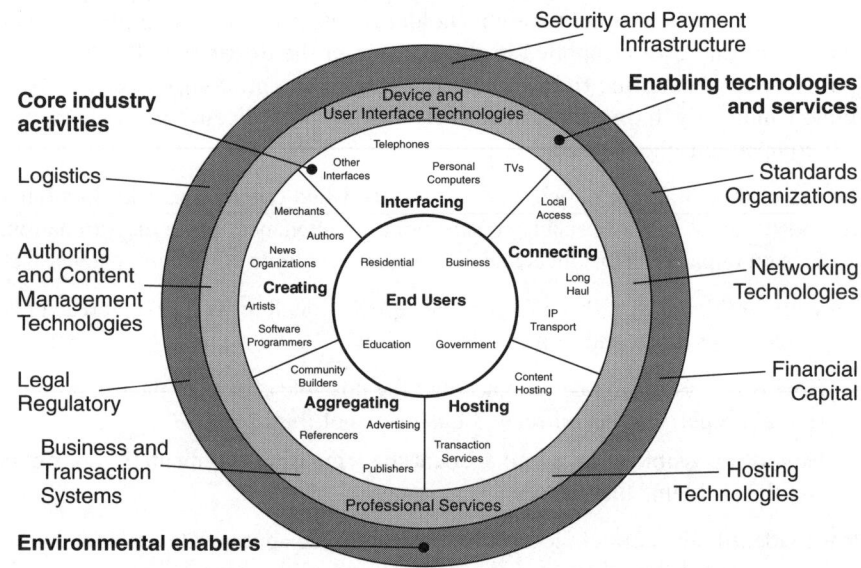

---

[3] See G Karnell, 'Rättskydd för exemplarframställning, offentligt framförande, visning och spridning vid elektronisk exploatering', in *Digitalisering och upphovsrätt* (Karnell, ed) (Stockholm, 1993), 14 (discussing electronic distribution of works in terms of the traditional value chain); *EU Copyright Green Paper*, 26–27 (recognizing that a decisive role may be played by people whose activities have not hitherto directly or immediately been affected by copyright laws).

[4] See for discussion *ECC Report 1999*, 173, 180.

[5] http://www2.echo.lu/condrinet/.

The network-based value chain has the following typical elements: **3.12**

1. There is an interaction between each level of the value chain. In order to maximize its success, each level must gain acceptance among other levels of the value chain.
2. Companies' goal or aim, at each level of the value chain, is to be the primary criterion affecting the choice of the end-user. The choice of the end-user is increasingly affecting the strength of the leverage position of each company.
3. Companies are increasingly changing their positions in the value chain. This may be because they consider the primary value and profit to be in another level of the value chain, or because they believe that through vertical integration they can better control the adoption of their primary product. As a consequence, all parties are increasingly dependent on the use and the usage terms of other parties' intellectual property rights.[6]

The outcome of this emerging new economic order is a market with a number of **3.13** parallel, competing and complementing interests and related intellectual property rights. As an indication of a general trend, the interdependency between companies is increasing in the network economy.[7] Consequently, the meaning of foreclosure and exclusion of prospective competitors is becoming more significant. The 'public interest' is increasingly identifiable through the interests of parties and therefore there is less need for the protection of an anonymous public interest.

In terms of intellectual property rights, the economic model is shifting from the **3.14** model of traditional proprietary sources of innovation and creativity, to the model best described as a web of links, 'the IPR network' of all kinds of intellectual property rights affecting the ability to compete and design a product.

Products in the field of information technology face increasing challenges relat- **3.15** ing to proprietary rights, primarily patents and copyrights. This may be illustrated as a 'network' of such rights, these networks having an increasing density of links.[8]

The manufacturer of a product has to decide how it will position its product in **3.16** this network. Further, by having its own intellectual property rights covering some of the technologies in the network, the intellectual property owner can

---

[6] At the same time, it is often more profitable for companies to innovate and create than imitate. See P S Segerstrom, 'Innovation, Imitation and Economic Growth' (1991) 99 Journal of Political Economy, 807, 808 (firms engage in imitation when there is only one leading firm, in the presence of two or more leading firms innovation is more profitable).

[7] Overall technical architectures are becoming increasingly important. If one element of technical architecture is used, there is a likelihood that one needs also to use the other elements of the same architecture. See eg L Lessig, *Code and Other Laws of Cyberspace* (New York, 1999) 127 for his code theory (computer codes may have a far more important role in providing exclusivity than copyright laws).

[8] See detailed discussion in respect of the fragmentation problem below in ch 5.

potentially have a powerful tool to control the actions available to the manufacturer to position its product in the network.

Balance between intellectual property rights, competition and external effects in network-based value chain

Difference between output of single undertakings and output of network

Reward of rights holder re-examined: impact of network effects

3.17　One of the leading assumptions in the network economy is that sales of one product or service may affect the sales of a number of other products or services. The availability of other products or services may also affect the sales of any single product or service.

The following illustrates this development. A consumer buys a computer, DVD drive, operating system and application software along with a modem and opens an account with an Internet operator. The consumer uses his computer to download music from the Internet and watch DVD movies. Since he has a number of friends with whom he likes to meet, he also buys a portable device on which he can download his favourite music for playback while he is not at home. What factors will affect the consumer's selection of these services and products?

Firstly, consumers are likely to choose equipment and an operator which enables them access to the Internet. In networks like the Internet, sometimes also called *actual networks*,[9] the users' choice of the network or e-mail provider is affected by their reliance on the ability of the network or the access provider to maximize their opportunities to interconnect with other users for a reasonable price.

3.18　After choosing equipment and service providers that enable them to access the network, they are likely to select an operating system, application software, portable device and a provider of music and DVD disks that enable them to download and play their favourite music and watch DVD movies. Since they probably would like to communicate with their friends or even share their DVD movies with their friends, their choices are likely to be affected by the choices of their friends and the information they get from the media. In this respect their choices are affected by existing virtual networks.

---

[9] M A Lemley and D McGowan, 'Legal Implications of Network Economic Effects' (1998) 86 California Law Review, 469, 488; D A Balto and R Pitofsky, 'Anti-trust and High-Tech Industries: The New Challenge' (1998) 43 Anti-trust Bulletin, 583, 585; M L Katz and C Shapiro, 'Network Externalities, Competition and Compatibility (1985) 75 American Economic Review, 55, 424; J Farrell and M L Katz, 'The Effects of Anti-trust and Intellectual Property Law on Compatibility and Innovation' (1998) Anti-trust Bulletin, 609. These networks are formed by products whose sole value lies in facilitating interconnection between a consumer and others who own the product. A typical example of an actual network is telephone or telefax. The primary benefit for the purchaser of an actual network product is access to other purchasers.

Virtual networks are formed by products whose inherent value increases with the   **3.19**
number of users of identical and/or interoperable goods. There are usually very
strong positive feedback effects tied to providing functional compatibility of such
products with other similar products. As an example, unlike the telephone or fax
system, even a single user may use a computer program. However, its value
increases as the number of users increases. Virtual networks may be created by
horizontal technical compatibility, by positive feedback in the form of complementary goods or services,[10] or even through a web of formal and informal
contracts, eg credit cards.

If a person is the only subscriber to a particular communications service, the   **3.20**
service has practically no value. If he is the only user for a particular type of
equipment or software product, the value of such program is limited. The value
of his DVD disk is even more limited if he can play it only on a particular type
of equipment.

If there is only one customer buying a particular movie recording, the value of the ability
to watch the recording to that buyer is generally less than if he could share that experience
with other people.[11] Also, the movie recording has little value unless there is equipment
that can display such recordings.[12]

Each new subscriber to the communications service and each new user of appli-   **3.21**
cations, such as word-processing software, increases the value of that utility to
the existing users. This increased value is indicated by the number of different
connections a user can make by using particular communications services and by
opportunities to share the same applications with other users.[13]

In a simple example, if there are 4 subscribers to a network, there are 12 separate communications connections available between them. If the number of subscribers increases to 5,
the number of available connections increases to 20. If the number of subscribers is 6, the
number of connections is 30; 7 subscribers produce 42 connections. The number of

---

[10] Software developers write more applications for the most popular operating system, users are
likely to use operating systems for which there are more applications available, the training costs for
the most popular programs are likely to be lower. See Lemley and McGowan, n 9 above, 491–492.
[11] This is an example of network effects that cannot be owned as compared to effects that can be
owned and controlled by someone. See S J Liebowitz and S E Margolis, 'Network Externality: An
Uncommon Tragedy' (1994) 8 Journal of Economic Perspectives, 133, 135–136.
[12] Movie recordings and related display equipment are examples of complementary products. See
M L Katz and C Shapiro, 'System Competition and Network Effects' (1994) Journal of Economic
Perspectives, 93, 93–94 (emphasizing the importance of availability of content for any introduction
of new display or play-back technology).
[13] This principle, known as 'Metcalfe's Law', has not been measured rigorously and has therefore
been suggested as an indication of the potential effects only. See Lemley and McGowan, n 9 above,
484; Balto–Pitofsky, n 9 above, 587–588; Katz–Shapiro, n 9 above, 424; W A Sheramata, 'Barriers to
Innovation: A Monopoly, Network Externalities, and the Speed of Innovation' (1997) Anti-trust
Bulletin, 937, 952; K Kelly, *New Rules for the New Economy: 10 Radical Strategies for a Connected
World* (Viking 1998) 23–25. The optimal network size occurs when the marginal benefits conferred
upon a new user (also to other users) equal the marginal costs of serving that new user.

connections Y subscribers can make if they are connected into the same network is $Y \times (Y - 1)$.[14] That means that 100,000 subscribers can make almost 10,000,000,000 (ten billion) connections.

3.22 Consequently, consumers make choices that are likely to maximize the value of their preferences: the choices that maximize their opportunities to communicate with their friends and to entertain themselves and their friends.[15] If one combination allows them to benefit from the choices made by other similar users more than other combinations, they are likely to choose that alternative. It is in the consumers' interest to make choices that allow them to maximize the combined value to themselves.

3.23 A major challenge to the successful choice between the existing balancing theories is that intellectual property rights may potentially be used to affect the value which an end-user derives. If there are a number of manufacturers and service providers, the way the rights holders exercise their exclusive rights may affect the ability of the user to benefit from the activities of other users and manufacturers. In anything involving communication, the ability or opportunity to benefit from the activities of other users is of essential value. There are numerous examples to support this:

Proprietary architectures of communications products may make them incompatible. Incompatibility makes it impossible for the user to communicate with other users or makes it possible to communicate only from a particular location.

Incompatibility of proprietary applications, such as word-processing software, may make it impossible for users to share their files with users of other manufacturers' software, or read files prepared by previous versions of the software with the new version of the software.

---

[14] Where Y is the number of subscribers connected to the same network.

[15] One sometimes also speaks about positive feedback effects. *Positive feedback effects* are increasing the value through economies of scale. As the number of customers increases, the average fixed costs are likely to decrease since the fixed costs are spread over a larger number of products. Positive feedback effects do not require any compatibility or connection to a network. They are a side effect of an increasing demand. See Lemley and McGowan, n 9 above, 495; Sheramata, n 13 above, 953.

Further, a distinction is sometimes made between *inter-system* and *intra-system* effects. Intra-system effects, such as the combination of a computer and the related software, do not necessarily imply direct network effects. It is important for any purchaser of a computer that there are software products available that can be run on the computer. The information of such availability is therefore relevant to the purchaser. The number of computers sold may signal that there is likely to be software and other components available on competitive terms.

One may also separate *indirect network effects*. Indirect network effects are present whenever complementary goods are more plentiful and less expensive as the number of users increases. M Katz and C Shapiro, 'Technology Adoption in the Presence of Network Externalities' (1986) 94 Journal of Political Economy, 822, 98–100. Indirect network effects are available in many industries, such as the video game industry where Sony, Sega and Nintendo sell their game master units at relatively lower prices than their software game consoles. S J Liebowitz and S E Margolis, 'Network Externality: An Uncommon Tragedy' (1994) 8 Journal of Economic Perspectives, 133, 135 (commenting critically on network effects theories arguing that network externalities may often be derived from the mere technological progress); Balto–Pitofsky, n 9 above, 592; Farrell–Katz, n 9 above, 609–610.

Music or video recordings that can only be played by using particular equipment or software, or cannot be played by using other software or equipment, affect the potential competition between equipment and software manufacturers since the users can or, in the latter case, cannot benefit from the body of existing recordings or equipment.

Extensive licence fee requests may cause the value of the network for a user to be reduced.

The case of peer-to-peer file-sharing networks illustrates the problem.[16] The **3.24** value of the peer-to-peer file-sharing network increases as more users join the network. The primary value such network provides for users is the ability to access a potentially unlimited number of digital music files in an organized manner, download them while online and obtain such digital music files free of charge or at a lower cost than CD disks conventionally distributed through record shops. Consequently, the value of the network is increasing because (1) the network provides immediate access to a much higher number of recordings than any conventional music distribution system, and (2) an external effect of such a network is that rights holders cannot effectively enforce their rights against private users who let others download music files from their computers. Such enforcement would be too costly to implement.

The problem is that to allow the rights holder to close the services would under- **3.25** mine the great value such a network may have to the users. The value of such networks for users is likely to cause such networks to emerge because there is a demand for them. In contrast, to permit users to continue unauthorized distribution of music files would undermine the justified property rights of rights holders to decide whether they want their music to be shared without any compensation. These interests have to be balanced in an effective manner that would maximize the net social value for society.[17]

The traditional view would be that a payment system would be established to **3.26** solve the dispute. The rights holders would establish their prices on the level that, taking into account their marginal costs, would maximize their revenue. However, without taking into account the effects of their pricing to the value of the network, the rights holders are likely to set the licence fees on the high side. In the network environment, the rights holder does not have any marginal costs, except for costs that are caused potentially by the payment system. The problem

[16] File-sharing networks are technologies the sole purpose of which is to allow consumers to share their music files with other consumers. They are sometimes called 'peer-to-peer' networks because there is a network architecture where all machines have equal status. This means that all stations can access data stored on all other workstations. In 2000, such technologies as Napster gained a lot of attention because of enforcement actions addressed against them by the music industry. In addition to Napster or Gnutella, another popular peer-to-peer technology, *Wired Magazine* listed in October 2000 a total of 25 other peer-to-peer network initiatives.

[17] The reward of each party is likely to equal their share of the total value added in the industry. Consequently, the reward is likely to be a combination of the value of the entire network and the value of an individual transaction. C Shapiro and H R Varian, *Information Rules—A Strategic Guide to the Network Economy* (Boston, 1999) 198–199.

is to find the optimum level for licence fees.[18] Since the number of users potentially increases at an exponential rate, any new users may allow the rights holders substantially to reduce their prices. Also, any increase in prices would potentially lead to a substantial loss of revenue as the number of users drops. The problem is to find an optimum level of pricing that would maximize the revenue for the rights holder and at the same time maximize the value of the network. Such an optimum level is presumed to result in low licence fees per transaction.

Network effects and balancing theories

3.27   Theories on network effects have long been researched and evolved with respect to actual networks, especially the traditional wire-based telephone industry. Early attempts to analyse and regulate network effects date back to the beginning of the twentieth century and the US telecommunications industry. However, the early theories were closely related to public utilities and monopoly industries. They also primarily focused on natural monopolies characterized by declining unit costs as the scale of the production is increased.[19]

3.28   Network theories gained new momentum with the emergence of new facilitating technologies, primarily silicon chips, computer software, fibre-optics cable and cellular telephone technologies. Since the 1980s, discussion has focused on the new dynamic possibilities of these network technologies in related industries. At the same time, it has been recognized that network effects and natural monopolies cannot be analysed using the same tools and criteria. The declining unit costs created by the increasing scale of production do not explain network effects.[20]

3.29   One of the essential elements of modern network effects theory is that *network effects are relevant in any technology or information content service provided that users can benefit from others using the same technology or service*.[21] This means that network effects are highly relevant in the computer industry where interconnection between different computers is increasingly necessary, in the software industry where the users have an increasing need to share their files with other users and also in the entertainment industry where the end-users are interested to use their copies in a number of different types of equipment. In any simple competition format, the product or technology with the highest market share is attractive to the user, because the manufacturer of such a product or the owner of the technology has the opportunity to gain experiences and feedback

---

[18]   See Farrell–Katz, n 9 above, 616–617 (the price a consumer is willing to pay depends on (1) his basic willingness to pay, (2) the goods' level of quality improvement and (3) the size of the network to which the goods belong). In the absence of actual information about the size of the network, consumers form beliefs. See also Kline, n 13 above, 55–56 (suggesting that the more a resource is used the more demand there is for it).

[19]   See some examples in *Melamed*.

[20]   F M Scherer, *Industrial Market Structure and Economic Performance* (Chicago 1980), 482.

[21]   J E Lopatka and W H Page, 'Anti-trust on Internet Time: Microsoft and the Law and Economics of Exclusion' (1999) 7 Supreme Court Economic Review, 157, 168–169.

from the highest number of users. Therefore, any single user may indirectly obtain the benefit from this network of users through better products.

The amount of experience and customer feedback available in traditional industries has, however, grown arithmetically, not exponentially, since the flow of information has not been arranged in networks but rather in a series of unilateral directions, one from users to manufacturers and a second one back from the manufacturer to the user.

Another element of the network effects theory is that *wherever network effects* **3.30** *are found, they tend to form self-reinforcing virtuous circles, in other words positive feedback conditions.* Each additional member (or subscriber) of the network increases the network's value which in turn attracts more members, initiating a spiral of benefits.[22]

VALUE

USERS   USERS

VALUE

This element has one consequence over other consequences: in traditional indus- **3.31** tries, the revenue of a company was largely related to whether the company made use of economies of scale in a more effective manner than its competitors; in the network industries, this is only one factor. Another factor is the efficiency of the network since customers are willing to pay a premium for an effective network at the same time as the company can benefit from economies of scale from the self-reinforcing nature of networks.

According to classical economic theory, it is presumed that a manufacturer will gain declining returns as the scale of economy increases. This means that the return per product is smaller in large-scale production than in small-scale production.

In the network economy, the returns per product may even increase since customers are willing to pay a premium for increased network effects.[23] Therefore, it is important to focus not only on the effects on the supply side (declining costs) but also on the demand side (increasing network value to customers).

Some commentators have suggested that because of this potentially huge differ- **3.32** ence between the values of different networks, companies could even subsidize

---

[22] 'Positive feedback makes large networks get larger', Shapiro–Varian, n 17 above, 13; Kline, n 13 above, 25.
[23] Lemley and McGowan, n 9 above, 484; W E Cohen, 'Competition and Foreclosure in the Context of Installed Base and Compatibility' (1996) 64 Anti-trust Law Journal, 535, 539–540.

users to join the network.[24] Also, if there are potentially a number of factors affecting this increased marginal return, such as patentees owning standards-related patents with royalty requests, it is not clear who should be entitled to the benefit of such additional margin. Is it a component supplier or a licensee, or the system manufacturer supplying the entire system or the complete product? Should it be possible to interfere with the distribution of this reward?

3.33   Finally, for the subject of this book, network effects have one more essential element. *It is advisable for a company in a network industry to focus its activities in creating and improving the network effects of its technology.* The downside of this strategic need is that in the competitive environment, by decreasing the opportunities for other companies to have their products or technologies benefiting from network effects, a company can support its own sales.

3.34   According to some theories, if a network is unable to obtain a sufficient base of users in the early period of its introduction, such a network has little prospect for subsequent growth or maintenance. Therefore, the survival of new networks depends upon consumer expectations about the prospective expansion and value of the new network.[25]

3.35   There are no clear rules on how network effects should be taken into account in legal decision-making. The actual economic effects of the theories are not entirely clear and the implications from case law have so far been inconsistent. Some commentators have suggested that when applying network effects theories to legal decision-making, the following factors should be taken into account: the nature and the strength of network effects, the evidence indicating the existence of network effects, the openness of the network, the significance of network effects in the industry, the nature of the relief sought and finally the other factors relevant for the legal rule in question.[26] Other commentators suggest that these factors should affect market definition and the characterization of particular conduct.[27] Practices that otherwise would be allowed may be condemned. Alternatively, practices that have traditionally been targets for intervention by the regulators may in the presence of the network effect be entirely justified and efficient.

3.36   In this book, it is recognized that the application of network effects theory may differ depending on the factual, economic and legal context where it is applied.

[24] See, M L Katz and C Shapiro, 'System Competition and Network Effects' (1994) 8 Journal of Economic Perspectives, 93, 100; consider also the practice of telecommunications operators giving subscribers free or subsidized telephones and Internet operators providing free access.

[25] Balto–Pitofsky, n 9 above, 588–589.

[26] Lemley–McGowan, n 9 above, 609–610 (recognizing that there probably cannot be any clear-cut rules but rather a set of balancing factors).

[27] Balto–Pitofsky, n 9 above, 594–595 (suggesting that the practice of artificially raising the barriers to entry may be subject to criticism).

The network effects theory is best applied as an indication of economic reality. The legal conclusions which take into account such economic reality may vary according to the background and the justifications of particular doctrines.[28] The ability to use indications of economic reality may be different in different jurisdictions. They may be undeveloped or they may be different for different doctrines, eg intellectual property laws and competition or anti-trust laws.

One outcome from network effects theory is clear. Modern anti-trust theory has **3.37** traditionally focused on price and output. A specific activity has been assumed to be relevant from an anti-trust or a competition law point of view only if it has had an effect on the price of the relevant products. Because of the close connection of price and output in economic theory, any activity that has output restrictions may affect price. Therefore such activities have also been subject to anti-trust scrutiny. The existence of external effects, such as network effects, may add new elements into the equation.

Even though a particular practice of using intellectual property rights does not **3.38** affect the price or output of goods, it may reduce the value of the network effects available to the user.[29] Therefore, even if the resulting price and quantity from a particular practice were the same, the value for the user may differ. Alternatively, even if a particular practice had an effect on price and quantity of supply, the value derived by the user through increased network effects may be substantially higher. Therefore, one of the propositions of this book is that network effects may justify either more liberalized or even more scrutiny of particular traditional anti-trust law doctrines.

In Europe anti-trust laws seem to be better equipped to respond to network exter- **3.39** nalities than the anti-trust laws in the US. The impact of the pure price theory has been less obvious in Europe. Rather, the required dominance may be found if the intellectual property owner can impede the maintenance of effective competition in a substantial part of the relevant market.[30] This may be the case if a firm is in the position to engage in particular activities irrespective of its competitors.[31]

The balancing theories described in the previous chapters have not had any **3.40** particular focus in the way values are created in particular industries. One of the key assumptions in the communications industry is that there is currently a shift from the traditional value chain to the network-based value chain. The efficiency

---

[28] Lemley–McGowan, n 9 above, 487.
[29] Sheramata, n 13 above, 969 (intellectual property secured by a monopolist in conjunction with network externalities can lead to barriers to innovation).
[30] *Deutsche Grammophon* [1971] CMLR 631, para 17.
[31] *United Brands v Commission* [1978] 1 CMLR 334; *Hoffman-La Roche v Commission* [1979] 3 CMLR 211; *Michelin v Commission* [1985] 1 CMLR 282. See for discussion M Meinhardt, *Die Beschränkung nationaler Immaterialgüterrechte durch Article 86 EC Vertrag* (Bern, 1998) 34–35; I Govaere, *The Use and Abuse of Intellectual Property Rights in EC Law* (London 1996), 111–112.

of a single company or the use of a single innovation or work is not the same as the efficiency of the underlying network. In the traditional value chain, it may well be argued that the intellectual property owner should be entitled to maximize its revenues from innovation or creation.[32] The harm or damage those practices may cause is limited. Everyone has their own proprietary products and consumers make their choices. The use of intellectual property rights may well be at the discretion of the rights holder.

It may be argued that the rights holder should be entitled to implement all kinds of use restrictions, eg discriminate between different customers by using its intellectual property rights and charge every customer a separate price. This would increase the output of inventions or works. The increased output would increase consumer benefits and the reward to the rights holder would also be maximized.[33]

3.41 However, in the network-based value chain, the consumer benefits are less attributable to the output of a single entity. Instead of and in addition to valuing the output and the price of a single product, it is increasingly important for the consumers to know how changes in price or output in one product affect the output and value of the underlying network.[34] Consequently, one must solve the potential conflict between the value derived by an individual company, the value of the entire network and the changes in value on the market of interrelated services and products. This does not necessarily change the legal analysis but it requires a consideration of all the effects of a particular practice.

3.42 This shift in value creation may justify a redefined balancing of the potential conflict between competing interests and goals. The goal of maximizing a reward for a single rights holder may compete with the goal of rewarding one or more other firms or the end-users who benefit from the value of the entire network. Furthermore, consumers may gain more benefit if none of these firms are given the freedom to maximize their reward in regard to intellectual property rights.

In respect of other types of property, with which analogies are so readily made, it is possible to establish a number of rules that balance the interests of property owners with the interests of the general public and other property owners.[35] These rules include safety rules for traffic, environmental rules and simple rules between neighbours. It is not generally

---

[32] See P J Nordell, *Rätten till det visuella* (Stockholm, 1997), 405 for a good analysis of justifications for limitations of copyright in the traditional value chain (suggesting that the justifications for limitations of copyright may depend on whether the particular use is motivated by the economic interests of the user). This book suggests that a network user always has an economic interest connected to the value of the network but that such interest may still justify restrictions.

[33] W K Tom and J A Newberg, 'Anti-trust and Intellectual Property: From Separate Spheres to Unified Field' (1997) 66 Antitrust, 167, 212; W S Bowman, *Patent and Anti-trust Law, A Legal and Economic Appraisal* (Chicago, 1973) 64.

[34] L Shapiro and H R Varian, *Information Rules—A Strategic Guide to the Network Economy* (Boston, 1999) 198–199.

[35] L Lessig, *Code and Other Laws of Cyberspace* (New York, 1999) 131 (if a private right is harmful to a collective good, then the state has no reason to create it).

argued that a person should have an absolute property right to drive a car recklessly fast in a residential area. Instead, it is clear that a public policy of avoiding traffic accidents is considered to be more important than the interest, sometimes even justified interest, of any car-owners to maximize the benefits of their property rights. The same applies to the use of real property in a manner that affects other people.[36]

External effects categorized

The models that discuss the effects created by particular business practices on others may effectively help to choose the correct interpretation or policy under existing balancing theories. In economic literature, such effects are usually referred to as 'externalities' or social benefits and costs. If some of the costs of a private producer are borne by another party, and where the producer does not compensate the other party, it can be defined that his activities cause social costs or externalities.[37]   **3.43**

Externalities and leveraging practices may be categorized in various ways. One possible categorization is based on the activities of the rights holder that have external effects. This method may be identified as *activity-based criteria*. By using activity-based criteria, it may be possible to identify externalities that are created or affected through the rights holder's *enforcement of intellectual property rights*. Typical examples of enforcement activities are refusals to license one's intellectual property rights or demands for licence fees. It may be possible to identify externalities that are created by limiting the freedom of contract partners through *restrictive contract terms* or by using particular *technical solutions* in the rights holder's own proprietary product designs.   **3.44**

If company A designs a product that combines different elements, in certain circumstances it may become impossible for competitors to compete by making functionally similar products combining different elements. The design choice of company A has an impact on such competitors' business.

Another example of superficially normal business activity is the refusal to license except on the condition that the licensee do an unrelated favour to the licensor.

If company B makes its patent licence conditional on the purchase of unpatented raw materials from the patentee, the competitors' ability to sell raw materials and the licensee's costs of raw materials may be affected as a consequence of the restrictive practice.

---

[36] Zoning requirements, environmental laws and rules protecting public order typically affect owners of real property.
[37] J W Schlicher, *Patent Law: Legal and Economic Principles* (1999), 2–3; M J Swygert and K E Yanes, 'A Primer on the Coase Theorem: Making Law in a World of Zero Transaction Costs' (1998) 11 Depaul Business Journal, 1, 17–18; K Rissanen, *Kilpailu ja tavaramerkit. Kilpailunrajoituslain soveltaminen tavarameikin yksilöimiin järjestelyihin* (Vammala 1978), 254 (the anti-trust laws justify intervention in otherwise lawful behaviour the consequences or effects of which are harmful).

3.45 Another possible categorization is to rely on *addressee-based criteria*. This method distinguishes between parties whose activities are affected by the intellectual property rights of the rights holder. It is possible to distinguish different addressees based on their roles in the value chain. Consequently, end-users, suppliers, distributors, interconnected or even unrelated third parties may individually be affected by a particular practice.

If telecommunications operator C requires all its suppliers to commit to royalty-free licensing of its patentable inventions as a condition for access to the operator's confidential system specifications, a telecommunications equipment manufacturer's incentives to innovate may be affected by such a practice.

Computer software is typically licensed separately to each individual computer. It is not possible, because of technical and contract restrictions, to acquire computer software on a single disk and use the software from that disk on multiple computers but only on one computer at a time without permanently installing it. This practice affects the ability of families to acquire a separate computer for each of their children because new computers require new copies of the same basic software products.

The practice of encrypting digital music files so that they cannot be copied onto any other play-back equipment other than the one onto which they were first downloaded makes the introduction of any new play-back technologies or equipment very difficult. This is because without being able to play existing collections, the end-user is not likely to buy new equipment. Consequently, the music industry's practice affects the business opportunities of the play-back equipment manufacturers.

3.46 Externalities may also be categorized according to the activities the rights holder's intellectual property rights affect. This method relies on *impact-based criteria*. A particular activity of a rights holder may typically have its impact on (1) the imitation of the protected feature; (2) the market of a related non-infringing product or service; (3) the market of the functionally complete product when the patent or copyright protects one of many components of such product; (4) the value derived by the user; or (5) the incentives of others to innovate.

Intellectual property rights have their most typical impacts on imitations. If patentee D has a patent on a feature that enables downloading of ringing tones on cellular telephones, others are excluded from manufacturing, selling, using and importing any cellular phones that contain such features.

If shopkeepers must pay copyright fees to rights holders in order to be able to keep their radios turned on, the number of listeners to radio stations' shows is reduced. This has an impact on the advertising revenue of radio stations.

Patentee E's royalty request for its component patent may have an impact on the supply of computers if the cumulative royalty for all necessary licences becomes excessive.

If end-user F may play its copy of the music recording only on particular equipment, it cannot benefit from the innovations in the play-back equipment industry and the value of its copy is thus reduced. Alternatively, if end-users can use their existing word-processing files with the new word-processing software, this may have an impact on the user's purchase decision.

Some legal implications of the above examples and categorizations are obvious, others are complex and to a certain extent unnoticed. In respect of every externality, there is always an action-based, addressee-based and impact-based element. All three elements are always parallel. **3.47**

The table below provides guidance for further study and strategy work. It is important to notice that one relationship or activity may justify different legal treatment than another relationship or activity. Enforcement activities against competitors to stop imitations may justify different legal treatment than a restrictive contract practice against end-users which has an impact on the market of non-infringing products.[38] **3.48**

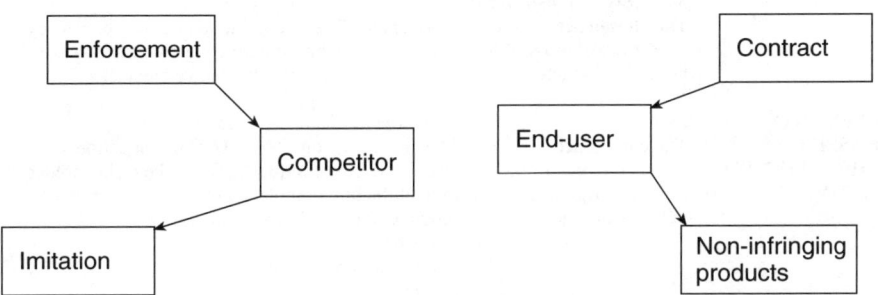

Even the simplest combinations of these elements provide sixty different possible external effects of patents and copyrights.[39] The issue of externalities becomes even more complicated because a particular practice may have various different impacts, it may affect various addressees and the rights holder may even develop various actions simultaneously. Also, the decision either to condemn or allow a particular practice necessarily affects the incentives the rights holder has available. If the incentives are reduced, fewer resources are presumably allocated to creation of new inventions and works. **3.49**

What does this mean in practice? How should intellectual property rights strategies be designed? One of the key messages of this book is that such strategy does not have to be limited to acquisition and enforcement of intellectual property rights. Rather, the strategy can be based on a broader concept. **3.50**

A software product serves as a useful illustration. Every designer of a commercial software product has to decide how to deal with interoperability. In order to **3.51**

---

[38] One may presume that the further away the effects of the practice are from the immediate production process, the more critical such practice is from the competition point of view. U Bernitz *et al, Immaterialrält* (7th edn, Stockholm, 1998), 142–143.

[39] 3×4×5=60.

MAIN ELEMENTS OF EXTERNAL EFFECTS	SUBGROUPS		
ELEMENTS BASED ON THE CHOSEN ACTION	*Enforcement* Rights holder seeks injunction or licence fees.	*Contracts Practices* Right holder conditions its licences upon various restrictions.	*Technical Solutions* Right holder integrates new features or uses proprietary interfaces.
ELEMENTS BASED ON THE AFFECTED PARTIES	*End-users* The chosen action affects end-users.		*Competitors* The chosen action affects the ability of competitors to compete on the same primary market.
	Suppliers and distributors The chosen action affects suppliers and/or distributors of the rights holder's products.		*Inter-related parties* The chosen action affects the parties supplying products that interact with the rights holder's products.
ELEMENTS BASED ON THE AFFECTED ACTIVITY	*Imitation* The chosen action affects the opportunities to imitate rights holder's products.	*Complete products* The chosen action affects the opportunities to manufacture complete products for which the rights holder's intellectual property or products are ingredients.	*Incentive* The chosen action affects the rights holder's incentive to innovate in the future.
	Non-infringing products The chosen action affects the opportunities to supply non-infringing products.		*Value derived* The chosen action affects the value derived from the object of the action.

be successful, a software product has to interoperate with components of the same system and some components of other systems. Since a software code is generally protected by copyright, its functionality can under certain circumstances be protected by a patent and at least some elements of the user interface can be protected by copyright, the designer of the software product may be in a position to use its copyrights and patents to control interoperability.

3.52   There are two basic alternatives in approaching the issue of interoperability: *proprietary* and *open*. An intellectual property rights strategy supporting the proprietary approach maximizes usability of the software in its dedicated environment but minimizes any possibility of using products other than those supplied by the same supplier.

3.53   There are a number of ways for attempting to implement a *proprietary* strategy. Software products may be designed with confidential external interfaces. Even a technical approach, such as this, may be implemented in a number of ways.

Firstly, it is possible to target this feature solely against end-users, and design the software so that a copy of it cannot be run on any system other than the dedicated computer hardware. Another alternative is to allow additional features, such as digital content, to be run with the software only if they are encoded to interoperate with the original software. A further possibility is to target the practice against competitors by deliberately making it difficult to design products that would interoperate with the software after it has been installed on the system. All these practices can be implemented because it would be an infringement of intellectual property rights to copy the technical design.

Instead of or parallel to proprietary product designs, it is possible to implement a **3.54** proprietary contract practice. This means that one agrees with the customer that the customer may only install the software on dedicated computer hardware, run only dedicated digital content on the software, or use it only in connection with some specified other products. This is possible if a company has intellectual property rights that without a licence would be infringed.

Finally, it is possible to use aggressive enforcement of intellectual property rights **3.55** in order to support proprietary strategy. This means the instigation of copyright and patent litigation against parties that do not comply with the desired strategy.

Alternatively, it is possible to implement an *open* strategy. This would involve **3.56** technical designs, contract practices and enforcement in order to keep interfaces open for anyone to use and design interoperable and even competing systems.

In practice, a successful intellectual property rights strategy contains both propri- **3.57** etary and open elements. It is uncommon to be successful by solely implementing either a proprietary or an open strategy. This is because in an extreme proprietary strategy, competitors and customers are encouraged to find alternative solutions. This is likely to lead to fragmentation of the market. It is often better to have a lower market share from a bigger market than a high market share in a small market. An extreme open business strategy is also challenging since others are encouraged to enter the market with competing interoperable products and the original designer risks losing some existing customers. Furthermore, it is sometimes necessary to use intellectual property rights in order to ensure that the proprietary strategies of other parties are not preventing the development of a rights holder's own open strategy.

External effects and entitlements

External effects re-examined: exercise of exclusive performance rights
Intellectual property laws define the rights, or 'entitlements', of the rights holder. **3.58** The following example illustrates the importance of initial entitlements in the

analysis.[40] The example is simple and involves a disputed legal issue. Therefore, it provides a useful tool for discussing the issue of entitlements in a way that may be applicable to more complex circumstances.

3.59 Any radio station broadcasting music needs to pay a fee to the copyright owner unless some promotional arrangements have been agreed. If A is a copyright owner and B is a commercial radio station that plays A's music in its broadcasts, B needs to pay a fee. That is a part of the exclusive right of the copyright owner. The fee is a necessary reward for A in order to encourage it to create more music. If B were allowed to play A's music without any cost, A's reward would potentially be reduced in an unacceptable manner.[41]

3.60 The analysis becomes more complicated if one adds external factors and costs into the calculation. Rights owner A may claim that, based on its exclusive right of public performance or reproduction, no shops, offices or even taxicabs may have their radios turned on. This is because the general public has access to these premises and the right of the shopkeeper publicly to perform A's music is different from the licence given to B to broadcast A's music.[42] Conventionally, A would

---

[40] The example is chosen because of the potentially important role various intermediaries may have in the emerging digital networks, eg 'streaming' of content or play-back of samples. If one is authorized to reproduce and distribute digital music files through the Internet, may one use intermediaries and do such intermediaries need to pay a separate fee to rights holders? Does one need to acquire a separate licence for public performance in order to be able to allow customers to listen to samples before downloading? The issue may be relevant because the reproduction right, distribution right and the right of public performance may all be administered by separate entities. See C-337/95 *Parfums Christian Dior SA v Evora BV* [1997] ECR I-6013.

[41] In Finland, see *KKO* 1992:55 (radio station was ordered to pay performers for the broadcasting of foreign music in radio shows); *Broadcast Music, Inc v Columbia Broadcasting System, Inc*, 441 US 1 (1979) (under copyright laws, those who publicly perform copyrighted music have the burden of obtaining prior consent).

[42] This is consistent with the copyright laws of most European jurisdictions. In Finland, Copyright Act § 2.3 and § 47 (amendment of Copyright Act 365/1997 establishing the right also for performing artists); *KM* 1987:7, 38–39 (public performance of music recordings may diminish work opportunities for artists); Finnish Supreme Court, *KKO* 1934 I 22 (restaurants); *KKO* 1968 II 81 (buses); *Finnish Copyright Council* 1990:14 (physical therapy institutes); 1995:19–20 (issue of compensation for performing artists); 1993:1 (issue of public performance); see for discussion P L Haarmann, *Tekijänoikeus k lähioikeudet* (Helsinki 1999), 94; K Harenko, *Copyright Question in the Digital Environment* (Helsinki 1999), 104–108. In Sweden, § 26 (f) of the Swedish Copyright Act; Swedish Supreme Court HD 27 March 1980 (master television in hotel rooms); HD 10 December 1986 (radio shops); HD 21 December 1988 (hospitals); see for discussion H Olsson, *Copyright. Svensk och internationell upphovsrätt* (7th edn, Stockholm 1998), 194; German Copyright Act § 20 and § 22. In the US Congress enacted in 1998 the Fairness in Music Licensing Act that added a new subparagraph (B) to s 110(5) of the US Copyright Act. The subparagraph provided that small establishments, such as restaurants, bars and grills, are exempted from paying royalties and licensing fees, or obtaining a rights holder's permission to play non-dramatic musical works over radio or television on their premises. In 1999, the European Union filed a complaint at the WTO dispute panel on behalf of the Irish Music Rights Organisation. On 5 May 1999, the WTO panel ruled that the Act failed to fulfil the requirements for general exemptions defined in Art 13 of TRIPS. See for report, *World Licensing Law Report* 07/00 (2000) ('WTO Issues Final Ruling In Music-Licensing Dispute') and also EU press release of 25 July 2001 (procedural agreement between EU and the US in order to define the compensation for European musicians). For discussion about Art 13 in general, see 144, p 54.

allow shopkeepers to have radios turned on upon the payment of a separate fee to A. The traditional balancing theories respond that such right is inherent to the exclusive right of the copyright owner and therefore entirely lawful and justified. It may also be argued that the combined reward potentially gained by the rights owner is higher than the potential harm caused to a single taxicab or shopkeeper. Also, it may be argued that the rights owner has a justified interest to be paid for the value gained by the shopkeeper from being able to keep the radio turned on.[43]

This conventional analysis fails to explain some of the external effects of A's **3.61** practice. An important effect of A's activity is passed to radio station B. B's advertising revenue depends on the number of people listening to the broadcast. If shops, offices or taxicabs may have their radios turned on only if they pay a fee to A, it is likely that, depending on the amount of the fee, several of them will keep their radios turned off. For B, this means fewer listeners and less advertising revenue. Less advertising money is therefore allocated to radio stations as compared with other potential advertising channels. This decrease of advertising revenue is an external effect of A's practice in using its property rights.[44]

The response of the traditional intellectual property doctrines, which focus on A's **3.62** reward and its justifications, does not necessarily respond satisfactorily to B's concerns to have as many listeners for its broadcast as possible.[45] A's activity is not likely to increase the price of music on the market. It also does not reduce the output of music in general. Consequently, under any of the conventional balancing theories, no limitations to A's rights are likely to be imposed. This may be because intellectual property rights theories have not been focused on the external effects the use of such rights may cause to third parties.

By using the combinations of potential effects identified in the table on page 96. A's contract practice against shopkeepers and taxicabs will affect the value they derive from the possibility of playing music in their premises.[46] A's reward will be increased by the

---

[43] Since why would a shopkeeper keep the radio turned on unless it attracts more customers and increases business. If the same shops played music themselves, they would have to pay for such public performance. Without any payment the shops would be encouraged to have radios turned on instead of paying the rights holders to play the music themselves. The same reason is less likely in case of taxicabs. See also G Davies, 'Copyright and the Public Interest' (1994) IIC Studies vol 4, 140; Z Chafee, 'Reflections on the Law of Copyright' (1945) 45 Columbia Law Review, 503, 505 (author should be able to control all the channels through which his work or any fragments of his work reach the market).

[44] Since the number of listeners is also likely to correlate with the number of records sold containing A's music, that practice may also have a cost to A. A may still decide to implement the practice. This may be because of other costs or benefits to A. The problem is the same as in the example involving discriminatory licensing fees on the use of music on television and radio.

[45] In the market conditions, B would be willing to pay less to A, if A's practice affects B's advertising revenue. However, if A is a monopoly organization as most collecting societies in Europe, the market mechanism is not likely to work satisfactorily since the cost of music is the same irrespective of the number of actual listeners.

[46] This presumes that shopkeepers and taxicabs compete with the music they play to customers (or to their employees).

share of the same amount.[47] A's contract practice against shopkeepers also affects the allocation of advertising resources to radio stations since the practice is likely to reduce the number of potential listeners to radio station B's shows.

A's contract practice against shopkeepers may further affect the value of record sales by A since less listeners are exposed to A's music. Finally, A's contract practice against shopkeepers may also affect the allocation of shopkeepers' resources between alternative goals or priorities.[48]

3.63 The effects on radio station B are clearly effects that rights owner A has no direct interest in taking into account. In general, without any intervention, the existence of externalities leads to a socially inefficient allocation of resources.[49]

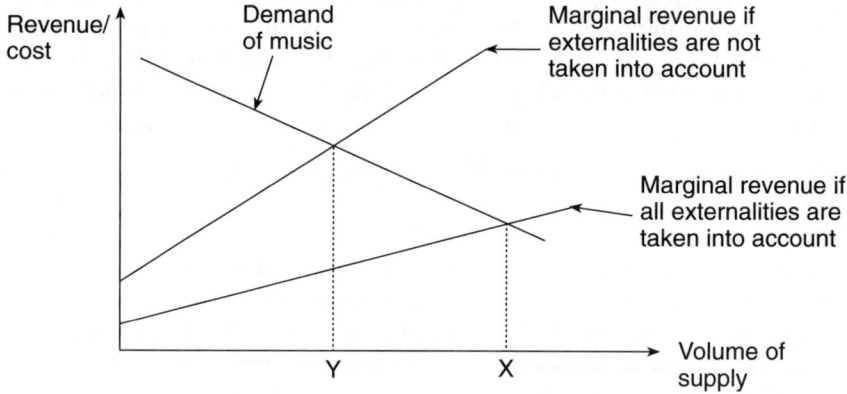

3.64 If rights owners decide to collect licence fees from shopkeepers and taxicabs, they are likely to experience a decline in marginal returns as they raise their licensing fees. Every increase in the licence fees is likely to cause some of the shopkeepers and taxicabs that were previously licensees to turn their radios off. This may also reduce the sale of records. Consequently, rational rights holders will establish their licence fees at a level (Y) where the marginal increase in total licence fees is equal to the marginal loss of income caused by such increase.

---

[47] In 1999 WTO/TRIPS ruling involving the 1998 Fairness in Music Licensing Act, the European Union identified that the non-American music industry would lose US$ 53.65 million and the US government estimated the same figure to be between US$ 416,000 and US$ 708,000 per year.

[48] Such effects, sometimes defined as pecuniary effects, do not normally justify any intervention. Pecuniary effects are natural effects caused by competition. The decision of a shopkeeper to use its resources to acquire a licence is a choice between competing goals or priorities made by the shopkeeper. Provided that such licence fees do not affect the supply of products on another market, such effect is inherent to the competitive process. See S J Liebowitz and S E Margolis, 'Network Externality: An Uncommon Tragedy' (1994) 8 Journal of Economic Perspectives, 133, 136–137; R H Bork, *The Anti-trust Paradox* (rev edn 1993, Chicago, 1978), 110–112.

[49] P A Samuelson and W D Nordhaus, *Economics* (12th edn, New York 1985), 715–716; see also G Prosi, 'Patents and Externalities' (1971) Zeitschrift für Nationalökonomie, 31, 63.

If rights owner A took into account all externalities, such as loss of advertising   **3.65**
revenue for the commercial radio station B, rights owner A would set its licence
fees at level X. The conclusion from the differences between X and Y is that the
existence of externalities causes rights owner A to demand what are not socially
optimum licensing fees.[50]

Naturally, the same mechanism also occurs in the case of positive externalities. If   **3.66**
the benefits of shopkeepers and taxicabs were substantial and rights holder A
would not be entitled to request licence fees from them, the rights holder may be
encouraged to supply less than the total social value that its contribution would
justify.

In traditional property theories, a few alternative solutions have been developed   **3.67**
to balance external effects caused by the use of a particular property. Primarily,
one tries to affect the motivations of the party causing the externality so that its
behaviour would be as close to the socially optimum level as possible.

Internalization of externalities
The first solution is to *internalize the external effect by giving one party a*   **3.68**
primary justification for its activities. If clear property rights are defined, the
socially optimum solution may be achieved through private negotiations.
Property rights are supposed to specify the benefits the rights holder is entitled to
derive and harms it is obliged to tolerate. They should also specify who must pay
whom to modify the actions taken by anyone. Consequently, the main justification for property rights is that they are an effective means to internalize benefits
and harms caused by particular practices.[51]

The popularity of this theory is largely attributable to Richard Coase and his   **3.69**
famous article for which he received a Nobel Prize in 1991. Coase suggests that
if the transaction costs between A and B were low, no intervention is necessary in
order to achieve the most efficient solution.[52] If there is a common interest
between the parties, they will find it and negotiate an agreement. However, the
intervention of laws may be necessary in order to identify the primary source of
liability. In our example, should rights holder A or radio station B be liable for
this external effect caused by A's practice?

If A is deemed not to be liable for external effects, it may still be in B's interest   **3.70**
to pay A in order to persuade it to let shops, offices and taxicabs have their radios

---

[50] See P Schonning, *Ophavsretten-mellum kulturpolitik och handelspolitik* (Århus, 1994), 112 (the
understanding among authors is that licence fees are reasonable from the point of view of cultural
politics).
[51] H Demsetz, 'Towards A Theory of Property Rights' 57 American Economic Review, 347,
349–350; R C Nordhaus, *Patent–Anti-trust Law* (2nd rev edn, Chicago, 1972), 88–89 (by giving inventors a sole property right to their inventions, the external economies of knowledge are internalized).
[52] R H Coase, *The Firm, the Market and the Law* (Chicago, 1998), 16.

turned on. The maximum amount B would be willing to pay is likely to be equal to the amount of the lost advertising revenue. A is likely to accept any amount that is close to its expected revenue with some eventual discount. Coase suggests that, in the absence of transaction costs, the initial allocation of liability does not affect the social cost to be compensated between the parties. It only affects the allocation of such costs between rights holder A and radio station B.

Externalities and entitlements

3.71   The key policy issue is then whether such costs caused by external effects would be allocated to the rights holder or the radio station. In the intellectual property field, this has to involve the balancing of the reward available to the rights holder and the interests of society to reward the investment made by the radio station. The simple response of emphasizing the long-term social value of innovation or creative work is not satisfactory. Also B's investment and eventual innovation and creativity are socially valuable and should be encouraged.[53]

3.72   In Scandinavia, Koktvedgaard investigated in 1965 the use of entitlements to solve the dispute between competing interests. In the US, Calabresi and Melamed in 1972 came up with essentially the same theory. According to these theories A, B and the shopkeeper may all have alternative justifications, and entitlements for their rights.[54] The strongest entitlement is a *property right*. It can be removed only if the owner agrees to remove it in a voluntary transaction. Under a property rule, a licence must be negotiated before engaging in an activity protected or restricted by a property rule. If A has a property right to stop the shopkeeper, B must persuade A not to use such right. A second form of entitlement is a *liability rule*. The entitlement is protected by a liability rule if the initial entitlement, A's exclusive right, may be removed by B or the shopkeeper by paying A money. Under a liability rule, a party may engage in an activity and acquire the necessary licences afterwards. The difference between a liability rule and a property rule is that under a liability rule injunctive relief is not available.

3.73   A third form of entitlement allows radio station B to have sole control over the broadcasting of its radio shows. Under this entitlement, rights holder A can stop the shopkeeper only if it manages to persuade B to allow the practice.[55] The

---

[53] R A Posner, *Economic Analysis of Law* (New York, 1998), 56 (wealth transfer affects the efficiency of market only if (1) it has the consequence of causing different entities to have different resource allocations, (2) the fees are so high that they have an impact on the general well-being of entities, or (3) transaction costs are high). Wealth transfer does not necessarily change allocation if radio stations pay more for their right to broadcast. See Coase, n 52 above, 172.

[54] G Calabresi and A D Melamed, 'Property Rules, Liability Rules, and Inalienability: One View of the Cathedral' (1972) 85 Harvard Law Review, 1089, 1092–1093.

[55] *M Witmark & Sons v Jensen*, 80 F Supp 843 (D Minn 1948) (the performing rights society's claim of royalties from movie theatres showing movies for which a copyright licence was already paid constituted copyright misuse). This method is frequently used when the balance is implemented in

fourth form of entitlement allows rights holder A to stop the shopkeeper but A must compensate radio station B. The entitlements three and four are actually property rights and liability rules protecting B against A. They may also be called B's *privileges* within the otherwise enforceable right of A. According to the static interpretation of the *Coase Theorem*, unless there are transaction costs, all these four alternatives are supposed to be equally effective. If there are transaction costs, the most effective solution is the one for which transaction costs are the lowest. Further, between liability rules and property rights, liability rules are presumed to be the most effective solution if transaction costs are high.[56]

Transaction costs are generally high when, due to the high number of transactions, their relative complexity and uncertain valuation favour collective treatment and administration. However, liability rules presume that where there are disagreements, courts or states would have the wisdom to establish the appropriate compensation.[57]

Compulsory licences administered by copyright collecting societies are a typical example of liability rules that have been imposed because of the high transaction costs involved in the negotiation of single licences. Licences are available collectively against a payment of a fee.

A party may also voluntarily give up its property right in favour of a liability rule. This happens frequently in the standardization organizations where members make commitments to grant patent licences against compensation or where there are patent pools or voluntary collecting societies.[58]

Balancing theories emphasizing property rights suggest that in order to maximize inventive or creative output, the rights holder should be given the relevant entitlement. In our example, that would lead policy-makers to assign rights holder A the entitlement to charge shopkeepers and taxicabs licence fees. Radio station B would then be able to negotiate with A some limitations to that right. Consequently, in recent years the scope of exclusive rights has systematically been extended to cover new positive externalities without taking into account any need for balancing negative effects.

3.74

intellectual property laws. See J Schovsbo, 'Ophavsrettens monopolproblemme', in *Ånd og rett, Festskift till Birger Stuevold Lassen* (Oslo, 1997), 25 (identifying industrial designs and computer programs as examples of balancing between competing entitlements (the need for compatible products and exclusive rights) by granting competitors an entitlement to copy elements that are necessary for compatibility); Coase, n 52 above, 17 (instead of creating a legal system of private transactions, the government may deal with the problem by setting limits to private rights).

[56] Calabresi–Melamed, n 54 above, 1110; R P Merges, 'Of Property Rules, Coase and Intellectual Property' (1994) 94 Columbia Law Review, 2655. See also Lemley, *Economics of Improvement* (1997), 1006–1007 (that entitlement rules force parties to reveal their preferences but there is no suggestion that a liability rule is preferable to a property rule); S N S Cheung, 'Property Rights and Invention' (1986) 8 Research in Law and Economics, 5, 14 (arguing that high transaction costs may make the protection inefficient).

[57] Merges refers to the problem of valuing the use of a play in a movie in *Sheldon v Metro-Goldwyn Pictures Corp*, 309 US 390 (1940); see Merges, n 56 above, 2664.

[58] R P Merges, 'Contracting into Liability Rules: Intellectual Property Rights and Collective Rights Organisations' (1996) 84 California Law Review, 1293, 1295, 1391–1393.

3.75 This book suggests that this policy may need some redefinition. The suggestion is based on a number of issues:

(1) lack of competition in the supply of licences;
(2) allocation effects that cannot be solved through private negotiation; and
(3) potential transaction costs and the irrationality of private behaviour.[59]

3.76 The conflicting interests of radio station B and rights holder A could be solved only through entitlements if the supply of music licences were competitive and no single party had any significant market power. If the supply of music to radio stations, shopkeepers and taxicabs were competitive, the rights holder would compete with other rights holders. Any practice to collect licensing fees above the socially optimum level would probably cause the radio stations, shopkeepers and taxicabs to favour (still popular) music that has lower licensing fees or no licensing fees at all. Even though such structure of collecting supports many efficiency-increasing and justified needs, the licensing of music is in many countries not competitive. There is no price competition between authors and artists. Consequently, *the existence of market power may achieve socially sub-optimum behaviour.*[60]

3.77 Even if the supply of music licences were competitive, the basic problem of transferring wealth to the rights holder from radio stations remains a fairness issue.[61] From society's point of view, this is justified if the resources are more effectively used by rights holder A than radio station B. Consequently, if the return from the allocation of resources to A is higher than the allocation of resources to B, A should be granted the initial entitlement. This involves increasingly complex calculations and a need for extensive background information. One can assume that demand flexibility has some significance. If the innovative or creative activities were not affected by the loss of revenue but rather the allocation of advertising resources were affected, the initial allocation should be reversed. Radio station B should potentially have the initial entitlement to control the use of its signal for public performances. Also, one possibility is to allocate the initial entitlement to the party with the greatest interest. If the potential revenue of A is higher than the harm to B, A should have the initial entitlement. *The comparison between marginal harms and benefits is therefore necessary in order to justify or condemn particular practices.*

[59] W P Heller and D A Starret, 'On the Nature of Externalities', in *Theory and Measurement of Economic Externalities* (ed Saylin) (London, 1976), 10, 20–21.

[60] S D Anderman, *EC Competition Law and Intellectual Property Rights* (Oxford, 1998), 249 (if a rights holder is entitled to appropriate what the market can bear, there must be a market to regulate such return).

[61] B Domeij, *Läkemedelspatent* (Stockholm, 1998), 34 (suggesting that private interest may lead to the most effective allocation of resources for those parties but that allocation may be different from the most effective allocation of resources from society's point of view).

Transaction costs cause the rational assignment of property rights to become even **3.78**
more difficult. Practical issues mean that the negotiation between A and B is not
likely to be without cost. The parties usually lack information about the respective values of the effects of a particular practice on each other.[62] This, together
with market power, may lead to irrational solutions.

The basic problem with the internalization of externalities is the multidimen- **3.79**
sional effects of the chosen solutions. With intellectual property rights, the issue
is not always only a simple resolution of external effects. Rather, the problem is
how to solve external effects created from a solution of another externality.
Consequently, the externalities created by internalization of externalities become
an increasingly significant issue.

External harms and entitlements
One possibility is to *impose the liability for external harms on the party causing* **3.80**
the costs. That would involve rewarding the rights holder only in accordance with
the net social benefit it produces. Consequently, rights holder A should be entitled to impose fees on shops, offices or taxicabs if it compensates B for the
reduced advertising revenues by for instance reducing the licensing fees from
radio stations. If the loss of such income is higher than the expected revenue for
A, A would probably decide that it will not charge the additional fees. According
to property theories, this is a justified outcome from the balancing of the different interests of A and B.

However, it is easy to see that this theory has not been widely used in any Western **3.81**
jurisdiction. This may be because the external effects caused by internalizing the
initial externality in intellectual property laws has not been extensively discussed
or analysed. No basic economic or theory objections are likely, other than possible transaction costs. The basic idea of granting the rights holder an entitlement
only to the net social value of a particular practice seems to be unobjectionable.
However, a method is still needed that would actually facilitate limiting the
reward to the net social value. A liability rule of the type introduced in the previous paragraph may provide some basis for workable solutions.

Inalienable entitlements
Another theory for solving the problem of external effects is the use of taxes and **3.82**
levies. This usually owes its source to the early lighthouse theories[63] and the works
of Pigou. The basic concept is that instead of relying on private negotiation

---

[62] For instance see n 48 above for differences in the market estimations for value of foreign music
played in US small establishments.
[63] Lighthouse theories were used to describe public goods problems. Lighthouses are necessary
establishments but it is difficult to have private parties pay for their use. It is possible to impose taxes
on any ships that visit particular ports but there the state runs the risk that particular ships will not visit
its ports.

practices, the ultimate costs caused by externalities are imposed on private parties by using levies and taxes.

3.83   If in the above example the state decides to regulate the relationship between A and B the state may implement a rule that any shopkeepers, offices and taxicabs can keep their radios turned on but a fee is collected from any manufacturers of radios. In property theory, it would be argued that the state made the entitlement inalienable.[64] Inalienable entitlements may generally be justified if they increase efficiency or secure equitable distribution of costs.[65]

3.84   Reflecting the historical trend, none of the current inalienable entitlements have their primary justification in the protection of third parties against external effects of intellectual property rights.[66] If the state decided to implement a separate fee, a levy, on all radio manufacturers in order to compensate A for the lost entitlement to collect money from shopkeepers, offices and taxicabs, this would harm the business of radio manufacturer C. What would be C's entitlement as compared to A and B?

3.85   A and B may argue that since every manufacturer would be paying a levy of the same amount, that would be a fair and non-discriminatory solution to the conflict between A and B. However, from C's point of view any levy will either raise the price of radios or reduce its profit margins. If C successfully raises its prices for radios without losing its profit margins, the higher prices for radios will lead to reduced sales and loss of profits. The lower number of radios on the market will also indirectly affect the number of listeners of B's radio shows and the sales of A's records.

3.86   Traditionally, asking who caused the harm would solve the issue. Is it C who manufactures and sells radios, B who broadcasts music or the shopkeeper who wants to have their radio on? A may respond by saying that it should not matter as long as they get their fair compensation. Another possibility would be to discuss whether there are some external harms caused by radio manufacturer C that they do not otherwise take into account.[67] States and courts have been

---

[64] Inalienable entitlements are controlled by states on the level of basic contract terms. In the intellectual property field, there are a few inalienable entitlements, such as non-transferability of moral rights, artists' right to royalty for further sales of their works and copyright levies imposed on consumer equipment. See § 53–54 of the German Copyright Act. G Schricker and P Katzenberger, 'Die urheberrechtliche Leerkassetten vergütung' (1985) GRUR, 87 (arguing strongly in favour of traditional levy schemes without discussing any of the external effects).

[65] Calabresi–Melamed, n 54 above, 1114.

[66] W Gordon, 'A Property Right in Self-Expression: Equality and Individualism in the Natural Law of Intellectual Property' (1993) Yale Law Journal, 1533, 1608. See also Gordon, 1543 (three most important human-based entitlements are (1) right to be free from harm, (2) right to have a share from others in times of great need, (3) free right to use the common.

[67] This is a typical form of inquiry when discussing environmental impacts of business practices. See also *Sony Corp v Universal City Studios, Inc*, 464 US 417 (1984) (no liability for contributory infringement if the product is widely used for legitimate, unobjectionable purposes).

increasingly reluctant to intervene in this type of complex economic analysis even though the importance of such analysis is becoming more and more significant. Instead, there is a general belief that the market will correct any misallocation caused by social costs.[68]

The issue of levies and taxes is also related to the correct bearer of such levies. **3.87** The tax or levy is likely to affect the allocation of resources between different goals or aims.

This may be illustrated through cellular telephones. If we assume a population of cellular phone users where 10% of users are willing to pay extra fees for the ability to download music onto their phones and use them as a play-back device, 60% think that they may use the feature if it were to be available without any increase in equipment prices and 30% are not likely to be interested at all. If no levies are imposed on cellular phones, the manufacturer is likely to include the feature in 70% of the phones. If levies are imposed, the manufacturer is likely to include the feature in 10% of the phones.

This introduction of fees or levies would have three effects: (1) competition on the market for play-back equipment would be limited, (2) provided that each user of a cellular phone paid the rights holder in order to obtain some materials for play-back, the market for musical works would be reduced, and (3) taxes from the sales of music to cellular phones would be reduced. Therefore, the output of cellular phones containing play-back features would be less than the socially optimum level.

The increasingly popular general assumption is that intellectual property rights **3.88** are property rights.[69] This assumption does not take into account that for most goods, entitlements are mixed. The allocation of entitlements between various parties also frequently reflects the idea of the fair or just distribution of wealth between those parties.[70]

In our example, the principal property right of A should not be challenged but the adverse effects of such right should be minimized. This may be implemented by granting B an entitlement to its right to broadcast its radio show without any intervention by A.[71] In

---

[68] G Calabresi, 'Transaction Costs, Resource Allocation and Liability Rules—a Comment' (1968) 11 Journal of Law and Economics, 67, 68; T J Brennan, 'Taxing Home Audio Taping', Economic Analysis Group Discussion Paper, 86, US Dept of Justice, Anti-trust Division, 1986, 29 (suggesting if levies cause harmful effects that is justified because consumers should pay for the benefits they gain).

[69] Merges, n 56 above, 2665–2667; G Schricker and P Katzenberger, 'Die urherberrechtliche Leerkassettenvergütung' (1985) GRUR, 87, 94 (constitutional protection for copyright in Germany).

[70] Calabresi–Melamed, n 54 above, 1093; Posner, n 53 above, 58 (if the problems of collecting correct information are disregarded, the combined values of interested parties may be maximized through more complex definition of property rights in a way that would take into account multiple interests); M A Lemley, 'The Economics of Improvement in Intellectual Property Law' (1997) 75 Texas Law Review, 989, 1069–1070 (divided property entitlements to encourage improvements).

[71] There may be a difference depending whether the practice is used within the primary coverage area of the radio station or outside it. Only the practice within the primary coverage area of the radio station may affect its advertising revenue. The practice outside the primary coverage area of the radio station may affect its possibilities to sell its signal.

practical terms, this would mean the formation of (1) something like an implied licence or similar concept that ties B's entitlement to B having paid A for the broadcasting right, or (2) imposing on rights holder A liability for the harm the practice causes to radio station B. The levies imposed on manufacturer C would not encourage any kind of efficiency but would work only as a statutory copyright tax with the same implications as any tax.[72]

3.89   The primary suggestion of this book is that *in the network economy, one should put increasing emphasis on the external costs a particular practice causes to parties other than those parties that are directly involved.* Furthermore, based on information about external costs, a more sophisticated allocation of entitlements should sometimes be provided in the place of the exclusive entitlement of the rights holder.[73]

External effects caused by fixed entitlements

Entitlements re-examined: utilization of patent exhaustion doctrine

3.90   The concept of external effects can be illustrated by another example, this time featuring patent law. The traditional doctrine of exhaustion provides that after the first authorized sale of a patented product the patentee's right has been exhausted: he may not impose any more restrictions on the use of the patented product or require licence fees from the subsequent purchaser or user of the products.[74] The same doctrine has also been applied where the licensee, and not the rights holder, has first sold the licensed product. In the increasingly complex value chain of the network economy, this simple rule can sometimes provide unexpected outcomes.

Patentee X licenses its patent to manufacturer Y. Manufacturer Y makes the product and sells it to customer Z who uses the product in his business activities. Patentee X, aiming to maximize its licensing profits, turns into customer Z and asks for royalty payments. Is X entitled to do that?

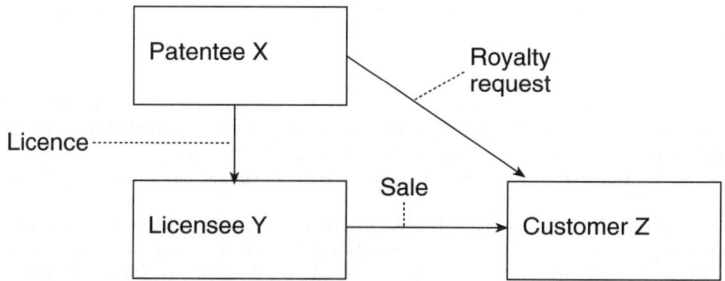

---

[72] L Kurlantzick and J E Pennino, 'The Audio Home Recording Act of 1992 and the Formation of Copyright Policy' (1998) 45 Journal of the Copyright Society of the USA, 497, 522–523.

[73] Consequently, this book does not suggest the politically correct outcome of balancing but only suggests that instead of one-dimensional arguments, a proper balance must be made between competing interests.

[74] For further analysis see ch 4, paras 4.24–4.39 below.

Based on the prevailing law, any expert familiar with the topic is likely to say no.   **3.91**
The right of patentee X has been exhausted by the first sale of the patented product by licensee Y. Why is this case then different from the previous example?
Why is the set of entitlements different? Some proponents of strong property
rights would certainly favour such a right. That would just provide additional
reward to patentee X and encourage it to innovate more. Naturally, any such right
would probably hurt licensee Y. Licensee Y would probably be able to sell less
products to customer Z. If licensee Y has agreed to acquire the necessary licences
for customer Z, he may even suffer direct financial losses as a consequence of
patentee X's additional royalty demands. However, as in our copyright example,
the harm caused to radio station B was not likely to be an issue for any policy-
makers. Why is this case different? By using the table introducing various externalities and leveraging practices, one may conclude that in patent law, the
patentee may generally not use its exclusive right against customers of the
licensee in order to derive additional value from them. The practice would also
affect the licensee and the supply of licensed products.

Some copyright experts respond that in the copyright example, rights holder A   **3.92**
was licensing different rights to radio station B than to the shopkeeper. The rights
licensed to the shopkeeper were never the subject matter of radio station B's
licence. However, patentee X's patent typically contains separate product and
method claims and the patent laws make a distinction between making, selling
and using. The licensed and utilized set of rights are not fundamentally different.
Customer Z is using the patented product for its intended purpose and the shopkeeper is consuming radio station B's show by keeping his radio turned on.

There are few differences between these two examples. Firstly, licensee Y and   **3.93**
customer Z have made a transaction, in this example a sale. Between radio station
B and the shopkeeper there is no contractual relationship. Does that imply that
entitlements are created through contracts?[75] If radio station B and the shopkeeper made a contract covering B's broadcasting to the shopkeeper's radio,
would that give entitlements to both B and the shopkeeper against rights holder
A? The likely answer is no. While contracts can create entitlements, B would not
be able to pass to the shopkeeper any more extensive entitlement than it had itself.
Again, it may be argued that if the patentee expressly limited licensee Y's entitlement, that should also limit customer Z's right. Still, in the absence of any
contract with the customer, customer Z's privilege to be free from any claims of
patentee X is likely to prevail.

Another difference between these two examples is that licensee Y is selling tangi-   **3.94**
ble goods while radio station B is sending a radio signal that is not tangible in the

---

[75] See M Koktvedgaard, *Konkurrencepraegede immetrialretspositioner* (Copenhagen, 1965),
203–206 for overview (suggesting that property rights are effective against anyone, while contract
rights may provide an exclusion).

strict traditional sense. If property rights protect both, it should not justify different treatment.

3.95 Consequently, it seems that entitlements may be different based on (1) the political choices made, (2) the type of property involved, and (3) whether the harmed or injured party has incurred transaction costs with the addressee of the rights holder's action. It seems *that the rights holder is entitled, at any time, to charge fees from different levels of the value chain that causes external harm at least to those of the rights holder's licensees that would like to sell or distribute their licensed contributions to such parties.* The simple conclusion is that the internalization of external effects through fixed entitlements is not necessarily a workable solution whenever the interests of more than two parties are concerned.[76]

3.96 In this respect patent laws seem to have traditionally been more sensitive to external costs. The external costs have been taken into account by establishing a *'per se'* rule of exhaustion by the first sale of products. This book suggests that in the copyright laws, it would be appropriate to pay more attention to the similar problem.

3.97 The further study of the subject can be illustrated by another example using the same parties. Patentee X is also a manufacturing business. Its product is a complicated system that uses several patents. Patentee X licenses its patent to licensee Y against a royalty of $0.10 for each licensed product. Licensee Y acquires all necessary other licences, manufactures the product and sells it in volumes to customers Z and V. Patentee X manufactures its own product and sells it to customers V and T in volumes.

3.98 What happens if customer Z indicates that it has a patent that both X and Y potentially infringe? Since customers V and T are their competitors, customer Z may decide to ask a royalty of $1.00 for each product. That will potentially increase the costs of her competitors and benefit it. The management of patentee X may contact customer Z and suggest that since both parties have one patent, the parties should make a royalty-free cross-licensing agreement. Customer Z may respond that it does not need any licence from patentee X since it buys all its products from licensee Y.

3.99 The traditional intellectual property theories are again not likely to provide any satisfactory answers to patentee X's concerns. Customer Z has a traditional privilege under patent exhaustion doctrine to be free from any claims of patentee X. Customer Z also has the right to maximize any gains he can derive from his

---

[76] J Schumann, *Grundzüge der Microeconomischen Theorie* (Berlin, 1984), 380 (suggesting that the existence of more than two interested parties may prevent optimum outcome through private transactions). See also W M Landes and R A Posner, 'An Economic Analysis of Copyright Law' (1989) 18 Journal of Legal Studies, 325, 327 (not shifting the risk may inhibit the development of the market).

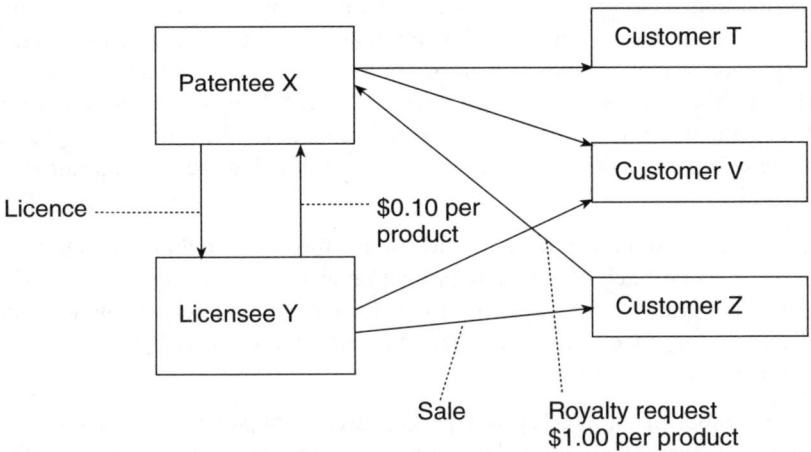

patent. One may also argue that its innovative activities should be encouraged and rewarded. However, customer Z's activity would certainly harm patentee X. If patentee X is in a position to raise its prices, customers V and T are likely to buy less. If the market price for goods is fixed, the royalty cost would cause a decrease in patentee X's profit margins.

According to some theories, customer Z will agree on a modest royalty rate or **3.100** royalty-free licensing if it expects to gain more from such an alternative than from maximizing its revenue.[77] Others suggest that in the network economy, customer Z would agree to the modest royalty if the consequent market growth and its market share are beyond its immediate royalty revenue expectations.[78] In this case, patentee X may still argue that the principal division of entitlements between it and customer Z is not reasonable. Customer X has its property right to its patent, the privilege of being free from patentee X's patent claims, the interest in foreclosing on its competitors and the interest in maximizing its revenues. The '*per se*' rule of exhaustion effectively limits the ability of patentee X to exercise its patent rights against customer Z.

Rebuttable entitlements
This book's author suggests that *the traditional fixed division of entitlements is* **3.101** *not necessarily adequate in an increasingly complex value chain.*[79] *Instead, rebuttable presumptions of entitlements should be used.* In more detail, it is

[77] G Bittlingmayer, 'Property Rights, Progress, and the Aircraft Patent Agreement' (1988) 31 Journal of Law and Economics, 227, 240–241.

[78] C Shapiro and H R Varian, *Information Rules—A Strategic Guide to the Network Economy* (Boston, 1999), 198.

[79] By rebuttable presumptions it is here meant 'an inference drawn from certain facts that establish a prima facie case, which may be overcome by the introduction of contrary evidence'. *Black's Law Dictionary*, 7th edn, 1999.

suggested that, in the field of intellectual property rights, any initial entitlement would be rebuttable by evidence showing that the use of such an entitlement by a party leads to externalities that are more harmful than the benefit to the rights holder or that such use leads to an irrational balance of hardships between the parties. After the initial demonstration of irrationality, the party relying on the initial entitlement could still justify its action by showing the inherent fairness of its activities.

3.102   In the battles between competing entitlements, this rule would allow intellectual property owners much of the same protection as the US business judgment rule allows to directors of the company. However, it would in a reasonable way force intellectual property owners also to take into account any social costs their activities may cause.[80]

3.103   In our example, customer Z's privilege to be free from patentee X's claims would be more efficient as a rebuttable presumption. Customer Z may have a strong privilege against the unilateral right of patentee X to exclude it or even ask it to pay royalties. However, if that right were rebuttable by patentee X showing that the outcome of such a privilege would not lead to a rational outcome, customer Z would have to show the inherent fairness of the situation in order to maintain its privilege. As a general presumption, the irrationality of the demand could be evaluated against the situation in which a party would not be able to rely on exhaustion or another similar privilege. The showing of royalty claims for technically necessary patents or other intellectual property rights with market power would in many cases be enough to rebut the initial presumption.[81]

3.104   In contract practice, this potential problem with customer privileges is, in the absence of any proper rule allowing the exhaustion doctrine to be rebutted, dealt with in various ways. Firstly, companies may be hesitant to license suppliers, eg semi-conductor manufacturers, because their customers may claim exhaustion. Secondly, companies are increasingly relying on combination patents and combination claims in order to leave them entitlements against exhaustion and customer claims.[82] Thirdly, companies are drafting termination clauses into their licensing agreements to facilitate defensive actions where there is a customer claim. Fourthly, companies are circumventing the initial privilege of the customer by,

---

[80] A concept of rebuttable exclusive rights had been previously advocated by at least F M Scherer, 'The Economic Effects of Compulsory Licensing', New York University Monograph Series in Finance and Economics (1977), 87 (suggesting weighing of benefits and costs).

[81] See I L Ayres and P Klemperer, 'Limiting Patentees' Market Power without Reducing Innovation Incentives: The Perverse Benefits of Uncertainty and Non-Injunctive Remedies' (1999) Michigan Law Review, 985, 1017 (suggesting that an increase of uncertainty in enforcement would increase substantially the social benefits without decreasing the patentee's profits).

[82] A combination patent is a patent 'granted for an invention that unites existing components in a novel way'. See *Black's Law Dictionary*, 7th edn, 1999. See R Jacob, 'Objectionable Narrowness of Claim', in *Principles of Patent Law* (Chisum *et al*) (1998), 974, 974–976 (discussing patent claims that, even though they disclose a component, claim the entire system).

instead of granting an express licence, agreeing not to sue the licensee. If properly used and enforced, most uses of this type of clause are entirely justified. The enforceability of contract clauses which have the effect of limiting the application of the exhaustion doctrine has sometimes been disputed. It has been argued that as exhaustion is protecting third parties, the parties may not limit its application in their contract. This author suggests that if a clause is drafted narrowly to provide the same effect as the doctrine of rebuttable initial entitlements, it should be enforceable.

In the prevailing law, the US has in place the largest number of legal structures **3.105** to balance the burdens between different parties. Primarily, the concepts of copyright fair use and misuse of patents and copyright appear to allow the balancing of different entitlements. In Europe the traditional copyright doctrines have been based on detailed lists of exemptions with rather flexible national legislative measures in place to correct any major deficiencies. However, the possibilities of any such corrective measures are increasingly giving way to detailed pan-European limits for any balancing actions. Also, TRIPS has considerably limited any balancing powers of national lawmakers. Therefore, it seems that some of the balancing power has to come from other sources, such as anti-trust laws, contract laws and traditional tort doctrines.

The rebuttable rule of initial entitlements would be consistent with the current **3.106** doctrines balancing the conflict between intellectual property rights and anti-trust laws. It would only enhance them. It would certainly conclude that market power is a prerequisite for anyone aiming to rebut the presumption. In our first example, if rights holder A had only a single song, radio station B would not play it any more if rights holder A required all the shopkeepers to turn off their radios. In our second example, if customer Z's patent is one of the many possible implementations, patentee X would simply use another implementation.[83] The issue of external costs and the need for balancing of hardships is paramount only if it is not possible effectively to compete without using intellectual property rights from a particular party.

In the US the federal Appeals Court used the reasoning of rebuttable entitlements **3.107** in its ruling in *Kodak III*. The court held that the plaintiff in the anti-trust litigation may rebut the presumption favouring the use of exclusive right. More specifically, it must be shown that the original business judgement of the rights holder was either 'pretextual' or 'does not legitimately promote competition'.[84] This author

---

[83] In the patent field, the potential problem may be that it is not always possible immediately to change a design and replace it by another design.

[84] *Image Technical Services, Inc v Eastman Kodak Co*, 125 F 3d 1195, 1212 (9th Cir 1997). See also *CR Bard, Inc v M3 Systems, Inc*, 157 F 3d 1340 (Fed Cir 1998) (patent misuse when the primary motivation for a technical change is to exclude a competitor); *United States v Microsoft*, 253 F 3d 34, 58–59 (DC Cir 2001) (if the plaintiff has provided prima facie evidence that a monopolist's conduct had anti-competitive effects and the defendant provides a pro-competitive justification—'a non-

suggests the broader use of rebuttable presumptions, not only in regard to monopolist conduct but also to support any significant balancing of external effects.[85]

3.108   In Europe the entitlements have been rebuttable under the proportionality test.[86] However, balancing has normally been made between free movement of goods and the exercise of intellectual property rights. Balancing with other interests is, however, not excluded.

3.109   In *Dior v Evora*[87] the European Court of Justice relied on the justification test that was essentially similar to the test proposed in this book. The European Court of Justice held that copyright may make it possible for a rights holder to control the marketing practices of third parties even in cases where such a third party is selling products lawfully. In such cases, the interest of the copyright owner in remuneration from the commercial exploitation of copyright must be balanced with the interest in allowing the reseller to market and sell the products in the normal course of business. In this particular case, the rights holder was relying on her copyright on the bottles of perfumes and on their packaging. The court concluded that a holder of copyright was not entitled to oppose the habitual use of the copyright by the reseller for the purpose of bringing to the public's attention the further commercialization of goods first fielded with the consent of the rights holder.[88]

Referring to our first example, both *Kodak* and *Dior v Evora* seem to suggest that balancing the interest of radio station B in maximizing its listeners with the interest of rights holder A in maximizing its revenue is appropriate. In our second example, the interest of the customer/patentee Z in maximizing its revenue could be balanced with its interest in using the product without the intervention of manufacturer/patentee X.

pretextual claim that its conduct is indeed a form of competition on the merits because it involves, for example, greater efficiency or enhanced consumer appeal'—the plaintiff must rebut that claim by demonstrating that the anti-competitive harm outweighs the pro-competitive benefit); *Atari Games Corp v Nintendo of America, Inc*, 897 F 2d 1572 (Fed Cir 1990) (an abuse may be found if sufficient power on the relevant market is present when a patent is used not only as a shield to protect an invention but as a sword to eviscerate competition unfairly); see, however, critically, R H Stern, 'Refusals to License Intellectual Property Rights and Monopoly Leverage' [1998] EIPR, 390, 394 ('pretextual' has significant content only if a patentee tries to compel the other party to yield to a demand that the patentee has no right to make).

[85] P Samuelson *et al*, 'A Manifesto Concerning the Legal Protection of Computer Programs' (1994) 94 Columbia Law Review, 2308, 2365, suggest a market-oriented approach for the protection of computer programs. That approach would involve tailoring the protection in a way that would provide the strongest protection of rights holders against imitators in the same market but would not grant similar protection for entities active in more remote markets; R S Katz and A J Safer, 'Copyright Misuse: Inconsistent Cases from the 1990s and Simple Formula for the 21st Century' (2000) 17 No 4 Computer Law 3, 7 (suggesting that a distinction is made between the market for which the exclusive rights apply and other markets in which the effects of a particular practice are visible); R A Posner, *Economic Analysis of Law* (New York, 1998), 56 ('in most cases, and without excessive cost, the courts may be able to approximate the optimum definition of property rights').

[86] See discussion above in ch 2, paras 2.123–2.137.

[87] C-337/95, *Parfums Christian Dior SA v Evora BV* [1997] ECR I-6013.

[88] See commentary and analysis in A Kur, 'The "Presentation Right"—Time to Create a New Limitation in Copyright Law?' (2000) 31 IIC, and above in ch 2, paras 2.130–2.132.

The problem with rebuttable entitlements is that their introduction into intellec- **3.110** tual property practice would be one further step towards 'individual intellectual property rights'.[89] In its most extreme application any decision involving the exercise of intellectual property rights would be subject to economic-related arguments involving reasonableness and the balancing of hardships. The existence of protection would no longer be an issue of principle since the actual scope would be tailored to individual cases.

This author suggests that individual intellectual property rights are already **3.111** increasingly created in copyright law when the economic activities of anyone involved in the media industry are intensively scrutinized. The ability to rebut initial entitlements is a necessary consequence of the expanding scope of new protected subject matter and increasingly complex value creation in the communications industry. Initial entitlements are a good solution for those situations for which they were first designed. For cases in which the initial entitlement or its particular exercise leads to extensive external harms, initial entitlements are sometimes not the appropriate solution.

Flexible liability rules

External effects may also be taken into account by favouring liability rules over **3.112** exclusive rights. Even though property rules are generally favoured for strong exclusive rights regimes, liability rules may be an alternative where there are not present the same interests as the strong regimes.[90] Therefore, it could be possible to balance social costs by implementing liability rules instead of property rules. In practice a liability rule instead of a property rule could be used to protect certain products, eg databases. However, at least in Europe, that approach has had decreasing support.[91]

Another possibility for protecting elements or activities other than the strong **3.113** 'cores' of intellectual property rights is to implement entitlements into laws based

---

[89] M Levin, *Immaterialrätten* (Stockholm, 1999), 126; P S Menell, 'The Challenges of Reforming Intellectual Property Protection for Computer Software' (1994) 94 Columbia Law Review, 2644, 2648–2649 (questioning the potential complexity of having every action equipped with 'externality meters').

[90] See J H Reichman and P Samuelson, 'Intellectual Property Rights in Data?' (1997) Vanderbilt University Law Review, 51, 148 (suggesting that an automatic licence may be ideal if the aim is to provide 'a minimalist, pro-competitive cure for chronically insufficient lead time'); M Lehmann, 'TRIPs, the Berne Convention, and Legal Hybrids' (1994) 94 Columbia Law Review, 2621, 2629 (suggesting strengthened unfair competition laws to protect computer programs); J H Reichman, 'Legal Hybrids Between the Patent and Copyright Paradigms' (1994) 94 Columbia Law Review, 2557–2558 (a liability regime would advance innovation more than the anti-competitive regimes of exclusive property rights); see also Menell, n 87 above, 2646 (rewarding all in accordance with their share leads to complex compensation issues); Merges, n 56 above, 2655 (suggesting the property rules with exclusive rights have been used quite effectively because they encourage parties to reduce transaction costs).

[91] See EU Database Directive (96/9/EY) (establishing property rights for databases).

on unfair competition or misappropriation. These laws traditionally provide flexible liability rules. In the US, this approach usually has its origins in *International News Services, Inc v Associated Press*.[92] This approach would actually provide entitlement to the initial investment subject to market conditions. In line with the suggestions of Reichman and Samuelson in respect of databases, such an entitlement could be based on the evaluation of the following arguments:

(1) amount of creation or invention appropriated by the user;

(2) nature of the appropriation;

(3) purpose of the appropriation;

(4) amount of initial investment;

(5) independence and amount of the user's investment;

(6) degree of similarity between products;

(7) proximity of markets;

(8) the speed of introduction by the user as compared to development time.[93]

3.114 The highly diversified national traditions where doctrines of unfair competition have been used to supplement intellectual property rights represent the main obstacle for the application of this doctrine internationally. The traditional German *Wettbewerbsrecht* has possibly the closest tradition of supplemental protection. The US tradition has been reluctant in its application of supplemental protections. Rather, federal intellectual property laws have pre-empted any such concepts under state laws.[94] The Scandinavian tradition, especially the Swedish and Finnish tradition, has many similarities with the American tradition.

---

[92] 248 US 215 (1918).

[93] See Reichman–Samuelson, n 88 above, 142–143.

[94] See *Bonito Boats v Thundercraft Boats*, 109 S Ct 971 (1989) (establishing federal pre-emption by holding that the state regulation of intellectual property must yield to the extent that it clashes with the balance struck by Congress in patent laws).

4

EXTERNAL EFFECTS THEORY APPLIED

Relevance of addressee/impact combination

Impact on imitating competitors

It can be easily seen that a rights holder may use intellectual property rights to **4.01** oppose imitations. The case law and commentaries have generally adopted the approach that any enforcement activities directed against competitors to stop imitations are privileged. This is the 'core' or 'specific subject matter' of any intellectual property laws. The courts and commentators are universally reluctant to overrule the legal presumption that activities with the sole aim of stopping imitations are privileged from intervention by anti-trust laws.[1] An innovator's most immediate concern is to enjoy the advantage of its innovation in the market for its product. Competitors in the same market threaten the activities of the rights holder in an immediate way.[2] This author supports this view.

The courts and enforcement agencies should not easily intervene if a particular **4.02** practice has nothing more than an effect on imitations by competitors. The limited duration of protection and protection against non-literal infringement have already been adjusted to balance the potential conflict between imitation and innovation. Therefore, also compulsory licensing schemes that can be applied against the rights holder merely at the request of imitators are both uncommon and generally not well-received by the courts, legislators and the international rights holders' community. The main exception to this rule is where there has been a deceitful or wrongful acquisition of the particular rights. Because of the high costs involved in intellectual property litigation, 'sham' litigation may, in the

---

[1] See above ch 2, paras 2.48–2.52 and 2.123; C Bellamy and G Child, *European Community Law of Competition* (5th edn, P M Roth ed) (London 2001), 644.

[2] P Samuelson *et al*, 'A Manifesto Concerning the Legal Protection of Computer Programs' (1994) 94 Columbia Law Review, 2308, 2418. Consequently, even the inability to supply the market demand should not justify compulsory licensing to competitors. For a different view see in Mentula *et al*, *Määräävän Markkina-asemas vaarinkaytto Kilpailuoikeudessa* (Helsinki 1998), 188; K Leivo and T Leivo, *Euroopan Yhteisön Kilpailuoikeus* (Helsinki, 1997), 357–358.

absence of any intervention, be effectively used to increase barriers to entry for small competitors. It may also cause them to divert into litigation resources that would otherwise be used in marketing or product development.[3]

Impact on secondary market

In general

4.03 There is a lot more uncertainty where a particular practice does not have its effects solely on imitating competitors. A company that is not actively selling its products on the same market as the rights holder does not immediately threaten the success of the rights holder. Intellectual property rights may still affect the activities of such companies. It is recognized that even though a rights holder may not be present in a particular market, it may still recognize business opportunities that it would like to make use of later. Consequently, protection is still justified. However, the more remote the market on which an innovation or work is used, the less justified is the exercise of the exclusive right to its full potential.[4]

4.04 Two simple charts can illustrate this. The first chart shows a static view frequently found in intellectual property statutes. Here, the protection of the rights holder does not have to be balanced against any competing interests. The second chart shows the situation in which it is recognized that the social value of the invention or work decreases the further away the activity is from the directly imitating activities.

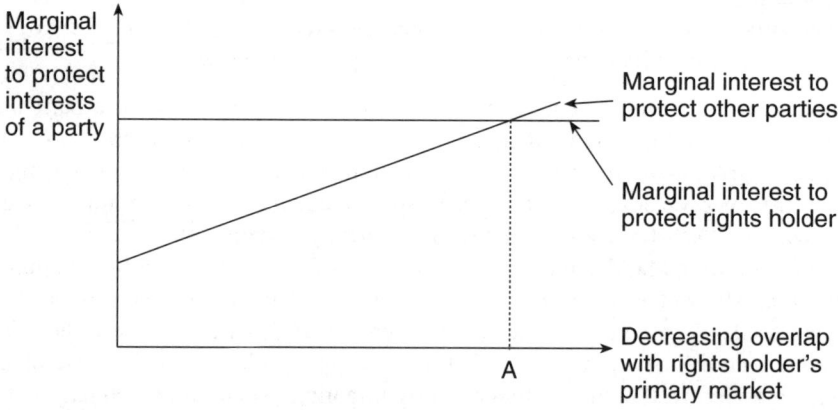

[3] In the US the leading case is *Professional Real Estate Developers v Columbia Pictures Industries, Inc*, 508 US 49 (1993) (the litigation is a 'sham' if it is objectively baseless in the sense that no reasonable litigant could realistically have expected success on the merits). See for commentary, R H Sinkfield and T L Houser, 'Patent Misuse and Anti-trust' (1999) 572 PLI/Pat, 383, 408.

[4] Samuelson–Davis–Kabor–Reichmann, n 2 above, 2418–2419; U Bernitz *et al*, *Immaterialrätt* (7th edn, Stockholm, 1998), 142–143 (one may presume that the further the effects of the practice are from the immediate production process, the more critical such practice is from the competition point of view).

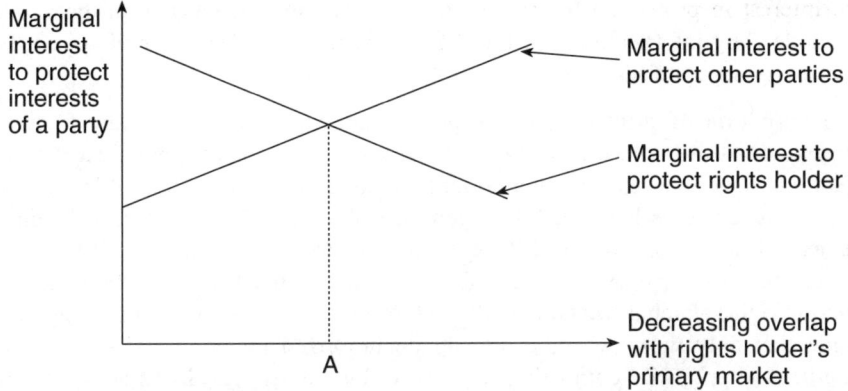

Marginal interest to protect interests of a party

Marginal interest to protect other parties

Marginal interest to protect rights holder

Decreasing overlap with rights holder's primary market

A

Table. If one presumes that the marginal interest to provide immunity for other parties against rights holders' leveraging practices increases as the overlap with the rights holder's primary market decreases, it is important to notice that the point (A) where such immunity is justified depends on the fact whether legal doctrines grant protection to the rights holder irrespective of the overlap with the rights holder's primary market (the first chart) or whether the protection decreases as the overlap decreases (the latter chart).

Consumers may value the services of an Internet service provider (ISP) partly **4.05** because it enables them to access digital music files. Similarly, a consumer may buy the particular music recording because the rights holder uses the network of the ISP to distribute it. Such a model of value creation is typical in the network economy. Neither of the parties may claim the exclusive role in value creation. How should the entitlements be distributed between the parties? The theory introduced in this book suggests that the initial entitlement of the rights holder to its copyright should not be disputed whenever the ISP is involved in the same primary market as the rights holder. Such is the case whenever the ISP establishes a service enabling the consumers to download digital music files from the server that ISP maintains.

However, if ISPs are not involved in that market but only in the market of provid- **4.06** ing access to the Internet, they are not competing with the rights holder. Such ISPs may compete with the rights holder for the popularity of consumers and the rights holder may potentially want to compete with the ISP on the market for delivery services, but the ISP is not competing on the market for music files. Even if technical copies of the works were created on the ISP's server whenever a consumer accesses digital music files through such an access point, the ISP's activity is not competing with the activities of the rights holder.[5] Consequently,

---

[5] H Laddie *et al*, *The Modern Law of Copyright and Designs* (3rd edn, London 2000), 1671 (reproduction rights cannot be infringed involuntarily since 'it is not machines which infringe copyright, but people').

the interest in protecting the rights holder is less significant than in the above example. Any intervention into the ISP's activities would have an effect on the market for separate services.[6]

4.07 The definition of primary and secondary markets is one of the key features presented in this book. It is recognized that such definitions are not always clear. If an end-user is accessing unauthorized digital content through an ISP's access point, how can one distinguish between primary and secondary markets? It may be argued that a copy in the ISP's system is a copy even though the ISP has no active control over it. According to this logic, the author has an exclusive reproduction right, which covers the work in all of its forms. The other possibility is to argue that only those who are making unauthorized material available on the Internet are primarily competing with the rights holder. The ISP's activities are only facilitating communication and its role is secondary. The author of this book suggests that the issue of providing protection against anyone making unauthorized copyrighted content available on the Internet is fundamentally different from the issue of extending similar protection against ISPs or equipment manufacturers that compete for the popularity of consumers only by providing them with technical services.

4.08 Another useful example involves spare parts. In the European discussion involving industrial designs,[7] elements that are necessary in order for the spare part to 'fit' in the place of the original part[8] and elements that are necessary in order for the same part to 'match' the original product[9] are exempted from the scope of the exclusive right. How would one justify this limitation by using the theory of primary and secondary markets? Is a manufacturer of spare parts imitating the rights holder on the primary market of spare parts or does the enforcement of the design right covering the original product potentially have an effect on the secondary market of spare parts? It is easy to recognize that the issue of 'must fit' and 'must match' involves design choices made in the original product. Such design choices may have an effect on the market of spare parts. In that sense, the limitation is made in order to minimize the effects on the secondary market of spare parts.

---

[6] Such intervention would potentially impede technological innovations that do not relate to the protected interests of the rights holder. See P Samuelson, 'Comments for Panel Session, in the *Boundaries of Copyright, its Proper Limitations and Exceptions* (Baukh *et al* eds) (1999), 76, 78–79 (listing search engines and filtering software as typical innovations that cannot be used without making technical copies).

[7] Directive 98/71/EC of the European Parliament and of the Council of 13 October 1998 on the legal protection of designs, [1998] OJ L 289, pp. 0028–0035.

[8] Art 7.1: A design right shall not subsist in features of appearance of a product, which are solely dictated by its technical function.

[9] Art 7.2: A design right shall not subsist in features of appearance of a product which must necessarily be reproduced in their exact form and dimensions in order to permit the product in which the design is incorporated or to which it is applied to be mechanically connected to or placed in, around or against another product so that either product may perform its function.

Consequently, this author suggests that at some point 'A' the interest to protect   **4.09**
third parties engaging in remote businesses exceeds the interest of society to
protect the exclusive right of the rights holder. At that point, the initial entitlement
of the rights holder should be rebuttable. However, there is a fundamental difference in the outcome depending on whether it is recognized that the social value
of the invention or work decreases as the activity involves more distant markets.
If that is not recognized, the exclusive right may cover activities that are more
valuable than the input of the rights holder.

The point 'A' may be established in the statutes as it has frequently already been   **4.10**
done. Consequently, a particular activity may be established that is not covered
by exclusive rights or is subject to particular safe-harbour rules that exclude the
activity from liability in particular circumstances. In recent years, the tendency
has been to tailor any limitations narrowly while at the same time expanding the
scope of protected subject matter. The problem is that activities beyond the point
'A' may provide attractive revenue possibilities. Also, legislation does not necessarily provide the flexibility to establish distinctions between different markets.
This may create situations in which the initial system of entitlements established
in intellectual property laws does not provide the proper balance. For such situations, the rebuttable entitlements are necessary.

It may be possible instantly to recognize cases and factual circumstances in which   **4.11**
intervention in enforcement activities has been justified. Firstly, one may refer to
the body of fairly recent case law in which the enforcement of intellectual property laws has been rejected if the practice has had its impact on a secondary
market or in general on *another market than the one on which the products
covered by the rights directly compete*. There appears to be a further distinction
between the sale of complete products and the licence to manufacture them, even
though the merits of such a distinction may be disputed.[10] The refusal to supply
complete products, or the refusal to license exclusive rights covering the product
on the same market in which the right has its primary use, or the product on the
related market for which the product is only a component for otherwise complete
products, may all be treated differently.

The rule seems to be visible in both the US and in Europe where courts are *per*   **4.12**
se hindered from intervening in the enforcement of intellectual property rights
against manufacturers in the same market where the rights holder also competes

---

[10] See *Musik-Vertrieb Membran GmbH and K-Tel International v Gema* [1981] 2 CMLR 44
(sound recordings are products even if they are protected by copyright); *CICRA and Maxicar v
Renault* [1988] 4 CMLR 265; *AB Volvo v Erik Veng (UK) Ltd* [1990] 4 CMLR 265. In the US, a
federal appeals court has rejected the merits of such a distinction. See *Image Technical Services,
Inc v Eastman Kodak ('Kodak II')*, 125 F 3d 1195 (9th Cir 1997), cert. denied, 118 S Ct 1560
(1998).

primarily.[11] However, if the enforcement action has an effect on allocation of resources on another market, this *'per se'* rule has been rebuttable.[12]

4.13 In *Kodak III*[13] the manufacturer of spare parts could not refuse to sell its patented spare parts to independent service organizations. The court held that a monopolist's refusal to deal is not justified if a jury finds that such refusal is pretextual. The initial presumption in favour of a rights holder's right to refuse to deal may be rebutted.

4.14 In *C R Bard, Inc v M3 Systems, Inc*,[14] the federal appeals court made a distinction between technical changes primarily justified by the need to improve the product and technical changes primarily addressed to harm competitors in another market for replacement parts.

4.15 In *re Service Organizations Antitrust Litigation*[15] the federal appeals court appears to have relied on the same test. The court denied the relief from independent service organizations. It held that a patentee could enforce its patents and copyrights against the infringing manufacturing by independent service organizations. Such organizations would have directly competed with the rights holder on the same market of spare parts that the exclusive rights covered.

4.16 Even though the outcome was different from *Kodak III*, it is possible to interpret the case as an example of a balancing test that under particular circumstances finds justification in favour of the rights holder.[16] The exclusive rights of Xerox covered the disputed parts and the element of the tying or otherwise arbitrary extension of the effects of the practice to another market was not as obvious as in *Kodak III*. Xerox was competing on the same market in which the exclusive rights were primarily exercisable and its competitors were infringing its intellectual property rights. Consequently, a rule finding a refusal to license any new innovations involving spare parts as 'pretextual' would have undermined the need to protect the innovations covering such parts. Rather, the burden of proof was on the defendants to show that the refusal was not justified.

---

[11] *Professional Real Estate Investors, Inc v Columbia Pictures Industries, Inc*, 508 US 49 (1993) (a sham infringement suit is a suit (1) which is objectively baseless, and (2) which conceals an attempt to interfere directly with the business relationships of a competitor). Consequently, the presumption strongly favours the justification of the rights holder.

[12] See S Anderman, *EC Competition Law and Intellectual Property Rights* (Oxford, 1998), 175 (discussing EU practice controlling spill-over effects on separate markets).

[13] *Image Technical Services, Inc v Eastman Kodak ('Kodak II')*, 125 F 3d 1195 (9th Cir 1997), cert. denied, 118 S Ct 1560 (1998). The controversial part of this case is the *dictum* that there is no difference between selling a patented product and the granting of a licence to manufacture it. Further, the concept of 'pretextual' refusal is subject to speculation. It is generally understood to mean that the refusal to deal was not truly based on a desire to protect intellectual property rights.

[14] *C R Bard, Inc v M3 Systems, Inc*, 157 F 3d 1340 (Fed Cir 1998) (patent misuse).

[15] *In re Independent Serv Organization Anti-trust Litigation*, 203 F 3d 1322 (Fed Cir 2000).

[16] As the balance was found in favour of the service organizations in *Kodak III*. It is recognized that, at the time this book was written, the proper interpretation of this case was unsettled.

Alcatel v DGI[17] illustrates the flexibility of the concept of copyright misuse[18]   **4.17**
whenever two separate markets can be identified. In *Alcatel v DGI* Alcatel had
licensed its proprietary operating system with restrictions that allowed the operating system to be used only in connection with Alcatel's network equipment. The
licence terms did not allow the operating system to be copied or disclosed to third
parties. A competitor, with the assistance of the network operator, copied the
operating system and designed its own products compatible with Alcatel's products. When the competitor's products were put into use, the operating system was
necessarily downloaded onto such products in order for them to function in
connection with other network elements.

The federal appeals court held that Alcatel's practice allowing customers to use   **4.18**
its operating system only in connection with the network equipment provided by
Alcatel constituted a misuse of Alcatel's copyright.[19] Independent providers of
network components could rely on such misuse even when they had directly
infringed the copyright by copying the operating system of Alcatel onto their
products in order to test them. The court came to the same conclusion in respect
of indirect copyright infringement of selling products that could only be used
together with unauthorized copies of Alcatel's operating system.[20] Without the
copying of Alcatel's operating system they could not have manufactured products
for the network previously provided by Alcatel.

The case appears to suggest that the enforcement of intellectual property rights is   **4.19**
not justified if such enforcement has its primary effects on another market than
the market of products protected by such rights.[21] The case is significant because
of its potential effects on competition between vertically and horizontally integrated business models.[22]

---

[17] *Alcatel USA, Inc v DGI Technologies, Inc*, 166 F 3d 772 (5th Cir 1999).

[18] See ch 2, paras 2.65–2.68 above for the definition of the misuse concept. See R S Katz and A J
Safer, 'Copyright Misuse: Inconsistent Cases from the 1990s and Simple Formula for the 21st
Century' (2000) 17 No 4 Computer Law, 3, 7 (suggesting a simple rule: (1) What is the market in
which copyright applies? (2) Is the rights holder trying to stifle competition on a separate market?).

[19] Compare with the European practice in *Windsurfing Int, Inc v E C Commission* [1986] 3 CMLR
489 (when patent for sailboards consists of two articles, a patent licence may not restrict dealings with
component parts).

[20] *Alcatel USA, Inc v DGI Technologies, Inc*, 166 F 3d 772, 793–794 (5th Cir 1999).

[21] In this case Alcatel's copyright in the operating system had its primary effects on the separate
market for expansion cards.

[22] *Alcatel v DGI* was the first case in which a court held that the traditional business model to
supply vertically integrated systems may successfully be challenged even without establishing any
monopoly power (or in practice, a *de facto* standard) on the market of system supply. The supply of
vertically integrated systems was for a long time and still, at the time when this book was written, is
the primary business model for many technically complex products. It is typical for the supply of such
vertically integrated systems that the software licensing terms for the operating system usually allow
it to be downloaded, copied and run on a number of equipment provided that such equipment is
provided by the supplier of the operating system. In the business of horizontally integrated markets,
typically PC markets, the licensing terms of operating systems allow it to be used only on a single

4.20   In Europe the effects of the practice have been balanced against other interests under the proportionality test. In *CICRA and Maxicar v Renault*,[23] the European Court of Justice held that the enforcement of design rights against anyone manufacturing products constituted the very essence of the exclusive right. However, the exercise of exclusive right may be prohibited under Article 86 of the EC Treaty[24] if it is used for arbitrary refusal to deliver spare parts to independent service organizations, to fix prices of such spare parts at an unfair level or in a decision to stop producing spare parts even though cars still remained in circulation.

4.21   In *Volvo v Veng*[25] the court relied on an analysis similar to that in *CICRA and Maxicar v Renault*, but developed it further. The court held that while arbitrary refusal to grant a licence to *import and sell* spare parts by a dominant undertaking is an abuse under Article 86, the refusal to license third parties to manufacture them, even in return for a reasonable royalty, cannot itself be regarded as an abuse of a dominant position.

4.22   In *Windsurfing International*[26] the provisions in the licence agreement were held to violate Article 85 of the EC Treaty to the extent that (1) the patent covered only a component part and the agreement attempted to control the complete product, or (2) the patent covered a complete product and the agreement attempted to control individual components.

Finally in *Magill*[27] the court held that television stations could not refuse to license their copyrights on the listing of their forthcoming programmes. Magill did not compete with television stations in their primary market of daily television programme listings but only in the separate market of weekly television programme listings. None of the exclusive rights of the television stations covered the weekly television listings but only the component parts necessary for weekly listings.

4.23   The court cited three separate grounds for its findings:

piece of equipment. A further licence fee is payable for any new equipment added to the network. Consequently, the Alcatel court seems to suggest that the licensing model of horizontally integrated systems is more justified than that of vertically integrated systems. See also D A Balto, 'Network and Exclusivity: Anti-trust Analysis to Promote Network Competition' (1990), 7 George Mason Law Review, 523, 523 (discussing the effects of network exclusivity). One possible approach is to discuss vertically integrated systems in terms of exclusive dealings.

[23]   *CICRA and Maxicar v Renault* [1988] 4 CMLR 265.
[24]   Art 82 of the Treaty of the European Union.
[25]   *AB Volvo v Erik Veng (UK) Ltd* [1990] 4 CMLR 265; see also *Eurofix Ltd v Hilti AG* [1989] CMLR 677 (the practice to sell patented nail cartridges had an effect on the secondary market for compatible nails).
[26]   *Windsurfing Int, Inc v E C Commission* [1986] 3 CMLR 489.
[27]   *Radio Telefís Éireann (RTÉ) and Independent Television Publications Ltd (ITP) v Commission ('Magill')* [1995] 4 CMLR 718.

(1) the refusal to license prevented the appearance of a new product,
(2) the defendants did not offer a similar product,
(3) there was a potential customer demand for such a product.

When balancing the competing justifications, the court held that the broadcasting activities as such and the publication of the stations' own proprietary television magazines were not enough to justify the practice. Instead, the court held that television stations reserved themselves the entire secondary market by excluding all competition when denying access to basic information, which is the raw material indispensable for the compilation of such guides.

Exhaustion
The exhaustion or 'first sale' doctrine of intellectual property rights is a tradi-   **4.24**
tional formal doctrine of solving problems arising on the interaction between intellectual property rights and competition. Exhaustion limits the effects of intellectual property rights on the secondary market. It has long been established that the rights derived from intellectual property protection do not extend beyond the first sale of the goods covered by such rights.

The subject matter of such rights, it has been said, does not go beyond such first   **4.25**
sale.

Consequently, it is considered self-evident that anyone may buy a car from a licensed manufacturer and may use it without any obligations to pay royalties to the patentee.

If one buys a compact disc from a record shop, one may play it a number of times and resell to third parties because the rights holder's exclusive right has been exhausted upon the first lawful sale.

The application of the doctrine, however, has been disputed in terms of its application to international trade due to the traditional territorial nature of intellectual property rights.[28]

In the network economy, this doctrine faces new challenges that may require   **4.26**
redefinition. Firstly, its application to the digital distribution of content has been challenged.[29] It has been suggested that the right to distribute a digitally distributed copy further should not exist because that would potentially facilitate counterfeit copying. The counter-argument has been that whenever a consumer is entitled to make a permanent copy of a digital file, that consumer should be entitled to the same rights as the purchaser of media that contains the same content. Secondly, in the increasingly complex value chain of the network economy, the

---

[28] See O A Rognstad, *Spredning av vorksexemplar* (Oslo 1999) 166 for motivations for the doctrine (identifying the doctrine as a solution to different interest conflicts: limitation of author's reward, society's interest in having copies available, interest of competition, balance between the purchaser of a copy and the author).

[29] Directive 2001/29/EC of the European Parliament and of the Council of 22 May 2001 on the harmonization of certain aspects of copyright and related rights in the information society, recital (29) (no exhaustion in respect of copies made by the users of online services); NII, 124 (no exhaustion upon transmission through networks because the original copy remains with the original owner).

application of the doctrine faces new challenges.[30] The doctrine may be used to maximize control over other companies' activities as well as to minimize their control. Both challenges have been initiated by the strategic choices some companies are attempting. The viability of these strategic choices is the topic of this chapter.

4.27 The doctrine essentially has a similar practical application both in Europe and in the US. However, the reasoning and the justifications for the doctrine are different in both places.

4.28 In the US, the Supreme Court applied the doctrine as early as in 1873.[31] The current application of the doctrine is best illustrated by the reasoning in *Mallinckrodt v Medipart*.[32] In *Mallinckrodt* a patented medical device was sold for 'a single use only'. The purchaser had the device prepared after each use and in practice used it multiple times. The Federal Circuit held in favour of the patentee while stating that such restriction was neither '*per se*' patent misuse, nor illegal under anti-trust laws. According to the Federal Circuit, the proper criterion is 'whether restriction is reasonably within the patent grant, or whether the patentee has ventured beyond the patent grant and into the behavior having [an] anti-competitive effect not justifiable under the rule of reason'.[33] It was relevant that the purchaser had positive knowledge of such restriction at the time it purchased the device, and the restriction was reasonable and not anti-competitive.

4.29 In Europe, the doctrine has evolved through national laws and through the decisions of the European Court of Justice. The current doctrines have established content.[34] The rights holder's right is exhausted by the first sale of the goods with

---

[30] See discussion in ch 3, para 3.12–3.16 above.

[31] *Adams v Burke*, 84 US 453 (1873).

[32] *Mallinckrodt, Inc v Medipart, Inc*, 976 F 2d 700 (Fed Cir 1992).

[33] Id at 708. If a device has practically no non-infringing uses, the limitation is likely not to be justified. *Met-Coil Systems Corp v Korners Unlimited, Inc*, 803 F 2d 684 (Fed Cir 1986) (establishing two requirements for implied licences by virtue of the first sale: (1) the equipment does not have any non-infringing uses, and (2) the sale must plainly indicate that the grant of a licence should be inferred). The similar is likely also in respect of first sales by a licensee, *Intel Corp v US Int'l Trade Commission*, 946 F 2d 821 (Fed Cir 1991) (Atmel did not infringe Intel's patents because allegedly infringing components had been supplied by Sanyo under its licence from Intel); *Intel Corp v ULSI Corp*, 995 F 2d 1566 (Fed Cir 1993) (ULSI did not infringe Intel's patents because allegedly infringing semiconductors were supplied by Hewlett Packard under its licence from Intel).

[34] See discussion above in ch 2, paras 2.35–2.36 and 2.125–2.132. *Centrafarm v Sterling Drug* [1974] 2 CMLR 480 (the patent right may not be exercised to prohibit the sale of patented goods in a member state if those goods have been marketed in another member state with consent); *Centrafarm v Winthrop* [1974] CMLR 480 (the same rule applies even if the prices of pharmaceuticals were different as a consequence of state action); *Musik-Vertrieb Membran GmbH and K-Tel International v Gema* [1981] 2 CMLR 44. The most extreme application of existence/exercise doctrine was probably in *Van Zuylen Freres v HAG AG ('HAG I')* [1974] CMLR 127 (one cannot rely on the exclusive right to prohibit the marketing of goods legally produced in another member state under an identical trade mark having the same origin but owned by a separate independent company); see after that especially *SA CNL-Sucal NV v HAG GF AG ('HAG II')* [1990] 3 CMLR 571 (effectively overruling *HAG I*);

the consent of the rights holder, irrespective of whether such first sale is made by the rights holder or a licensee.

Most exhaustion cases involve patents. In copyright cases, it is important to make **4.30** the distinction between the various rights an enforceable copyright provides for the author. It is also relevant to make a distinction between the copyright and the physical copy of a work of authorship. Only the right to distribute a physical copy may be exhausted, not the copyright as such, containing reproduction rights or performance rights.

In the network economy, companies face an increasingly more common situation **4.31** where different companies own the relevant intellectual property rights. It is usual that these intellectual property rights are owned by someone who has made a substantial investment in the development of such intellectual property, provided that the entity has also invested in the adequate protection of such rights through intellectual property protection systems.

Companies owning relevant intellectual property rights are increasingly compa- **4.32** nies whose primary activities are on a traditionally different level of the value chain than the company whose activities the exclusive rights affect. Alternatively, the potential users or licensees of the technology are increasingly found on a different level of the value chain as well. Consequently, in the network economy it becomes increasingly important to define the proper application of the exhaustion doctrine. This is because both exhaustion and the lack of it may be used for leveraging.

Firstly, the territorial limitations of this doctrine are not discussed in detail in this **4.33** book. Territorial divisions of markets and the consequent price discrimination are viable leveraging strategies for companies. The problem with territorial application of the exhaustion doctrine is that it may delay the emergence of global electronic commerce. The limitation of exhaustion may also have significant effects on the electronic commerce market for goods protected by intellectual property rights. This is because without exhaustion a customer in one geographic territory may potentially only acquire goods from that territory and not from other territories. The location of the supplier potentially remains a relevant factor and the opportunities for all kinds of intermediaries to engage in global e-commerce irrespective of their location may be diminished.

Secondly, any use restrictions or limitations on exhaustion may be used to facili- **4.34** tate control of the value chain. Such control is an effective form of leveraging. For instance, the limitation to use digital content distributed through the Internet only on specified terminal equipment is a viable means for the content industry

Pharmon BV v Hoecst AG [1985] 3 CMLR 775 (no exhaustion by compulsory licensing). See also *Microsoft*, BGH 6 July 2000–IZR 244/97 (the licence terms allowing OEM customers to redistribute software products only in connection with hardware were held unenforceable).

to control the introduction of new equipment. If the users may not use their digital content files on any equipment they like, equipment manufacturers become dependent on content providers. This is due to the fact that new equipment cannot be introduced if there is no content available. Alternatively, if users may use their existing digital content files on new equipment, the introduction of such new equipment would be controlled by the willingness of the users to use such content files on new equipment, not solely on the content providers' willingness to provide such content.

4.35 Consequently, it is in the interests of the content providers to argue that any use restrictions are valid and enforceable. It is in the interests of the equipment manufacturers and users to argue for the existence of the exhaustion doctrine. Due to the vertical integration of the content industry, operators and equipment manufacturers, there is also a third interest group of equipment manufacturers that may benefit from the possibility of excluding some of their competitors from introducing innovative new equipment.

This issue frequently raises controversies. It has been an established right of an author under copyright laws to control any new uses of his or her work of authorship. Therefore, it is sometimes claimed that if consumers were able to use the works on any equipment, that would potentially limit authors' control over the work.[35] Furthermore, it has been argued that it is important for the authors to be able to charge for every new use of their work. In the absence of that right, their reward potentialities would be seriously diminished.

The counter-argument to this has been that the laws have not allowed the author to control the use of a physical copy of the work after it has been first sold. Therefore, why should such a right be allowed in the network economy of digital works? The right to control new uses has covered only the right to reproduce the work in different forms and display or distribute them in a new form. The right to view, play or run the digital form of the same work on a different machine is not within that traditional right. The former argument has been targeted at the relationship between the author and the producer, the publisher or the distributor, whereas the latter argument deals with the relationship between the author and the end-user.

4.36 In most parts of the world, the exhaustion of copyright in the case of digital distribution remains unsolved. However, in Europe the EU Copyright Directive established some new limitations the implications of which are not entirely clear. According to the EU Copyright Directive, copyright is not exhausted if a user accesses the work through online services.[36] If this means that copyright is exhausted only if the user is licensed to make a permanent physical copy, there is

---

[35] J C Ginsburg, 'Authors and Users in Copyright' (1997) 45 Journal of the Copyright Society in the USA, 1, 1.

[36] Recital (29): 'The question of exhaustion does not arise in the case of services and on-line services in particular. This also applies with regard to a material copy of a work or other subject matter made by a user of such a service with the consent of the rightholder.'

no significant change in the law. However, if the new rule means that there will be no exhaustion whenever a copy is acquired through online service providers, this change may have significant business implications.[37] Since the EU Copyright Directive contains a number of limitations of the exclusive right, such as private copying, the actual implication of this change in the law remains to be seen. Also, it is obvious that the lack of exhaustion may violate anti-trust laws if the rights holder tries to benefit from it in an abusive way. However, the decision, reasoned with anti-piracy concerns in mind, was a remarkable deviation from the traditional rule of almost '*per se*' treatment of these restrictions in Europe.[38]

Thirdly, if a company asks for patent royalty payments from other companies or charges them with patent infringement, such a company is increasingly facing a threat of a patent counterclaim targeting their own business. This reflects the widely used strategy to use patents defensively and primarily to use them for counterclaiming.   **4.37**

If a company has already licensed its patents to a supplier of the party claiming its patents against such company, this strategy is less viable due to the patent exhaustion doctrine. A party asserting its patents may possibly claim that it does not need any licences because its suppliers already have a licence, or in the absence of a licence may in its intellectual property indemnity obligations have taken the responsibility to acquire any necessary licences. From the target companies' point of view, it may be unfair to be a target for patent claims at the same time as the claimant benefits from the innovations that, if the claim were known, would not have been licensed.   **4.38**

Companies have taken some initiatives to solve this potential problem. The most typical method is to exclude combinations prepared by the licensee's customers from the scope of the licence.

Another method is to exclude from the scope of the licence any components or elements, the designs of which have not been prepared by or for the licensee. This may apply to the design provided by a supplier or the customer of a licensee.

Yet more typical methods include an express exclusion of sales to some customers from the licence or rather the right to terminate a licence in the event of a patent claim from a particular customer.

The last frequently used effort is not to license a particular party but only to agree not to assert the patents against such party. The actual effect of such 'non-assertion clause' is assumed to be the avoidance of the exhaustion doctrine.[39]

---

[37] Because copies acquired through online service providers or on physical media would be treated differently.

[38] See eg in Germany, *Microsoft*, BGH 6 July 2000–IZR 244/97 (any end-users buying software directly should obtain the same benefits as if the software were pre-installed in the computer by OEM manufacturers).

[39] See ch 3, para 3.104 above.

4.39 The enforceability of these methods depends on a case-by-case analysis under the rule of reason. Under the rule of reason analysis, the specific facts, effects and motivations may be taken into account. Such motivations and effects may be presented in the following table:

TYPICAL LIMITATION OF SCOPE OF LICENCE	UNDERLYING MOTIVATION	POTENTIAL COMPETITIVE EFFECT
The customer of the licensee is not licensed to use the products.	Collect royalties	Provides control over licensee's customers = > royalty payments by the customers will limit the ability for a licensee to expand its business.
		May increase returns from licensing.
	Protect own business	Normally justified and pro-competitive but extensive practical application may discourage licensee's customers to innovate.
Termination of a licence if customer of a licensee sues for infringement.	Protect own business	May be justified and pro-competitive but may also discourage the licensee's customer to innovate.

Impact on end-users

Opposing imitations

4.40 It is self-evident that the practices used by the rights holder may have an impact on the end-user. Firstly, *practices that are solely aimed at stopping the end-user from becoming an imitator* are usually approved. Consequently, contract terms may be imposed that do not allow the end-user to reproduce the protected product, or, in the case of copyrighted works, do not allow the end-user further to distribute or publicly perform the product.

It is customary to limit the right of the customer to install software only on one computer or central processing unit (CPU). Consumers are not authorized to rent or publicly perform movies sold as video cassettes or DVD disks. Their licence terms typically limit their usage to the immediate household of the consumer.

4.41 Technical means, such as copy protection devices, are therefore generally justified in order to avoid imitation.

Technical protection means may for instance make it impossible for the user to forward digital content to other users. This is justified because without such technical means there is a risk that either the original user or the recipient of a copy will retain a copy for which the rights holder has not received any compensation.

Intellectual property laws protect the rights holder against imitations and the **4.42** enforcement of such rights does not normally raise any particular concerns.

However, the law generally protects end-users against abusive uses of intellectual **4.43** property rights. Also, some practices that may superficially have the justified goal of protecting rights holders against imitations may have a parallel effect in some related markets. In such cases, two rules are applicable. Firstly, the practice may be evaluated in terms of the balancing tests introduced above. Alternatively, there may be a consideration of whether there are any less restrictive practices available to achieve the same end.

Normal use
The first category of abusive uses covers *restrictions that do not allow the end-* **4.44** *user to make normal use of the product*. The definition of the normal use of the product as such does raise some particular questions. Normal use of a product is the use for which it is intended and for which the end-user had a reasonable expectation to use the product. This book discusses only restrictions that are based on intellectual property rights. Potentially, if end-users do not comply with particular restrictions imposed, they would be infringing the underlying intellectual property right.

Typical end-user restrictions are restrictions on the time, scope or place of the use. For instance, beta versions of computer programs typically are licensed only for a limited period of time. Patent licences may only be granted under product claims even though a licence under the method claims of the same patent may be necessary in order effectively to use the resulting product.

Contractual restrictions on physical products that do not allow end-users to make **4.45** repeated use of the product in their possession may sometimes be held to be abusive. However, the tendency is to increase the freedom of the parties to agree on any kind of limitations rather than to limit such freedom.[40] In the US, in *Mallincrodt v Medipart*,[41] the defendant had refurbished and re-used medical devices that, according to the sales terms, were only for single use and should have been disposed of afterwards. When the plaintiff sued for patent infringements, the court discussed whether such limitation was within the patent grants.[42]

---

[40] *ProCD Inc v Zeidenberg*, 86 F 3d 1447 (7th Cir 1996) (the enforcement of a shrink-wrap licence was not pre-empted by the US Copyright Act).

[41] *Mallinckrodt, Inc v Medipart, Inc*, 976 F 2d 700 (Fed Cir 1992).

[42] The reconstruction of the product is but not the repair of the product, 976 F 2d 700, 709. See also *Lummus Industries, Inc v D M & E Corp*, 862 F 2d 267, 272 (Fed Cir 1988); *Aro Mfg Co v Convertible Top Replacement Co*, 377 US 476, 480 (1964) (even repair of an unlicensed device constitutes an infringement).

It concluded that such limitation was not illegal as a matter of law. Rather, any anti-competitive effects of such a practice should be balanced by evaluating whether such limitation is justified under the rule of reason.[43]

4.46 For copyrighted products, such as software, one business practice is to provide licences that only allow use that is limited by time or the number of occasions on which the product is used. Frequently, limitations are effectively enforced by technical means that cause the product to cease working after the limitations are met. The purpose of such practices is to introduce a product to the users so that they can make their purchase decision. The limitation is enforced in order to stop the end-user from making use of the product beyond the originally agreed purpose. These practices have normally not raised any concerns, provided that the end-user has been aware of such restrictions. However, such practice, going beyond the use of beta versions, may also have an effect on other markets than the primary market. In that case, the balancing of interests is necessary.

4.47 In Europe, some normal uses of software have been identified in the EU Software Directive.[44] Consequently, every end-user may make such copies from the original software products that are necessary in order to use the product or to maintain the product in working condition.

4.48 For music and movies, a disputed issue is whether back-up copies and copies that allow the licensed work to be played or viewed at different times ('time-shifting') or on other personal equipment ('equipment-shifting') are a part of the normal use. The proponents of 'strong' intellectual property rights suggest that this is not necessarily the case since the value for the end-user is enhanced by this possibility. End-users that make copies for other play-back equipment could therefore be asked to pay more than those who use only a single piece of equipment. The counter-argument is a practical one: consumers are not likely to acquire multiple copies of the same work. Consequently, any limitations on such use are likely to be seen by consumers primarily as an attempt to limit normal 'fair' use. In Europe, the issue has partially been solved through exemptions involving private copying.[45] In accordance with the Copyright Directive, the copying of computer programs is not subject to private copying exemptions.

Selection of suppliers
4.49 The second category of abusive use covers *restrictions that limit end-users' ability to select other suppliers for related products and services*. These practices also

---

[43] *Mallinckrodt, Inc v Medipart, Inc*, 976 F 2d 700, 708 (patent owners should not be in a worse position, by virtue of the patent right to exclude, than owners of other property used in trade). Safety concerns and prevention of injury to the public have been held as justified interests.

[44] Council Directive 91/250/EEC of 14 May 1991 on the legal protection of computer programs [1991] OJ L 122.

[45] There is the ongoing dispute over the fact that the definition of private copying may in some jurisdictions extend beyond copies facilitating the normal use of the lawfully acquired original copy.

have an effect on markets other than the market for the product of the rights holder. Typical abusive contract restrictions imposed on end-users are tying arrangements that create lock-in effects.[46] A contract practice may require that a software product is licensed only on the condition that support and maintenance services are acquired at the same time. A software product may be licensed only on the condition that it is run on equipment purchased from the same supplier.

Buyers of products may be locked in to one supplier. There may be a lack of stan- **4.50** dards and, where there are intellectual property rights, an end-user may find that he can only buy replacements, spare parts and enhancements from the original supplier. Even though suppliers may compete for customers making their first purchase, after the first decision there is no competition where there is such a restriction. Economists have had diverse views on the effects of such a situation. Those users who have already made their choice and are locked in, as well as any companies willing to supply them, usually favour the lock-in to be 'opened' by public policy decisions. Companies with large installed customer bases usually consider the lock-in as justified. In the market for new customers, the lock-in may increase competition, causing first-time customers to favour the current situation.[47]

In Europe there is something of a tradition in solving such problems within intel- **4.51** lectual property laws. In the US the intellectual property misuse doctrine has also sometimes been used.[48] However, it should be remembered that exclusive supply terms as such are widely accepted and in the absence of market power do not raise any particular concerns. Any lock-in or tying should therefore not be a concern if an exclusive supply agreement in the same situation was not a concern.

Possibilities to compete
The third category of abusive uses covers *restrictions that limit the ability of the* **4.52** *end-user effectively to compete with the rights holder*. These restrictions are often limitations in quantity, price or sales channels and other 'downstream' competition.[49] Alternatively, they may limit the end-user's ability or incentive to innovate. The possibilities to abuse customers are already limited by provisions in intellectual property laws.[50] Anti-trust laws under certain circumstances are used to intervene in rights holders' practices. Examples of such restrictions are contract terms that expressly restrict the customer's right to use the product to

---

[46] These issues are discussed in more detail in ch 4, paras 4.132 and 4.148–4.162.

[47] J Farrell, 'Standardisation and Intellectual Property' (1989) 30 Jurimetrics Journal 35, 38.

[48] *Lasercomb America, Inc v Reynolds*, 911 F 2d 970 (4th Cir 1990) (licence terms restricting licensees' right to aid others to develop competing software constituted a copyright misuse on which a competitor could rely even though it was not the party to the licence).

[49] Also *extensive claims for compensation by a rights holder* may be abusive. However, the topic of extensive compensation is discussed below in ch 4, paras 4.98–4.123.

[50] M A Lemley, 'The Economics of Improvement in Intellectual Property Law' (1997) 75 Texas Law Review, 989, 1000 (discussing limitations motivated by the need to encourage improvements).

develop his own accessories, spare parts or services. Requests that tie the use of the product to other products supplied by the same supplier may also be identified as abusive.

4.53   The principal right of the rights holder freely to establish contract terms with licensees is generally presumed. However, any practices used by the rights holder, even the amount of licence fees, should be balanced against other interests. The practice of the rights holder should always be justified. At a practical level, 'coercion' of customers is relevant only if it crosses a certain threshold. If the practice not only affects the behaviour of the customer but also affects separate markets, it should be subject to a more critical assessment.

4.54   This is consistent with the current practice in the US. Anti-competitive effects that are not '*per se*' violation of law are reviewed in accordance with the rule of reason. The normal practice seems to be to evaluate whether the practice is within the exclusive rights or otherwise justified.[51] In Europe, the Technology Transfer Block Exemption provides detailed guidance.

Grant-backs

4.55   Intellectual property grant-backs are a traditional way of protecting business against leveraging and fragmentation. In the network economy, complete products potentially contain an increasing number of intellectual property rights. The cost of acquiring the necessary licences is therefore increasing. It is not surprising that companies try to minimize any need to pay licence fees to their customers. Contract terms requiring a licence grant-back are effective tools for this purpose. However, grant-back provisions may also facilitate other business purposes. The treatment of grant-back provisions has many similarities in the US and in Europe, including, however, the same deficiencies. A typical grant-back provision requires the licensee, as a condition of the licence, to grant back a licence of a specified scope to the licensor to use the licensee's technology: 'The Licensee agrees, under its intellectual property rights to technology ABC, to grant the Licensor a licence to make, use, sell, offer to sell, import or otherwise field the Licensor's products.'

4.56   If successfully implemented, a grant-back provision effectively minimizes the risk that the licensee of technology could prevent the licensor from supplying products that contain an improved version of the technology. In the network economy, grant-back provisions have some new uses and new possibilities.

4.57   There may be various reasons for requiring a grant-back licence. The most typical one is the protective interest of the licensor to avoid a situation in which the licensee could either block the licensor's own development or claim other intellectual property rights against the licensor. It is important for a licensor to avoid

---

[51] *Mallinckrodt, Inc v Medipart, Inc*, 976 F 2d 700 (Fed Cir 1992).

such a situation since the licensee may otherwise use its position to foreclose the licensor. Another motivation of the licensor may be to use the licensee for testing and further development of the technology. Since the licensee has its own motivation for investing in further development, the licensor will benefit from those efforts as a 'by-product'.

A grant-back provision is a typical clause in all open-source software terms. Typically it requires the licensee to grant back any modifications made in the original software code. Without such a clause, any licensee could benefit from the original open-source software but exclude others from using its improvements. This could potentially be detrimental to the further development of the product in the open-source format.

This clause is also used in connection with commercial proprietary software products and in connection with patent licensing. It serves the same purpose but the effects may be slightly different. While the licensor becomes protected against the claims of the licensee, the licensee may still be exposed to the claims of the licensor.

It is evident that a stand-alone grant-back clause seldom raises any issues of **4.58** competition. Most concerns from the anti-trust law point of view relate to the interest of the licensor to secure access to any future developments the licensee may produce. Such access may potentially reduce the licensee's interest to innovate.[52] Another problem is that, while minimizing the risks for the licensor, the licensee's business may become vulnerable against intellectual property rights claims from the licensor or its customers. Grant-back licences are usually subject to the rule-of-reason analysis. This requires an examination of the specific facts of the case.

In the US the use of the rule-of-reason test was established as early as 1947 in **4.59** *Transparent-Wrap Machine v Stokes & Smith*.[53] Where there is an exclusive grant-back clause, in combination with other practices, it may still be found to be illegal.[54] In the 1970s grant-backs were one of the US Department of Justice's nine banned practices for licence agreements. In the 1980s and 1990s the enforcement agencies' position shifted considerably. The 1995 *IP Guidelines* of the FTC and DOJ is one of the best examples of this shift of position. According to the 1995 *IP Guidelines*:[55]

If the Agencies determine that a particular grant-back provision is likely to reduce significantly licensees' incentives to invest in improving the licensed technology, the Agencies will consider the extent to which the grant-back provision has offsetting competitive

---

[52] R H Stern, 'Refusals to License Intellectual Property Rights and Monopoly "Leverage"' [1998] EIPR 390, 395 (discussing General Electric's practice in the 1940s of requiring grant-back licences as a condition for licences to its controlling patents, and the consequent challenge the DOJ based on the reduced incentive to innovate).

[53] *Transparent-Wrap Machine Corp v Stokes & Smith Co*, 329 US 637, reh denied, 330 US 854 (1947).

[54] *Copperweld Corp v Independence Tube Corp*, 467 US 752 (1984).

[55] 1995 *IP Guidelines*, at 20, 743–745.

effects, such as (1) promoting dissemination of licensees' improvements to the licensed technology, (2) increasing the licensor's incentives to disseminate the licensed technology, or (3) otherwise increasing competition and output in a relevant technology or innovation market. In addition, the Agencies will consider the extent to which grant-back provisions in the relevant market generally increase licensors' incentives to innovate in the first place.

4.60 In the traditional industrial economy, the courts in the US generally emphasized several factors as a part of the rule-of-reason analysis.[56] Such factors included:

- whether the grant-back is exclusive or non-exclusive;
- if exclusive, whether the licensee retains the right to use the improvements;
- whether the grant-back precludes, permits or requires the licensor to grant sublicences;
- whether the grant-back is limited to the scope of the licensed patents or covers inventions which would not be dependent of the licensed patent, ie would not infringe the licensed patent;
- duration of the grant-back;
- whether the grant-back is royalty-free;
- the market power of the parties;
- whether the parties are competitors; and
- the effect of the grant-back on the incentive for developmental research.

4.61 In Europe grant-back provisions have usually been defined as an improvement grant-back. Such grant-back provisions have been allowed if they are reciprocal and non-exclusive.[57] As early as in *Raymond/Nagoya*,[58] the European Court of Justice held that the requirement to assign ownership to improvements violates Article 85(1) of the EC Treaty. Exclusive grant-back provisions are treated in a similar way.[59]

4.62 In the network economy of the communications industry, motivations of companies, the effects of their conduct and the consequent application of these principles may be different. There are a few essential issues to examine.

4.63 Firstly, the variety of different grant-back alternatives and their typical areas of use have substantially increased. Secondly, the incentive to innovate is not easily affected by a patent grant-back since the actual implementation of a patented solution typically requires additional know-how in order to be effectively implemented. Since a licensee that is required to grant a licence back still can compete

---

[56] I K Gotts and H W Fogt, 'Clinton Administration Expresses More Than Intellectual Curiosity in Anti-trust Issues Raised by Intellectual Property Licensing' (1994) 22 AIPLA Quarterly Journal, 1, 14.

[57] Commission Regulation (EC) No 240/96 [1996] OJ L31/2 on the application of Art 85(3) of the Treaty to certain categories of technology transfer agreements, Art 2(1)(4); S D Anderman, *EC Competition Law and Intellectual Property Rights* (Oxford 1998), 109.

[58] *Raymond/Nagoya* [1972] CMLR D45; see also *Royon v Meilland* [1988] 4 CMLR 193.

[59] *Velcro SA v Aplix SA* [1989] 4 CMLR 157.

by using its ability to implement the actual product design and the opportunity to be the first to introduce new features, the effect on the incentive to innovate is limited.

Thirdly, in the network economy, the success of a new solution is increasingly **4.64** dependent on customers accepting it to be the best solution. Therefore, in the communications industry, companies tend to be prepared to share their innovations in order to maximize any network effects. Fourthly, companies are increasingly interdependent and unwillingness to share any innovations is a sign of a potential leveraging position rather than of a desire to protect one's innovations.

Finally, the market power of a patentee is higher if a technically necessary patent **4.65** is licensed than if another patent is licensed. Whenever technically necessary patents are licensed, the anti-trust or competitive law scrutiny of grant-back provisions is supposed to be more stringent because the patentee has more market power. In the contract practice of the communications industry, the variety of typical grant-back clauses and their typical areas of use are set out below.

An *improvement grant-back licence* is a licence under which the licensee grants **4.66** the licensor a licence to any improvements the licensee develops in the licensed technology. Improvement grant-back licences are a traditional method of securing that, whenever the licensee uses the licensed technology as a base for developing more advanced proprietary solutions, such solutions are shared with the licensor. A typical effect of a broad improvement grant-back licence is that the licensee is effectively providing development work free of charge for the licensor as a partial compensation for the licence. Therefore, an improvement grant-back licence is sometimes used to outsource to licensees at a minimum cost some further development activities.

An improvement grant-back licence is a part of any basic licensing model agree- **4.67** ment and subject to frequent analysis and comments. The improvement grant-back has some equity reasoning built into it. Rights holders frequently argue that if they license a competitor, the competitor may use the licensed technology, develop a more advanced solution based on that, and exclude the rights holder from using it. In order to avoid that, rights holders typically favour grant-back licences in their licence agreements.[60]

None of the major companies involved in the communications industry easily **4.68** accepts improvement grant-back licences. They are more frequently used in other fields in which new technologies are still primarily based on proprietary features. In addition, such licences are not necessarily effective in achieving the desired result unless they are properly tailored. These concerns are based on the following factors.

---

[60] See discussion of 'serial model of innovation' in ch 1.

4.69 Firstly, companies are reluctant actively to inform the licensor of any improvements. Where the improvement is a simple modification to the code or design, the grant-back is of limited value without this positive reporting. Also, any active reporting obligation easily forces the company to release the technical development phase it is engaged in. Therefore, such grant-back facilitates not only the technical flow but also the leakage of other information. Secondly, in the network economy, the flow of information is one of the key success factors and any company paying for information is reluctant to allow the licensor to benefit free of charge from the investment of the licensee. Rather, apart from the blocking risk, it is sometimes considered that any sub-contracting of actual development should be expressly agreed on and not be built into a licensing agreement in the form of a grant-back. Thirdly, any licence to the patented solutions actually blocking the development of the licensor is more properly tailored in a narrower way. Consequently, in the communications industry, grant-back licences are increasingly tailored differently.

Royalty-free software licensing programs such as open-source licensing programs or public-domain licensing programs Linux, Mozilla and Gnu use traditional grant-back provisions. Typically in these licences as a condition for the royalty-free licence the licensee is required to grant a licence to all modifications and/or derivative works based on the original work. The philosophy behind such licensing programs is to involve the licensee community in the further development of the initial program. As a return for grant-back of improvements, the licensee may use the improvements of other users. In that sense, the aim is pro-competitive.

4.70 An *anti-blocking grant-back* is a grant-back clause aimed at granting a licence for a licensor to use those intellectual property rights of a licensee that would otherwise block the licensor from further developing the licensed technology.[61] It may typically be used to cover licences to interfaces and other elements of the technology that the rights holder would expressly like to maintain open for anyone or at least a particular company to continue further development. A typical effect of an anti-blocking grant-back is the preservation of network effects created by such an interface or component. Anti-blocking grant-back clauses typically specify in detail the elements of the licensed technology that are subject to the grant-back. If the grant-back is primarily for software copyright, the grant-back clause requires a licensee to grant a licence to any modifications of the specified software code. The other alternative is to require that certain parts of the code may not be modified in order to ensure compatibility with other licensees and the licensor. If the grant-back is primarily for patents, the grant-back requires a licensee to license any patents that are based on a specified element or contain it. The word 'based on' contains some ambiguity. In most cases, it can be understood as referring to the introductory part of the patent claim. The term 'contain' is

---

[61] *OECD Report*, 21.

usually understood as a patent that contains the specified part as one of the elements of a patent claim.

A *protective grant-back* is used to protect the licensor from any patent claims by **4.71** a licensee. This type of grant-back typically has an equitable background: if a licensee has a patent counterclaim, it should make it before and not after it has been granted a licence. The underlying idea behind this is that by signing the licence agreement, the parties are presumed to have settled their potential patent disputes. The scope and use of such a protective grant-back licence may vary.

The broadest protective grant-back covers any licensee's innovations. It effec- **4.72** tively ensures that the licensee will not be able to raise its patents against the licensor. A more limited grant-back extends only to the licensee's patents that cover the licensor's products in which the licensor uses the licensed technology. This type of grant-back is based on the idea that both parties are part of the same IPR network.[62] Another possible scope of a grant-back is to extend it to any patents relating to the same technology as the licensed technology. This scope does not extend to anything beyond the licensed technology, even though it may be eventually used by the licensor in its products. Finally, the scope of the protective grant-back licence may require the licensee to grant a licence to the licensor under all the licensee's technically necessary patents and/or commercially necessary patents.[63]

A *pick-licence* is sometimes used when both parties conclude that any future **4.73** patent disputes are not desirable but they cannot agree on the scope of the licence or grant-back. Therefore, an added clause is used to solve the issue, stating that in addition to the defined scope of licensed patents, either party or both parties may additionally 'pick' an agreed number of patents and have them licensed to it. This clause recognizes the interdependency of the parties in the network economy. However, the parties may still gain exclusive rights to their innovations without any licensing obligations.

Feedback licensing is increasingly used when a licensor wishes to engage other **4.74** parties in the development and testing of its products. A typical feedback licence simply states that if a company provides ideas and suggestions for the other company in relation to the products of that company the recipient company may use such ideas and suggestions.

If a customer telephones the help desk of a software supplier, the supplier usually wants to be certain that it can use the identified problem, create a solution and provide such solution for all of its customers. A feedback licence facilitates this.

---

[62] For the definition of IP network, see above in ch 3, para 3.14.

[63] See *Integraph Corp v Intel Corp*, 3 F Supp 2d 1255 (N D Ala 1998); M O'Rourke, 'Striking a Delicate Balance: Intellectual Property, Antitrust, Contract, and Standardization in the Computer Industry' (1998) 12 Harvard Journal of Law & Technology, 18 (using the attributes of an improvement grant-back to oppose defensive grant-back).

4.75 Feedback licences are increasingly used with early adopters, beta users, co-operation partners and customers that may have access to confidential proprietary technology. The core of this licence is that its scope is not dictated by the scope of the licensor's disclosure but rather by the scope of the licensee's disclosure.

4.76 This author suggests that the traditional rule relating to improvement grant-backs is not necessarily applicable to other types of grant-back. Rather, the anti-competitive elements of an improvement grant-back term are not necessarily found in other types of grant-back licences. Such licences may also have a number of pro-competitive elements and motivations, such as decreasing fragmentation, maintenance of compatibility and protection of immunity against infringement claims.

Relevance of chosen action

Enforcement of intellectual property rights

Overview

4.77 The rights of the rights holder to enforce intellectual property rights are generally presumed to be immune from the intervention of anti-trust laws. As discussed above, this presumption has sometimes been rebutted in Europe and in the US provided that there has been a clear interest to rebut the presumption.

4.78 As stated above, the right to enforce intellectual property rights against imitators has been subject to the highest degree of protection. If the effects of enforcement have been evident in activities other than imitations, the above presumption may be more likely to be rebutted by the interest in (1) protecting customers against abusive uses, or the interest in (2) encouraging competition on some related markets.[64]

4.79 It seems that anti-trust courts are quite reluctant to intervene in enforcement activities but instead, the issue of enforcement is likely to be 'internalized' into intellectual property rights themselves.[65] Consequently, typical enforcement problems may be resolved within the doctrines dealing with protected subject matter, scope of protection and limitations of protection. However, it is as evident that even if the intellectual property doctrines adequately take into account all categories of possible conflict situations, the intervention of anti-trust laws for certain practices may still be justified.

---

[64] *Atari Games Corp v Nintendo of America, Inc*, 897 F 2d 1572, 1576–77 (Fed Cir 1990) ('patent owners may incur antitrust liability for enforcement of a patent known to be obtained through fraud or known to be invalid, where license of a patent compels the purchase of unpatented goods, or where there is an overall scheme to use the patent to violate antitrust laws').

[65] See discussion in ch 2, paras 2.48–2.52.

Refusal to license

The right of the owner of intellectual property rights to exclude others is funda-   **4.80**
mental. A refusal to license is a powerful tool that enables the rights owner to
maximize the full potential of the exclusive right. Consequently, it is also an
effective tool for leveraging. There are several early examples to illustrate this.[66]
Of special concern for this book are the legal limitations of such refusals. In
particular, if the value of the increased network effects to the manufacturers and
users of particular products is higher than any benefit to the licensee from a
refusal to license, there may be some economic justification to rebut the right to
refuse.

The obligation to grant licences to competitors is frequently considered as nulli-   **4.81**
fication of that right. Therefore, there is widespread reluctance in regard to any
obligations to license, especially in the form of compulsory licensing.[67]
Compulsory licensing creates the situation where the rights owner cannot enforce
its copyright or patent against a party that would otherwise infringe them.
Compulsory licensing can either be royalty-free or a party obtaining a compulsory licence may be required to pay a licence fee to the rights holder. In addition
to a plain compulsory licence, a party may sometimes be required to provide
access to some particular information, such as technical drawings or interface
information.

Some proponents of property theory consider any compulsory licensing as inter-   **4.82**
vention into private property rights. Consequently, compulsory licensing of
patents is, according to the TRIPS, Article 31, strictly limited.[68] The compulsory
licensing of copyrights through national copyright collecting societies has had a
broader application. The primary justification for compulsory licensing in the
copyright field has been the need to control the fragmentation of rights.

---

[66] F M Scherer, *Industrial Market Structure and Economic Performance* (Chicago 1980) 452
(suggesting that the unwillingness of James Watt to license his steam engine patent in the 1790s may
have delayed the introduction of locomotives and steamboats).

[67] According to Areeda, compulsory licensing may only be a remedy for some anti-trust violations,
since otherwise the rights holder would be 'robbed' of any incentive to develop the invention. P E
Areeda and H Hovenkamp, *Anti-trust Law: An Analysis of Anti-trust Principles and their Application*
(Vol III, rev edn, Boston 1996) § 705c.

[68] Art 31 lists twelve conditions for compulsory licensing: (1) a licence shall be considered on its
individual merits, (2) the user should make an effort to obtain a licence directly from the rights holder,
(3) the scope and duration must be limited to the specified purpose, (4) a licence shall be non-exclusive, (5) a licence shall be non-assignable, (6) a licence shall be for the supply of the domestic market,
(7) a licence shall be terminated if circumstances change, (8) adequate remuneration is payable for the
rights holder, (9) the validity of the licence shall be subject to judicial review, (10) the remuneration
shall be subject to judicial review, (11) in the case of anti-competitive practices, the user does not have
first to request a licence from the rights holder and the licence does not have to be limited to domestic markets, and (12) if a licence is granted for patents blocking improvements, such a licence is
subject to (i) the improvement being a significant one, (ii) cross-licensing the improvement to the
rights holder and (iii) being non-assignable.

4.83 Under property theory, the refusal to license is closely related to the idea that the rights holder's entitlements are a property right. The fundamental idea of property rights is that they allow the owner to exclude others from using the property.[69] Another possibility would be to provide rights holders' entitlements under liability rules. Liability rules would provide that the rights holder may not prohibit others from using the property but can only ask for just compensation.[70] A third possibility is that the initial entitlement is based on property rights but in certain circumstances the rights holder agrees to liability rules.[71]

4.84 The current presumption strongly favours the property rule as the entitlement for intellectual property rights. In the US, there is a vast amount of case law indicating that there must be more than a mere unilateral refusal to deal in order for the courts to order compulsory licensing.[72] In Europe, a similar body of law has been established.[73]

4.85 The restrictions imposed against compulsory licensing do not impede the ability to intervene with one's right to exclude competitors whenever such right is used in an improper manner.[74] This means that unenforceability of intellectual property rights is recognized as a remedy against misuse or abuse of intellectual property rights. The challenge is then to identify circumstances that amount to misuse or abuse of rights. At a theoretical level, a distinction is made between the right to exclude others in general and limitations of such a right in circumstances where the use of the right is not consistent with other rules of law or other interests of society.

---

[69] See ch 2, paras 2.79–2.110 and ch 3 above for analysis and discussion.

[70] See J S Turner, 'The Nonmanufacturing Patent Owner: Toward a Theory of Efficient Infringement' (1998) 179 California Law Review, 204 (suggesting that society should use liability rules for patents whenever such use would maximize social welfare).

[71] R P Merges, 'Contracting into Liability Rules: Intellectual Property Rights and Collective Rights Organizations' (1996) 84 California Law Review, 1391–1393 (promoting the system widely used by collective collecting societies and standardization organizations).

[72] *Continental Paper Bag Co v Eastern Paper Bag Co*, 210 US 405, 429 (1908); *Dawson Chemical Co v Rohm & Haas Co*, 448 US 176, 215 (1980); *Data General Corp v Grumman Systems*, 36 F 3d 1147 (1st Cir 1994); *Genentech v Eli Lilly and Co*, 998 F 2d 931, 949 (Fed Cir 1993), cert denied, 114 S Ct 1126 (1994); *Miller Insituform v Insituform of North America*, 830 F 2d 606, 609 (6th Cir 1987); *SCM Corp v Xerox Corp*, 645 F 2d 1195 (2d Cir 1981); *United States v Westinghouse Electric Corp*, 648 F 2d 642 (9th Cir 1981).

[73] *AB Volvo v Erik Veng (UK) Ltd* [1990] 4 CMLR 265; in Finland Setec, Kilpailuvirasto 5.2.1997 61/95/dnro 580 (making a rather unique suggestion that the inability to supply market demand would justify intervention). See also H Laddie, P Prescott and M Vitoria, *The Modern Law of Copyright and Designs* (3rd edn, London 2000), 1520 ('It is now well-established that the owner of an intellectual property right does not have a dominant position simply because he can prohibit third parties from marketing products which would infringe that right'); P Virtanen, *Määräävan Markkina-aseman Kontrollointi* (Jyväskylä, 2001), 443–445.

[74] See also TRIPS, Art 8(2) (measures against abuse of intellectual property rights authorized); J A Franco, 'Limiting the Anti-competitive Prerogative of Patent Owners: Predatory Standards in Patent Licensing' (1983) 92 Yale Law Journal, 831, 847 (suggesting that a refusal to license which is against social efficiency should be condemned).

One may use several alternative approaches to solve this potential conflict **4.86** between the various interests. Firstly, under anti-trust and competition laws, the doctrine of essential facilities has been used to balance the interests of property owners and their competitors. Secondly, it may be possible simply to reduce the scope of the substantive right to exclude in order to achieve the desired result. In the US, the doctrine of intellectual property misuse as a defence to infringement claims has been developed.[75] In other parts of the world, no similar concepts have emerged but traditional compulsory licensing laws have largely produced the same outcome. Thirdly, it may be concluded under anti-trust or intellectual property laws that the right to exclude others should be limited only if the exercise of such right is not justified after balancing it with other important interests in a specific case.

A balancing of interests as suggested in this book may be the most appropriate **4.87** approach (1) when creating new legislation and (2) when analysing individual practices. In the network economy, there are several relevant circumstances that increase the importance of this issue: (i) the refusal to license may delay or stop the emergence of a standard; (ii) in the absence of a standard, consumers cannot benefit from network effects; (iii) the 'circular model of innovation'[76] is unable to function, the production of a new innovation is delayed and the cost of creating a new innovation potentially increased.

The issue of refusal to deal has been discussed most in the case law involving **4.88** spare parts. In Europe, cases such as *Volvo v Veng*[77] established quite early that intellectual property rights do not justify a refusal to sell product parts if such a refusal is not justified in the absence of such rights. In the US, the issue has been much debated in connection with *Image Technical Services Inc v Eastman Kodak Co.*[78]

In general, in the US compulsory licensing may be a part of an anti-trust remedy. **4.89** Sometimes, also the unenforceability of intellectual property rights may result from other doctrines, such as the misuse doctrine, even though such relief is practically excluded in the absence of a 'sham'[79] or 'pretextual'[80] conduct.[81] In other parts of the world the misuse doctrine has not been applied.

---

[75] See ch 2, para 2.65–2.68 for discussion.

[76] See explanation in ch 1.

[77] *AB Volvo v Erik Veng (UK) Ltd* [1990] 4 CMLR 265.

[78] 125 F 3d 1195 (9th Cir 1997), cert denied, 118 S Ct 1560 (1998) (*'Kodak III'*). See also *Eastman Kodak Co v Image Technical Services Inc*, 504 US 451 (1992) (*'Kodak II'*).

[79] *Professional Real Estate Investors v Columbia Pictures Industries, Inc*, 508 US 49 (1993).

[80] *Image Technical Services, Inc v Eastman Kodak*, 125 F 3d 1195 (9th Cir 1997), cert denied, 118 S Ct 1560 (1998) (*'Kodak III'*).

[81] See the Patent Misuse Reform Act of 1988 (no misuse may be found by the reason of refusing to license or use any rights to the patent) 35 USC § 271 (d) (1988).

4.90   The essential facilities doctrine is a highly disputed doctrine that is still frequently cited as the primary solution for balancing the potentially harmful effects of the refusal to license intellectual property rights. If applied in its basic form, the doctrine establishes a '*per se*' rule that under certain circumstances, the refusal to license may be rebutted without any further balancing of justifications. Consequently, the high standards of the required circumstances have made the scope for the application of this basic form of doctrine extremely limited. Therefore, and because of the complexity of the related case law, by 'essential facilities', one usually refers to the totality of circumstances that may make it unlawful to refuse to deal.

4.91   The essential facilities doctrine was first developed in the US in early cases such as *Terminal Railroad* and *Associated Press*.[82] The doctrine is based on cases discussing the unilateral refusal to deal under Section 2 of the Sherman Act. The US Federal Courts have analysed refusal to deal cases either by expressly referring to the doctrine or just applying similar reasoning without necessarily any explicit reference.[83] In *Otter Tail Power Co v the United States*, the US Supreme Court ruled that a dominant firm that controls an infrastructure or an asset that other companies need to make use of in order to compete has the obligation to make the facility available on non-discriminatory terms.[84] In *MCI v AT&T*, the US Seven Circuit Court designed a four-step test for determining whether access should be granted to a particular facility on the basis of the essential facilities doctrine:

(1) control of the essential facility by the monopolist;
(2) a competitor's inability practically or reasonably to duplicate the essential facility;
(3) the denial of the use of the facility to a competitor; and
(4) the feasibility of providing the facility.[85]

The consequent US case law contains a variety of cases and circumstances but none of those cases involve the use of intellectual property rights.[86]

4.92   In Europe, as in the United States, the essential facilities doctrine has been developed through the case law. However, the ECJ has not explicitly applied the doctrine as such. Rather, the case law has evolved in the form of a justification

---

[82] *United States v Terminal Railroad Association*, 224 US 383 (1912), *Associated Press v United States*, 326 US 1 (1945).

[83] See K Glazer and A Lipsky, 'Unilateral Refusals to Deal under Section 2 of the Sherman Act' (1995) 63 Antitrust Law Journal, 753–754; D J Gerber, 'Rethinking the Monopolist's Duty to Deal: A Legal and Economic Critique of the Doctrine of "Essential Facilities"' (1988) 74 Virginia Law Review, 1069.

[84] *Otter Tail Power v the United States* has been said to be the first case where the US Supreme Court applied the essential facilities doctrine. *Otter Tail Power Co v The United States*, 410 US 366 (1973).

[85] *MCI Communications Co v AT&T*, 708 F 2d 1081 (7th Cir 1983), cert denied, 464 US 891.

[86] See *Intergraph Corp v Intel Corp*, 3 F Supp 2d 1255 (N D Ala 1998) (Intel not allowed to cut the supply of information related to its upcoming integrated circuits).

test under Article 82 of the Treaty of European Union (sometimes together with Article 86 when a state monopoly is involved) starting with some of the ECJ's early 'refusal to deal' cases. In the case law, it was established quite early that a refusal to deal does not of itself constitute an abuse of a dominant position. Such abuse will only be found in the presence of other factors, such as, for example, where a denial to supply would put the competitor out of business and eliminate competition in a related market.[87] The doctrine involving intellectual property rights was developed further by the ECJ in *Volvo v Veng*[88] and *Renault*.[89] These two decisions demonstrate the ECJ's reluctance to interfere with the rights of the rights holder where refusals to deal are motivated by the interest to stop competitors imitating.

In *Volvo v Veng* the court held that 'the right of the proprietor of a protected   **4.93** design to prevent third parties from manufacturing and selling or importing, without its consent, products incorporating the design constitutes the very subject matter of exclusive rights. It follows that an obligation imposed upon the proprietor of a protected design to grant to third parties, even in return for a reasonable royalty, a licence for the supply of products incorporating the design would lead to the proprietor thereof being deprived of the substance of his exclusive right . . .'.[90] In *Renault*, decided on the same day, the ECJ confirmed the judgment given in *Volvo*.[91]

In *Magill*[92] the ECJ concluded that, *first*, the broadcasting companies' refusal to   **4.94** supply 'basic information by relying on national copyright provisions thus prevented the appearance of a new product, a comprehensive weekly guide to television programmes, which the appellants did not offer and for which there was a potential consumer demand'. *Second*, the refusal was arbitrary in that it was not associated with either the TV listing's broadcasting or publishing activities. *Third*, by denying access to this information the broadcasters could reserve to themselves the secondary market for weekly television guides by excluding all competition on that market.

The ECJ's judgment in *Magill* has been considered by some as an acceptance of   **4.95** the application of the essential facilities doctrine to intellectual property anti-trust cases and to anti-trust cases in general. The ECJ formulated the requirements for

---

[87] Case C6-7/73 *Instituto Chemioterapico Italiano SpA and Commercial Solvents Corp v Commission* [1974] ECR 223 (refusal would eliminate a competitor); Case C27/76 *United Brands Co v Commission* [1978] ECR 207, [1978] 1 CMLR 429 (cannot stop supplying a long-standing customer who abides by a commercial practice, if the orders placed by that customer are in no way out of the ordinary); Case C22/78 *Hugin v Commission* [1979] ECR 1869 (no objective reason to cut off supplies because of technical reasons).

[88] Case C238/87 *Volvo v Veng* [1988] ECR 6226.

[89] Case C53/87 *CICRA v Renault* [1988] ECR 6039.

[90] *AB Volvo v Erik Veng (UK) Ltd* [1990] 4 CMLR 265.

[91] Case C53/87 *CICRA v Renault* [1988] ECR 6039.

[92] Cases C-241-242/91P and C-242/91P *Radio Telefís Éireann and Others v Commission* ('*Magill*') [1995] ECR I-743. See also discussion in ch 4, para 4.21–4.22 above.

imposing on a dominant firm an obligation to supply as follows, referring to them as exceptional circumstances: (1) the company has control of 'indispensable' material where its refusal prevents the appearance of a new product for which there is a potential demand; (2) there are no justifications for such a refusal; and (3) the dominant company has an intention to reserve a secondary market for itself by excluding all competition from that market.

4.96 This author suggests that the doctrine of essential facilities is not helpful in explaining the holding in the light of the subsequent case law. Rather, *Magill* may be interpreted to establish, in line with the previous body of case law, the need to balance the justification for enforcing intellectual property rights with other important interests.[93] Under specific circumstances the justification for enforcing intellectual property rights may be rebuttable. The case establishes that it is of relevance for the outcome of the balance whether the refusal to license has its primary effect on imitation or on separate markets.

4.97 Under external effects analysis, *Magill* can be differentiated from the other cases citing it but with a different outcome. In *Magill* the effects of the practice were visible on a separate market in a way (total exclusion) that was not justified. In subsequent case law, this element of effects on other entities may be identified as a factor in the explanation.

4.98 This analysis was followed by the European Court of Justice in *Dior v Evora*.[94] The ECJ held that copyrights might make it possible for a rights holder to control the marketing practices of third parties even in cases where such a third party is lawfully selling products. In such cases the interest of the copyright owner in remuneration from the commercial exploitation of copyright must be balanced with the interest in allowing the reseller to sell the products in the normal course of business. In this particular case, the rights holder was relying on its copyrights on the bottles of perfumes and on their packaging. The court concluded that a holder of copyright was not entitled to oppose the habitual use of the copyright by the reseller for the purpose of bringing to the public's attention the further commercialization of goods first fielded with the consent of the rights holder.

4.99 In the *Tiercé Ladbroke* judgment,[95] the Court of First Instance first considered the grounds for '*per se*' unenforceability established in *Magill* to be cumulative.[96] In particular, this case shows the relevance of market definition in the application of the *Magill* test and the essential facilities doctrine. If the products are in the same market and the competitor is imitating, the enforcement of intellectual property

---

[93] See similar view by J Temple Lang, 'European Community Antitrust Law—Innovation Markets and High Technology Industries'. Speech before Fordham Corporate Law Institute, 17 October 1996.

[94] *Parfums Christian Dior SA v Evora BV*, C-337/95, [1997] ECR I-6013. See also ch 4, paras 2.130–2.132 and 3.101.

[95] Case T-504/93 *Tiercé Ladbroke v Commission* [1997] ECR II-923.

[96] D Fitzgerald, 'Magill Revisited. *Tiercé Ladbroke SA v The Commission*' [1998] 4 EIPR, 154, 154 (suggesting cumulative nature of arguments).

rights is more justified than against firms in a separate market having an effect on that market.

The *Tiercé Ladbroke* case relates to a denial to license the right to broadcast **4.100** sound and pictures of French horses (French sound and pictures) in Belgium. Tiercé Ladbroke, a Belgian betting shop, requested the owners of the intellectual property right to license to it the right to broadcast French sound and pictures in Belgium. The companies refused to license Tiercé Ladbroke.

In its decision, the Court of First Instance upheld the Commission's definition of **4.101** the relevant market as the Belgian market for the transmission of sound and pictures of horse races in general, and not only French sound and pictures, as argued by the applicant. The CFI based this reasoning on the fact that, at the material time, in Belgium there was at least one more product, the sound and pictures of British races, which was interchangeable in terms of its technical characteristics and use. Furthermore, the CFI considered that the televised sound and pictures of horse races was the ancillary market and the taking of bets was the principal market.[97]

The Court of First Instance distinguished *Magill*, as in this judgment the domi- **4.102** nant company's intention was to reserve a secondary market by excluding all competition from that market. In contrast with the facts in *Magill*, Tiercé Ladbroke was already established and dominant in the main betting market, whereas the *sociétés de courses* were not present in that market. Consequently, the refusal to license did not have any detrimental impact on the betting market.[98]

Consequently, this author suggests that rather than analysing refusals to license **4.103** solely under the essential facilities doctrine or other similar artificial and disputed theories the external effects analysis provides a more practical solution. The rights of the rights holder to refuse to license should be respected unless the effects of such refusal are not justified.

Excessive licence fees
The primary competitive effect of intellectual property rights is the increase they **4.104**

---

[97] Fitzgerald, n 96 above, 160 (explaining sound and pictures to be an upstream market and betting the downstream market).

[98] See subsequently Case C-7/97 *Oscar Bronner GmbH & Co KG v Mediaprint Zeitungs- und Zeitschriftenverlag GmbH & Co KG* [1998] ECR I-7791 (the refusal to deliver competitors' newspapers not an abuse of dominant position). In *Oscar Bronner*, the ECJ confirmed that the holding in *Magill* was limited to specific circumstances. See, however, S D Anderman, *EC Competition Law and Intellectual Property Rights* (Oxford 1998), 211 ('There I little doubt that the decision in *Magill* means that Art 86 [of EC Treaty] reaches more widely in the realm of the exercise of IPR'). See also EU Commission's action against IMS Health (Case COMP D3/38.044 *NDS Health/IMS Health*: Health, Interim Measure, 3 July 2001) (interim action against the abuse of dominant position upon the refusal to license a copyrighted system of dividing Germany into 1,860 sales areas because the system had become a standard in Germany for reporting pharmaceutical data), interim measures suspended by the Court of First Instance on 10 August 2001, Case T-184/01 R).

sometimes cause to end-users' or competitors' costs. Accordingly the strength of such rights may be determined by the ability to affect the costs of a competitor. This is normally not of any concern: it is equal to the fair return for the rights holder. It is only fair that an artist is paid for his song and the inventor is compensated for his invention.

4.105   In the competitive market the compensation of a rights holder may be determined in various ways. It may reflect the amount of required work,[99] the scope of licensed use, the market value of the work or invention or the expected revenue of the licensee. Since a typical outcome of an arm's-length negotiation is a balance of all these methods, 'standard' rates are seldom reliable. Rather, they sometimes provide useful benchmarks for further negotiations. Normally, private negotiations lead to optimum results that reflect the balances between the parties. However, if the market is not competitive, private negotiations may lead to a less than optimum result. The further division of such potential costs into the following categories illustrates circumstances that may justify intervention.[100]

4.106   First, licensing is often an alternative to a company's own development or creation. Therefore, the costs of creating an alternative competing solution may be taken into account when analysing a particular royalty structure. This presumes that it is possible to create an alternative solution within a reasonable timeframe. Secondly, if a company does not take a licence, it may lose business opportunities or may decide to invest its resources in some alternative activity. Therefore, a rational licensee takes into account the cost of lost opportunities where it cannot enter the market. The value of a lost opportunity is normally calculated by taking into account any alternative opportunities. Thirdly, any licensing involves direct costs in terms of licence fees. Consequently, the potential licensing cost needs to be taken into account in case the owner of intellectual property rights agrees to grant a licence under their exclusive rights.

4.107   Purely technical factors and realities dictate the cost of an alternative solution, including the risks related to the quality of complex engineering work. However, such costs are greatly affected by the strength of intellectual property rights. If the protection provided by intellectual property laws is extensive, the investment required in order to prepare an alternative non-infringing design is higher. This element of intellectual property laws is controlled by principles such as inventive step, doctrine of equivalence, the minimum amount of originality required under copyright laws, fair use and other limitations and exemptions from patent and copyright protection. Typically, if licences were available, a company would take a licence if the cost of 'designing around' and the lost opportunity resulting from the absence from the market were both higher than the cost of the licence.

---

[99] This is typical for R&D subcontracting and in general 'works for hire'.
[100] An example of patent licensing is used. However, there are no significant objections for using the same arguments for copyright licensing fees.

Determining royalty rates is usually at the owner's discretion. 'A patent empow- **4.108**
ers the owner to exact royalties as high as he can negotiate with the leverage of
that monopoly.'[101] Therefore, one of the viable strategies of a licensor is always
to maximize licensing revenues and, under traditional doctrines, the courts tend
to accept that. This principle is based on the presumption that a willing licensee
does not take a licence if it is too expensive. Rather, they will not enter the market
(Alternative B) or develop their own alternative design (Alternative A). Typically,
a rational licensee is assumed to be in a position to evaluate all these alternatives.
When evaluating the different alternatives, a risk factor is assumed to be attached
to the calculation.

The problems with this approach in the network economy are best illustrated by **4.109**
a simple example involving a traditional licensing situation and the licensing of
standard-related essential patents.

EXAMPLE: EFFECTS OF STANDARDIZATION

A typical model for using the cost of designing around, the cost of the lost opportunity and
the cost of a licence: a patentee requires the payment of a licence fee of 5%. The sales
during the next five years are expected to be between US$ 50 million and US$ 200 million.
The industry average operating profit is 8% but depending on the market share, the profit
can vary between 3 and 15%. The estimated cost of an alternative design[102] would be US$
5–7 million with a potential delay in the introduction causing the loss of sales of US$ 5
million.

- If the estimated own development cost has a 10% probability of being US$ 8 million, a
  50% probability of being US$ 6 million and a 40% probability of being US$ 5 million,
  then the weighed average estimated cost of an alternative design $A = US\$ 5.8 M$.
- If the estimated operating profit has a 30% probability of being US$ 30 million, a 50%
  probability of being US$ 8 million and a 20% probability of being US$ 2 million, then
  the average weighed estimated cost of the lost opportunity $B = US\$ 13.4 M$.
- If the estimated royalty cost on estimated sales has a 30% probability of being US$ 10
  million when the sales are US$ 200 million, a 50% probability of being US$ 5 million
  when the sales are US$ 100 million and a 20% probability of being US$ 2.5 million
  when the sales are US$ 50 million, then the average weighed estimated cost for a licence
  fee $C = US\$ 6.0 M$.

---

[101] *Automatic Radio Company v Hazeltine*, 339 US 827, 830–834, reh denied, 340 US 846 (1950);
Brulotte v Thys Co, 379 US 29, 33 (1964); R C Nordhaus, *Patent–Antitrust Law* (2nd rev edn,
Chicago 1972), 217 ('Generally, royalties need not be reasonable'). See also eg *American Photocopy
Equipment Company v Rovico, Inc*, 384 F 2d 813 (7th Cir 1967) (the jury finding that royalty of 12%
on patented copying machine equal to 24% of the patented part was not misuse of patent was not
clearly erroneous); C Holmes, *Intellectual Property and Anti-trust Law* (West Group 2000) 24–3
(discussing 'exorbitant and oppressive' limitation 7th Circuit had applied previously in the same
case).
[102] The cost of alternative design is presumed to include any risk factors, such as the lack of qualified design engineers, risk of delayed design times and risk of design quality. It is recognized that for
a company it is difficult to evaluate these figures objectively, except at the high level.

4.110   Consequently, a rational company would not take a licence since the cost of making an alternative design is less expensive than the estimated cost of the license (A < C).[103] However, if the patentee's solution is adopted into the standard, the licensee will not have the opportunity to prepare its own design. Instead, the standard specifies the design everyone must use in order to comply with the standard. As a consequence of the standardization, the company must only calculate the estimated operating profit that would be lost if one cannot supply the market and compare it with the licensing cost. Based on the above example, the increase of the leverage caused by the adoption of a patented solution in the standard is evident.

4.111   In the normal licensing situation, a rational licensee never accepts a licensing proposal if the cost of such a proposal exceeds the cost of an alternative design. Therefore, the ability or opportunity to prepare an alternative design is an important safeguard for controlling extensive royalty demands. Being able to make an alternative design not only affects the royalty rates; it may also affect the royalty structure, the royalty base and the willingness to accept grant-back provisions. If the cost of alternative design is taken into account, the royalty structure frequently reflects the cost of an alternative design. Terms such as paid-up options and decreasing royalty rates tied to sales and time are common.

4.112   In the licensing of essential patents, there is no such safeguard. Since the standard specification dictates the solution to be used, it is not possible to make an alternative design.[104] Consequently, the negotiation position of any owner of an essential patent is substantially stronger than the position of the owner of a patent outside standardization. In fact, the theoretical ability of a patentee to collect revenue from licensees using technically necessary patents is, when compared to a normal licensing situation, much higher than the net increase of operating profit. The net increase of operating profit may be calculated from the estimated operating profit by deducting the value of alternative revenue possibilities and the typical cost of preparing an alternative design.

4.113   This potential problem of extensive royalties is best illustrated by using technically necessary patents as an example. Standardization rules out formally any viable use of alternative designs. However, the same issue is also emerging more and more outside formal standardization. The licence fees claimed by music publishers and collecting societies for music licensing may also be influenced by the market power those entities have. This is due to the increasing interdependency between them. Interdependency of manufacturers, innovators and creators of copyrighted digital content is typical in the network economy. The problem is also typical for the 'circular model' of innovation. The problem rarely occurred

---

[103] Provided that the probabilities used in the example are risk neutral.
[104] Except if the standard is amended accordingly.

in the traditional 'serial model' for innovation since the economy was, in this model, primarily reliant on single sources of innovation.

For the network economy, the primary policy question is whether the patentee **4.114** should be allowed to make full use of its increased leverage? In particular, can a patentee maximize royalty revenue from technically necessary patents and other intellectual property rights that may have the same effect because of *de facto* interdependency of innovators and creators? For further analysis of this question the following analytical structure is useful. Firstly, it could be assumed that the minimum amount of outside intervention is always preferred. Therefore, if workable safeguards exist, avoiding intervention by lawmakers, courts or government agencies should be the preferred option.

Secondly, the safeguards preventing extensive royalty requests may be different **4.115** depending on (1) whether the patentee is in the same business as the licensee, (2) whether the patentee is in a related business in the converging information industry, (3) whether the patentee is a user of the technology, or (4) whether the patentee's sole interest is in the licensing business. It is useful to recognize the different roles since the roles may reflect different motivations. While the underlying motivation of a company is not formally of primary relevance in the analysis of competitive effects,[105] such motivation may help in understanding the various effects of typical behaviour.

Thirdly, the answers that the existing reward models provide might be of rele- **4.116** vance. The existing models are primarily designed to define royalty rates in a typical 'serial model' of innovation. Nevertheless, they are still the primary source for courts and several licensing bodies.

Fourthly, the problem of cumulative intellectual property costs should be **4.117** discussed since they are typical in the network economy. Fifthly, the economic consequences of various alternatives dealing with this 'increased reward potentiality',[106] as it may be called from the intellectual property owner's point of view, should be discussed. Finally, any less restrictive alternative models should be taken into account.

If a patentee is in the same business as the licensee, the patentee usually has a few **4.118** alternative motivations or strategies. It may be in the interests of the patentee to increase the costs of a licensee to the level where the licensee cannot effectively compete against the patentee. In the increasingly competitive environment, even small differences in the cost structures of competitors may have a substantial impact on the success of the companies. Therefore a strategy based on the *interests in excluding competitors* is a viable alternative.

---

[105] Simply because companies are presumed to compete vigorously against each other.
[106] The potential net increase of operating profit.

4.119   In the absence of the ability to 'design around', high royalty rates are a viable offensive strategy. This may effectively be implemented by charging as high a licence fee as possible by using the increased leverage discussed above, namely the licensee's potential net increase of operating profit. The likely problem with this is that such an increase of net operating profit is not a consequence of the patentee's innovation. It is primarily due to the standardization activity and the resultant increase in the market potential. This is almost always unrelated to the qualities of one particular technical element of a complex system.

4.120   There are a few safeguards to prevent this. For a manufacturing patentee, they form alternative strategic approaches. Firstly, in the network economy, a viable new market is likely to require several suppliers. Therefore, some patentees are likely to limit their royalty requests in recognition of the necessity of having several companies successfully supplying the same market. This safeguard may be identified as the *market-making interest*.

4.121   Secondly, if a patentee is a manufacturer in the same market as the licensee, it increasingly faces the risk of not being able to avoid the use of other manufacturers' patents. The increase of such risk is dictated by the interdependency of the companies in the network economy. If a patentee maximizes its revenue from a particular patent, at the same time it increases the risk that it can be subject to similar requests by other parties or the licensee. Therefore, the patentee is likely to limit its royalty demands, either unilaterally or in return for a cross-licence or grant-back licence. This safeguard may be identified as the *protective interest caused by interdependency*.

4.122   If an intellectual property owner is engaged in a related converging industry,[107] it may have an interest in excluding companies from a particular market, it may also have market-making interest and protective interdependency interests. In addition, the owner may also have the *interest to control*.

4.123   The interest to control licensees in a related converging industry is a partial consequence of the interdependency of companies. For a particular intellectual property owner, it may be important that companies in the other converging industries adopt the technology or content that such a licensor prefers. A licensing policy of a software developer is easily affected by their interest in promoting the adoption of its solution. The licensing policy of a computer manufacturer or communications equipment manufacturer may be affected by the fact whether the technology used by the licensee is the same as or at least interoperable with

---

[107] By a related converging industry, it is here meant the relationship between eg the communications industry and the software industry, the computer industry and the media industry, and the software industry and the media industry. It is typical that the companies involved in these industries have an increasing interest in either supplying the other industries, using the products of the other industries, integrating elements of the related industries in their own products or even competing with the related industries.

(or alternatively different from or not interoperable with) the technology of the rights holder.

Consequently, the interest to control may drive the owner to reduce royalty requests.[108] This is likely to happen if the entire technical solution adopted by the licensee is in the interests of such rights holders. Alternatively, the interest to control may encourage the request of extensive royalties. Such a request may be motivated by the rights holder's desire to discourage the adoption of particular technologies, eg as a consequence of particular standardization activities, the result of which has not been satisfactory for the rights holder. **4.124**

If the rights holder is the supplier of the licensee, it may still have other motivations. The rights holder may have a primary interest in preserving the licensee as a customer. Therefore the rights holder is likely to reduce royalty demands. Any rights holder may have a similar motivation with respect to closely co-operating companies. This is primarily dictated by the fact that the other party provides the rights holder with something that creates some leverage against the rights holder. This may be called the *co-operation interest*. **4.125**

If the rights holder is the customer of the licensee, the rights holder may have a market-making interest and a co-operation interest. In addition, it may also have an interest to raise the costs for its competitors. In many industries, suppliers indemnify their customers against infringements of intellectual property rights. As a consequence of this, it is sometimes thought, high royalties required by one customer are likely to affect the price of the equipment for other customers for the same supplier. This motivation may be referred to as an *interest indirectly to raise competitors' costs*. The viability of it is based on the assumption that the supplier can control the price. If competition or powerful customers primarily affect the price of the equipment, any high royalty requests based on this motivation will primarily affect the profitability of the supplier. **4.126**

Finally, if the rights holder's sole business is licensing, their only interest is to maximize licensing revenue. Therefore, this motivation is referred to as *an interest to maximize licensing revenue*. The problem with these rights holders are that unless there are any other safeguards, such licensees have an interest to use leverage to obtain the entire potential net operating profit increase. To achieve their targets, such licensees may have an additional interest to increase the number of licensees. This motivation, which can be referred to as an *interest to have everyone licensed*, may influence the willingness of the rights holder to settle its royalty rates at a lower level. Consequently, the different motivations possibly involved can be summarized in the following table: **4.127**

---

[108] In addition to a number of restrictive licence terms limiting the behaviour of the licensee.

MOTIVATION	TYPICAL IMPLICATION	PRIMARY USER
1. Interest to exclude competitors	Extensive royalty requests against competitors	Manufacturer from its competitors
2. Interest indirectly to raise competitors' costs	Extensive royalty requests from suppliers	Customer from its suppliers
3. Interest to maximize royalty revenue	Extensive royalty requests from any licensee	Rights holder that does not have any other interest
4. Interest to control	Royalty rates are used to encourage or discourage adoption	Anyone
5. Market-making interest	Reduced royalty rates are used to facilitate the interest of the critical minimum number of suppliers	Manufacturers and users from each other
6. Protective interest caused by inter-dependency	Reduced royalty rates or non-monetary com-pensation	Manufacturers from other manufacturers
7. Co-operation interest	Reduced royalty rates caused by common co-operation interests	Anyone
8. Interest to have everyone licensed	Tailored deals to encourage everyone to sign	Anyone

4.128   In the US the only case reported to intervene with the royalty rate has been *Rovico*.[109] In the issue involving interlocutory injunction, the court held that the injunction against Rovico was erroneously issued because of an 'exorbitant, oppressive royalty, involving the bulk of the industry'. However, on remand, the district court found no violation on the basis of the royalty rate and the appeals court affirmed this.[110]

4.129   In the case law of the European Court of Justice, excessive prices in connection with intellectual property rights have been discussed in a few cases. To some extent the legal doctrine supports the rule that the rights holder may maximize returns only if there is a market to control such returns.[111] However, there is no case law in support of this. *Coditel II*[112] established that a dominant rights holder

---

[109] *American Photocopy Equip Co v Rovico, Inc*, 359 F 2d 745 (7th Cir 1966).
[110] *American Photocopy Equip Co v Rovico, Inc*, 384 F 2d 813 (7th Cir 1967).
[111] S Anderman, *EC Competition Law and Intellectual Property Rights* (Oxford, 1998) 249.
[112] *Coditel v Ciné Vog Films* [1983] 1 CMLR 49 ('*Coditel II*').

does not violate Article 82 by claiming licence fees that exceed a fair return for investment. In *SACEM*[113] the court held that licence fees in one member state may not be substantially higher than in other member states. However, apart from discrimination, the relevance of claims directed against the absolute amount of licence fees is constantly disputed. In *Parke Davis*[114] the mere fact of the higher price was not enough to find an abuse. In *Deutsche Grammophon*, the court essentially gave a similar ruling.[115]

Contract practices

External effects beyond an interest in excluding imitations are generally subject to more critical treatment if they are caused by contract practices than by some other practices. This is because section 1 of the Sherman Act and Article 81 of the Treaty of European Union authorize intervention in contracts and combinations that restrict competition. The same provisions are not applicable to other practices. **4.130**

In the US, contract practices are evaluated either under '*per se*' rules or under the rule of reason. In recent years the application of the rule of reason has been favoured over '*per se*' rules. In Europe, the application of Article 81 does not recognize the existence of rule of reason as such.[116] However, before applying Article 81, the courts evaluate all applicable circumstances in order to establish whether the practice limits the competition.[117] If such a limitation can be established, the practice is *per se* illegal, unless exempted under Article 81(3). **4.131**

This book does not discuss the particular practices in any detail. It only suggests that external effects of particular practices may have an effect on their treatment. **4.132**

---

[113] *Ministère Public v Tournier* [1991] 4 CMLR 248 ('*SACEM*') (fees imposed by national collecting societies may indicate an abuse of dominant position if they are appreciably higher than in other member states).

[114] *Parke Davis v Centrafarm* [1968] CMLR 47 (the higher sales price as such is not an abuse of dominant position but it can have a meaning in the analysis); *Sirena v Eda* [1971] CMLR 260 (although the price level of the product may not itself necessarily be enough to indicate abuse, it may, however, if unjustified by any objective criteria, and if it is particularly high, be a determining factor).

[115] *Deutsche Grammophon* [1971] CMLR 631 (the difference between the controlled price and the price of the product re-imported from another member state does not necessarily indicate an abuse of a dominant position; it may, however, if unjustified by any objective criteria and if it is particularly marked, be a determining factor in such abuse). See also *Philips Electronics NV v Ingman Ltd*, English High Court, Chancery Division, Patents Court, 13 May 1998; [1998] 2 CMLR 1185.

[116] See T Ackermann, *Art 85 Abs 1 EGV und die Rule of Reason* (Bonn 1997) 263.

[117] *Bayer AG v Süllhöfer* [1990] 4 CMLR 182 (the court must determine whether, taking the positions held by undertakings concerned on the market for products in question, the clause is of such nature as to restrict competition to an appreciable extent); Bellamy and Child, n 1 above, 77–78 (identifying two practices: (1) through analysis of the economic context surrounding the agreement, and (2) by focusing on the terms of the agreement itself). Anderman, n 111 above, 35 (the effect and the intention of the agreement or practice is relevant in determining whether or not Art 81 is applicable). See for discussion in Germany, M Kretzer, *Immanentetheorien im Kartellrecht. Methodische Fehlentwicklungen im Wirtschaftsrecht* (Kehl 1992), 69–70.

A practice that does not have any effects beyond the justified protection against imitations is not limiting competition in the sense of either Sherman Act, section 1 or Article 81 of the Treaty of European Union.

4.133   In Europe the Commission has provided block exemptions that limit the application of Article 81 only to such practices that limit competition. The block exemption for technology transfer agreements in particular provides a framework for the treatment of particular practices.[118] The *IP Guidelines* in the US generally provide a similar framework.[119]

Intellectual property and effects of technical design

Integration

4.134   The skilful combination of technologies is one of the drivers of technological development. The most successful companies are not necessarily those that make the initial technological advances. Rather, success may be driven by the ability to use technical advances in the way that the users are likely to adopt. The success of the technology is always tied to the success of the products using such technology. However, the quality of the underlying technology has not been the only, or even the necessary, factor explaining the success of products. The list of obvious modern combinations is long. There are such simple combinations as a radio and a clock, the result being the clock radio. There are more complex examples. Modern computers contain an increasing number of features, such as multimedia, Internet access and telephone capabilities. Cellular telephones have an increasing number of combined features such as calendars and clocks. Word-processing software has spell-checking features included in it. In the near future, a vast share of all communications equipment is going to have the capability to access the Internet and to play back music and other content.

4.135   Consumers are increasingly requesting new features to be included in their favourite products. Alternatively, they are replacing their previous products with products that have better features or a greater number of useful features. Consumers consider the integration of new features to be one major form of technical development affecting their choice of suppliers.

---

[118] Commission Regulation (EC) No 240/96 ([1996] OJ L31/2) on the application of Art 85(3) of the Treaty to certain categories of technology transfer agreements. However, the conformity of the practice with Art 81 does not preclude the application of Art 82, *Tetra Pak Rausing SA v EC Commission* [1991] CMLR 334.

[119] In the US, the practices within the patent grant or scope of copyright protection are generally excluded from intervention. Unless restrictions are *per se* illegal, they are covered by rule-of-reason analysis. In Europe, even a practice that is within the 'scope of protection' or 'specific subject matter' may be blacklisted. See for discussion L Pehrson, 'Forhallandet Mellan immaterialratten och Konkurrensbergränsningsratten inom EG, EES och Sverige', in *Vennebog til Mogens Kotvejgaard* (Stockholm, 1993), 385, 393.

According to some marketing studies, products that do not have the newest features are considered to be commodities for which consumers are not willing to pay a premium. However, not all new integrations of features are successful. Sometimes the new features are not considered to be advancements compared to the existing products. This is usually explained as reflecting the saturation of the market.[120]

Integration and combination are part of ongoing technical competition. **4.136** Integration is seldom self-evident and is easy in the sense that anyone can do it in a limited period of time. If a company has the capability of integrating and combining new features into its products faster and better than anyone else, it may gain a substantial competitive edge on the market. Through that skill and capability, the company may gain a dominant position. Should this development be a concern for policy-makers, those drafting anti-trust, competition law and intellectual property law or enforcement agencies?

The analysis of external effects is useful here. It may be easily identified that it **4.137** may be possible to integrate and combine features using a number of practices. Firstly, functionality of a product may be enhanced by adding new technical functions to it. If a radio is integrated into a clock, the result is a clock radio. The resulting product is likely to appeal to people that would like to wake up by listening to their favourite music rather than listening to the ringing tone of the clock. It may be easily recognized that such a practice has its primary effects on competitors in the clock market. As clock radios become increasingly popular, the manufacturers of traditional clocks may lose markets. They are tempted to make their own versions of clock radios or they may focus on the customer segments that cannot readily use clock radios, for instance by manufacturing travel versions of clocks.

Another possibility is contractually to tie together two or more products and sell **4.138** them only in a package. For example, MP3 software could be added to a clock-radio package. If a person already has a clock radio he may complain that the manufacturer is engaging in an illegal tying practice because he is forced to buy an unnecessary clock radio in order to get the MP3 software.

In the US the legal treatment of tying has a long history involving intellectual property rights primarily because of the long-lasting presumption of market power derived from copyright and patents.[121] This history is not discussed in this book in any detail.

The current definition of tying makes it an anti-trust violation in the US only if (1) there are two separate products, (2) the customer takes the second ('tied') product not on its merits but only because he must take it in order to obtain the desired ('tying') product, either at all or on favourable terms, (3) the supplier possesses economic power over the

---

[120] This is because the integration no longer adds value to the attributes that customers primarily value. C M Christensen, *The Innovator's Dilemma—When New Technologies Cause Great Firms to Fall* (Boston, 1997), 39–42, 165.

[121] See analysis above in ch 2, para 2.10–2.25.

tying product, (4) the arrangement has the potential for 'foreclosing' or blocking competitors from the market, and (5) not an insubstantial part of the market is affected.[122]

In Europe Article 81(1) lists as limitations to competition obligations those that are unrelated to the transaction. Consequently, tying of unrelated objects is blacklisted for all block exemptions.[123] Under Article 82, unrelated obligations are also mentioned as examples of abuse of a dominant position.[124]

4.139 Economic analysis of tying usually concludes that tying is not likely to have anticompetitive effects unless there is economic power in the market of the tying product.

The issue is controversial since there has been a development emphasizing the deficiencies of the old '*per se*' treatment of tying. At the same time there has been high profile concrete enforcement action against Microsoft, based on Microsoft's intent to integrate an Internet browser[125] into its Windows operating system. In the US Microsoft provided to the court examples of a number of benefits that the user obtains through such integration.[126]

4.140 The new issue is the notion that integration or tying may have effects beyond the competitors and customers who directly experience the effects of the practice. Traditionally, it has been considered whether the effect of tying is to expand the monopoly of the monopolist into the new market of tied products or whether it is just making the initial monopoly position stronger.[127] In the network economy, there is no need to monopolize. It is enough that it is possible to 'tip the scale' by gaining initial market acceptance.

4.141 A starting point often taken is that each company may design such products as it thinks the market would like to buy. The *autonomy* of the company to compete is one of the principles that should not be easily intervened with. This has also been the starting point of the majority of commentators and courts addressing the issue.[128]

---

[122] P E Areeda, *Antitrust Law. An Analysis of Antitrust Principles and Their Application* (Boston 1991), § 1702, 30–31.

[123] No enforcement of these provisions has in recent years been reported under Art 81. See also Bellamy and Child, n 1 above, 551–552 (no violation if indispensable for the exploitation of the patent).

[124] See *Eurofix Ltd v Hilti AG* [1989] CMLR 677 (abuse of dominant position to sell patented cartridges for nail guns only on the condition that the customer also buy nails for such cartridge); *The Community v International Business Machines* [1984] 3 CMLR 147 (abuse of dominant position because of bundling mainframe computers and operating software, and mainframe computers and memory); in Finland *Digital*, Kilpailuvirasto 13.10.1993 dnro 4/359/92 (maintenance of hardware and software updates).

[125] See also EU Commission's press release of 30 August 2001 (Statement of Objection extended to cover the integration of Media Player into Windows).

[126] See discussion of those benefits in W H Page and J E Lopatka, 'The Dubious Search for Integration in the Microsoft Trial' (1999) 31 Connecticut Law Review, 1251, 1256–1258.

[127] L Kaplow, 'Extension of Monopoly Power Through Leverage' (1985) 85 Columbia Law Review, 515, 520; R C Feldman, 'Defensive Leveraging in Anti-trust' (1999) 87 Georgetown Law Journal, 2079, 2079.

[128] W A Sheramata, 'New Issues in Competition Policy Raised by Information Technology

The next logical step is to ask whether it makes a difference if it is possible to   **4.142**
combine two products or features by integrating them into one single product or
by packaging them together and selling them at a single price.[129] Similarly, it is
possible to ask whether it makes any difference whether the customer is forced[130]
to buy a particular combination of features by using legal tools, such as contract
terms, or by integrating the features into a single product.

The obvious conclusion is that there is no fundamental difference between these   **4.143**
methods. The method used to combine two initially separate products should not
lead to a different legal treatment. It is easy to see that at the practical level of
enforcement, this has still resulted in different treatment. Except for the enforcement action against Microsoft in the US, integration of new features into a single
product has not been treated as tying, simply because there has not been 'a package of two separate products'.[131] The US Appeals Court for DC Circuit discussed
this issue in *US v Microsoft*.[132] The court made a distinction whether a product
'combines functionalities (which may also be marketed separately and operated
together) in a way that offers advantages unavailable if functionalities are bought
separately and combined by the purchaser.'[133] Judge Wald, in his concurring
opinion, would have used the evidence on whether there are separate markets for
component parts as an indication whether the market thought there were substantial efficiencies to be gained.

Industries' (1998) 43 Anti-trust Bulletin, 547, 556. See, however, Page–Lopatka, n 126 above,
1271–1273 (suggesting that consumers should not be forced to accept an integration they do not
want). The deficiencies of this approach as a controlling criterion are easy to identify by generalizing
the issue: should any integration by a company with market power be rejected if there are consumers
who do not like it?

[129] One could eg ask whether it makes a difference if a car has integrated tyres or tyres that one can
easily change and replace. Consumers would anyway like to buy their cars with the tyres included in
the same package. See *Data General* (using this example) and *Kodak I* (refusing to accept that tyres
and cars are always the same product). Further, this presumes that there is an existing independent
market for the combined technologies.

[130] This is sometimes referred to as the element of 'coercion'.

[131] See P E Areeda *et al*, *Anti-trust Law. An Analysis of Anti-trust Principles and their Application*
(Vol X, Boston 1996), 207 (the test is whether (1) products are commonly sold separately, and (2)
whether such separate sale is more efficient than the sale together); see also ibid, 224 (a product is an
integration if (1) two or more items are integrated in a way that has not been done before, or (2) previously separately sold items operate better if they are integrated by the manufacturer and not the end-
user) and ibid, at 268 (rejecting tests that focus on whether items are useless without the other item
or whether both items are needed).

[132] *US v Microsoft*, 147 F 3d 935 (DC Cir 1998).

[133] Id at 948. Those dissenting would have used a balancing test where 'the greater the evidence of
distinct markets, the more of a showing of synergy Microsoft must make in order to justify incorporating what otherwise would be an 'other' product into an 'integrated' whole. If evidence of distinct
markets is weak, then Microsoft can get by with a fairly modest showing . . .' (although perhaps not
the minimal showing required by the majority). Id at 950. See also J E Lopatka and W H Page,
'Antitrust on Internet Time: Microsoft and the Law and Economics of Exclusion' (1999) 7 Supreme
Court Economic Review, 173 (suggesting that obvious efficiencies exist that support integration) and
United States v Microsoft Corp, 253 F 3d 34, 92 (the separate product test is a poor substitute for net
efficiency from newly integrated products).

4.144 Different legal treatment is a consequence of legislation. It is usually not possible to intervene in unilateral action unless there is an attempt to monopolize the market or abuse of a dominant position.[134] Only if there is a contract or other concerted action, do the laws justify intervention in any practice limiting competition.[135]

4.145 There may be two main kinds of market effect as a consequence of the combination. Firstly, in the original product's primary market the usefulness of that product is increased.[136] As a consequence competitors are not necessarily able to make the same combination. This inability may be a consequence of their lack of skills, lack of resources or intellectual property rights blocking them from making such combinations.

4.146 Secondly, in the secondary market of the product that is being combined with the primary product,[137] the combination may exclude other suppliers of that product or feature. This risk is higher if there is not a substantial number of other customers except those customers that prefer or are forced to buy the combined product. Therefore, in order to compete effectively, any other supplier of the 'tied' product should enter the market of combined products. However, it is possible that they are blocked or 'foreclosed' from being able to make the same combination. Such an inability to make the same combination may be due to their lack of skills, lack of resources or the intellectual property rights stopping them from making such combinations.

4.147 It appears that the *inability of competitors to make the same combination should be a concern only if such inability is caused by factors controlled by the party making such combination.* The anti-trust or competition laws should not be applied if the inability of the competitors to make the same combination is primarily due to factors beyond the control of a single party. Factors controlled by a single party and factors built into the structure of the market may be categorized as follows:

---

[134] S 2 of Sherman Act, 15 USC § 2: Every person who shall monopolize, or attempt to monopolize, or combine or conspire with any other person or persons, to monopolize any part of the trade or commerce among the several States, or with foreign nations, shall be deemed guilty of a felony. S 82 in the Treaty of European Union: Any abuse by one or more undertakings of a dominant position within the common market or in a substantial part of it shall be prohibited as incompatible with the common market in so far as it may affect trade between Member States. See also *Copperweld Corp v Independence Tube Corp*, 467 US 752 (1984) (the conduct of a single firm is covered by § 2 alone); C Bellamy and G Child, *European Community Law of Competition* (5th edn, P M Roth, ed, London, 2001), 46–47.

[135] S 1 of Sherman Act, 15 USC § 1: Every contract, combination in the form of trust or otherwise, or conspiracy, in restraint of trade or commerce among the several States, or with foreign nations, is hereby declared to be illegal. Art 81 in the Treaty of European Union: The following shall be prohibited as incompatible with the common market: all agreements between undertakings, decisions by associations of undertakings and concerted practices which may affect trade between Member States and which have as their objective or effect the prevention, restriction or distortion of competition within the common market.

[136] Using the anti-trust and competition law terminology, the market of the tying product.

[137] Using the anti-trust and competition law terminology, the market of the tied product.

EXAMPLES OF FACTORS CONTROLLED BY A SINGLE PARTY	EXAMPLES OF FACTORS BEYOND THE CONTROL OF A SINGLE PARTY
Intellectual property rights covering either the 'tying' or the 'tied' product provided that such rights are controlled by a party	Intellectual property rights controlled by third parties
Essential elements (facilities, local loops, raw materials and components) controlled by a party	Initial investment required (machines, components, raw materials and skilful employees)
Contract practices locking customers	Customer preferences

There are a few necessary additional definitions. Firstly, in the network economy, **4.148** it is not always easy to recognize or identify which is the primary market and which is the secondary market. This is due to the interdependency of companies and the tendency of particular companies to compete in a number of markets. Under this suggested conclusion, it is not necessary to make this distinction. One of the key issues is whether a company controls assets that prevent competitors from making a particular combination of two potentially separate features.

Secondly, the distinction should be made between assets that are the core of such **4.149** combination and assets that are used as components for the combination. Sometimes, a particular combination may be innovative or creative. Therefore, a patent or copyright may protect such combination independently of its component parts. Combinations protected by such intellectual property rights may be subject to a different treatment. The competitive concerns are not necessarily different but if the combination itself is the primary element protected, it could be asked whether the inventor or creator should be entitled to the appropriate reward, namely the limited exclusivity granted by the intellectual property laws.[138] This would be similar to the analysis by the court in *Microsoft*,[139] except that this would establish a quality test for the advantages that combined functionality provides over the component parts being sold separately. Under this test, intellectual property rights preventing competitors from being able to make a similar combination must protect these advantages.

Finally, the legal criteria for treating combinations should not condemn them *per* **4.150** *se* if there is a finding that a party controls assets that may potentially be used to

---

[138] See, however, *Windsurfing Int, Inc v EC Commission* [1986] 3 CMLR 489 (a patent on the surfboard combining a rig and a sailboard did not justify licence terms which limited the right of purchasers to purchase replacements for individual component parts).
[139] 147 F 3d 935, 948 (DC Cir 1998).

foreclose or prevent competitors from making the same combination. Rather, any legal remedy should only be subject to the actual finding that a party is using such position to foreclose competitors. There must be a finding that a party is actually not allowing competitors access to such assets on reasonable terms. Such reasonable terms should not limit their ability to compete. In addition, anything other than substantial harm or damage to competition should not be subject to treatment, thus some kind of *de minimis* rule is appropriate.[140]

4.151 This suggested approach might obviously be subject to criticism as it limits the rights of intellectual property owners freely to make use of their intellectual property rights. Proponents of 'strong' intellectual property rights may claim that this would seriously limit the available reward and discourage innovation and creativity. This theory does not have that kind of aim and effect except whenever a party is using its intellectual property rights in leveraging. In those circumstances, the harm to competition resulting from not being able to intervene is presumably greater than the loss resulting from the restriction on the individual intellectual property owner.

4.152 This proposed theory seems to provide a reasonable working solution for making a distinction between leveraging and normal competition. Only leveraging should be a concern to policy-makers. Leveraging can only take place if a company is making use of some tools, such as proprietary assets, that are under their sole control. As a practical example, Microsoft argued during the anti-trust trial against the US Department of Justice that their practice of combining Windows and the Internet browser was not different from the normal practice of companies when integrating new features in their products. One could argue that because of the market share of Windows and the intellectual property rights Microsoft owned in Windows, other manufacturers of Internet browsers were foreclosed from making the same combination between the operating system and a browser. In that sense, Microsoft's position was different from a typical integration.

4.153 The same analysis could be applied in the cellular telephone market. Digital phone technologies are standardized. There are so-called second-generation digital cellular phone standards, such as GSM, IS-136, PCT and IS-95. There will emerge third-generation cellular standards. Should it be permitted that technologies compliant with both second- and third-generation standards be integrated into the same phone even if there are probably going to be manufacturers making only second- or third-generation phones? The proposed analysis suggests looking into whether a company controls intellectual property rights or other assets that could block someone from making the same combination. If there are such assets,

---

[140] See *United States v Microsoft Corp*, 253 F 3d 34, 65–67 (DC Cir 2001) (plaintiffs had to show prima facie evidence that the integration of new features into Windows harms competition and defendants had to show that there are justifications for such integration other than protecting its operating system monopoly).

policy-makers should explore the practices that allow others access to those assets. There should be no such concerns if others have the ability or opportunity to make the same combination.[141]

Compatibility

Compatibility is one of the most important practices of an individual company affecting other companies in the network economy. It is important because compatibility provides access to an installed base of competitors' customers. Consequently, debates over compatibility reflect the battle between companies over future sales to existing customers.[142] **4.154**

Two products are compatible if they can be used together. If they cannot be used together, they are incompatible.[143] If several products work together, they form a network. Access to network effects is one of the primary attributes of successful business in the network economy. By using intellectual property rights, it may be possible to control the potential of the competitor to benefit from network effects. This can be implemented by using (1) patents that cover interfaces; (2) copyrights that cover implementations of particular interfaces; and (3) trade secrets that cover the information necessary in order to manufacture any compliant product. **4.155**

In industries in which network effects are significant, there is increased likelihood that a single firm may come to dominate the market and maintain that dominance. Intellectual property rights have a significant effect on achieving and maintaining a dominant position. In particular, to the extent intellectual property rights cover network standards, a considerable amount of permanent market power may be attributed to them.[144] **4.156**

It is often the case that in industries involving network effects users will naturally tend to gravitate toward using products that are compatible with products already owned by the greatest number of other users. For this reason, a firm that initially has the largest number of users may become dominant. Such a firm may then **4.157**

---

[141] Standardization practices and the appropriate royalty levels are discussed more in detail below.

[142] M L Katz and C Shapiro, 'Product Introduction with Network Externalities' (1992) 40 Journal of Industrial Economics, 55, 55.

[143] J Farrell, 'Standardisation and Intellectual Property' (1989) 30 Jurimetrics Journal, 35, 36. The issue of compatibility is important in various businesses. See generally J Schovsbo, 'Som Skabt for hinanden—Immaterial-og Konkurreneretlig beskyttelse af Kompatible Produkter' (1997) NIR, 16, 16 (discussing spare parts, building blocks and accessories in terms of their design); J Schovsbo, *Graensefladesporsmä/Mellem immaterialretten og Konkurreneretten* (Copenhagen, 1996), 163. In this book, the particular focus is compatibility that allows two or more products to interact together.

[144] M A Lemley and D McGowan, 'Legal Implications of Network Economic Effects' (1998) 86 California Law Review, 469, 523; J Farrell and M L Katz, 'The Effects of Anti-trust and Intellectual Property Law on Compatibility and Innovation' [1998] Anti-trust Bulletin, 609, 610–611; P S Menell, 'An Epitaph for Traditional Copyright Protection of Network Features of Computer Software' [1998] Anti-trust Bulletin, 651, 651 (control of interface specifications and other network features has been the key to market dominance).

have an incentive to adopt competitive strategies that support a single standard by preventing the products of rivals from achieving compatibility. Where it chooses to do so, or if the costs of guaranteeing compatibility across networks are high, the products of rivals can become relatively less desirable to users. Sometimes this takes place irrespective of the fact that they appear to be of comparable (or possibly even higher) quality from a purely 'technical' standpoint. When the dominant firm's product becomes the standard for the industry, firms that are developing alternative standards may find it difficult to compete effectively.[145]

4.158 The strategic use of compatibility may have various effects. Since there is a tendency to favour one dominant network, incompatibility may limit competition. If others cannot supply the dominant network, a single company may sometimes gain monopoly returns. Since this possibility is recognized, companies are increasingly competing vigorously (1) to become dominant, and (2) to either maintain incompatibility or to achieve compatibility.

4.159 Compatibility may also neutralize competitive advantages. Companies with the largest installed base of customers may have an advantage: customers are likely to buy enhancements, spare parts and replacements for existing products. If products are compatible, there is only one big network. Manufacturers compete in such a network to supply the existing customer base of their competitors.[146]

4.160 Compatibility of products usually requires access to interface information. Other important issues are therefore copyright protection for interface information and the licensing strategies which companies use. These are sometimes combined in the discussion involving various technical protection means that, *de facto*, can impede anyone from extracting information in order to manufacture compatible products. Finally, it may be asked whether there should be any difference between the treatment of compatibility between different independent systems and within component parts of a single system. This discussion has tended to focus on the issue whether intellectual property rights should be limited in order to promote compatibility.[147]

4.161 Firstly, none of the commentators seem to use network effects theories to support stronger intellectual property rights. This is because intellectual property rights

---

[145] N Rubinfeld, 'Competition, Innovation, and Anti-trust Enforcement in Dynamic Network Industries', Speech before Software Publishers Association Meeting (1998), 5–6.

[146] Farrell–Katz, n 145 above, 611 (suggesting that the degree of compatibility may significantly affect supplier profit and consumer welfare); W E Cohen, 'Competition and Foreclosure in the Context of Installed Base and Compatibility Effects' (1996) 64 Anti-trust Law Journal, 535, 536–539; R J Kauffman, J McAndrews and Y M Wang, 'Opening the "Black Box" of Network Externalities in Network Adoption' (2000) 11 Information Systems Research, 61, 61 (suggesting that the higher the installed base of customers one has the less likely a company is to adopt a new more effective network).

[147] There are a number of analyses such as Lemley–McGowan, n 144 above; Farrell–Katz, n 144 above; Farrell, n 47 above.

can effectively be used to prevent the sale of compatible products. The primary arguments supporting denial of access to the interface information are based either on the argument that any such access would discourage companies from innovating or on the theory that such access is an intervention in private property rights. Commentators recognize that new technologies require 'sponsors' that have economic incentives to drive them into industry standards. Intellectual property rights may provide the appropriate form of incentive for sponsors to emerge.[148]

At the same time it is also recognized that intellectual property rights may affect **4.162** whether compatibility can be unilaterally imposed or blocked. If there are exclusive rights, a single company may block compatibility. In the absence of such rights, other companies may unilaterally exercise their exclusive rights to impose or block compatibility.[149] As a consequence, it may sometimes be privately advantageous for a company to support incompatibility even though it was socially advantageous to achieve compatibility.[150] However, it is also suggested that forcing or imposing compatibility may have adverse effects on incentives to innovate and cause a decrease in competition in research and development.[151] Secondly, the unlimited application of reverse engineering is not broadly supported.[152] Reverse engineering is primarily supported when it is necessary in order to gain access to network effects. Network effects are primarily available whenever there is a standard.

Thirdly, even though reverse engineering is allowed, the manufacturer of the **4.163** original equipment is still likely to have some benefits over anyone relying on reverse engineering of products. The legal structure around the issue is uncertain and involves a risk of litigation. Furthermore, reverse engineering may be covered by contract terms that, at least in the US, may according to some courts nullify the right to reverse engineer. Also, companies increasingly have patents over interfaces. In patent law, there are no similar doctrines of fair use to those found in copyright law to authorize limited reverse engineering. Sometimes reverse engineering may be difficult and costly, and the results uncertain. Finally,

---

[148] M L Katz and C Shapiro, 'Technology Adoption in the Presence of Network Externalities' (1986) 94 Journal of Political Economy, 822, 824.

[149] Farrell–Katz, n 145 above, 612–613.

[150] S J Liebowitz and S E Margolis, 'Should Technology Choice Be a Concern of Anti-trust Policy,' (1996) 9 Harvard Journal of Law and Technology, 283, 45.

[151] Farrell–Katz, n 144 above, 641–642 (admitting that compatibility may also increase such competition if it opens markets for companies that were not otherwise successful even with superior technologies); Farrell, n 47 above, 36–37 (suggesting also a potential loss of variety).

[152] See B Sheffner, '*Alcatel USA, Inc v DGI Technologies Inc*' (2000) 15 Berkley Technology Law Journal, 25, 46; P S Menell, 'Tailoring the Legal Protection of Computer Software' (1987) 39 Stanford Law Review, 1329, 1371. 'Reverse engineering' means a method of obtaining technical information by starting with the publicly available product and determining what it is made of, what makes it work or how it was produced. McCarthy's *Desk Encyclopedia of Intellectual Property* (2nd edn, Washington DC 1995).

by introducing frequent updates, the manufacturer of the original product may maintain their lead times. Consequently, companies still have a number of ways at least to increase costs of competitors to achieve and maintain interoperability.

4.164   In order to enable compatibility, some commentators have argued that any interfaces should be beyond intellectual property protection.[153] According to more limited views, the necessity to achieve interoperability should be a defence to any intellectual property infringement claim. This latter view would recognize that some features using interface information may be patentable and any extension of this exclusion to such features would be unreasonable. Licensing is also a broadly used solution to achieve compatibility. Especially if patents are involved, licensing is the most common (at least) current solution to achieve compatibility. Licensing allows the rights holder potentially to extract all surpluses gained from compatibility and therefore it has its limitations as a solution.[154] Finally, the possibility to design an adapter that makes a product compatible is sometimes recognized. Adapters or converters may allow a competing design to be used and sold to the existing base of customers.[155]

4.165   While in Europe limited provisions in statutes cover compatibility, the case law in the US has provided some interesting rules. The courts have relied either on fair use, excluded the interfaces from the protected subject matter or alternatively accepted a copyright misuse defence whenever the copyright owner has tried to use its copyright to prevent the sale of compatible, but otherwise non-infringing products.

---

[153] See T C Vinje, 'The Final Word on *Magill*' (1995) NIR, 156, 166; Farrell, n 47 above, 47; Farrell–Katz, n 144 above, 645–650 (suggesting that limited protection of interfaces or anti-trust enforcement are alternatives); Sheffner, n 152 above, 46 (suggesting that copyright should be unenforceable when it prevents a competitor from a market for compatible but non-infringing products); P S Menell, 'An Analysis of the Scope of Copyright Protection for Application Programs' (1989) 41 Stanford Law Review 1045, 1103–1104; Menell, n 144 above, 679; R B Lande and S M Sobin, 'Reverse Engineering of Computer Software: The Anti-trust Issues' (1996) 9 Harvard Journal of Law and Technology, 237, 273 (finding hostility of courts against efforts to use contract practices or copyright laws to oppose reverse engineering). *Lotus Development Corp v Borland Intern*, 49 F 3d 807 (1st Cir 1995), aff'd, 116 S Ct 804 (1996), reh'g denied, 116 S Ct 1062 (1996) (menu commands were unprotected methods of operation).

[154] M L Katz and C Shapiro, 'Product Introduction with Network Externalities' (1992) 40 Journal of Industrial Economics, 55, 72 (licensing affects the distribution of wealth within the industry but, provided that licensing is effective, not the actual allocation). The problem with this conclusion (based on the Coase Theorem) is that licence fees affect the allocation of resources within single licensees and it can indirectly affect the allocation between competing functions.

[155] M L Katz and C Shapiro, 'Network Externalities, Competition and Compatibility' (1985) 75 American Economic Review, 424, 434 (referring to Honeywell making a program that made its mainframe computers compatible with IBM mainframe computers in the 1960s); J Farrell and G Saloner, 'Converters, Compatibility, and the Control of Interfaces' (1992) 40 Journal of Industrial Economics, 9, 9 (if we had converters that could translate from one version to another, standardization would be less important).

Firstly, the right of the rights holder to make its products incompatible is in prin- **4.166**
ciple accepted. There is no general obligation to make compatible products.[156]
Consequently, products may be designed which are backwards incompatible[157] or
unilaterally incompatible.[158] Such incompatibility is usually imposed because the
designer expressly wishes to force existing customers to change from their existing products to new products. If the users of existing products supplied by a
competitor or by the manufacturer could use their existing products the customer
would have no incentive to buy the new product.

However, sometimes a change made in the product to make the competitor's **4.167**
product incompatible may amount to misuse of intellectual property rights. In *C
R Bard, Inc v M3 Systems, Inc*,[159] the patent holder changed its 'gun' device used
to take samples of body tissue. The competitor could no longer provide replacement needles without infringing the patent. The court held that the defendant had
to show that the change was made for the purpose of injuring competitors in the
replacement needle market, rather than for improving the operation of the gun.

Secondly, despite the principal right to design incompatible products, the right of **4.168**
intellectual property owners to use their exclusive rights to prevent others from
making compatible products has frequently been challenged. A typical case
involves a product and spare parts, enhancements or accessories for such a product. The cases tend to draw a balance between different interests and justifications.

The first category of cases involves products that necessarily need to copy a **4.169**
particular part of another product in order to be interoperable. Typically, particular bits of software programs need to be exactly the same. If the correct order of
the bits is not known the necessary information needs to be acquired. In Europe,

---

[156] *United States v Microsoft Corp*, 253 F 3d 34, 65 (DC Cir 2001) ('a monopoly does not violate
the anti-trust laws simply by developing a product that is incompatible with those of its rivals').

[157] *Backwards incompatibility* may be illustrated by the examples in the software industry. The software product is backwards incompatible if the new version of it cannot interact with the older version
of the software or other previous third-party software products. Backwards incompatibility is partial
if the product interacts with the older versions but the users of older versions cannot interact with that
new version. In addition to the software industry, backwards incompatibility may be found also in the
telecommunications industry, where the new more advanced standards are sometimes not compatible
with old technologies.

[158] *Unilateral interoperability* is best illustrated by computer software the user of which can use
other computer software with it or read files prepared by other equivalent software products.
However, this interoperability may be unilateral in the sense that the users of other software products
cannot read the files prepared by that particular software product or use it together with their primary
product.

[159] *C R Bard, Inc v M3 Systems, Inc*, 157 F 3d 1340 (Fed Cir 1998). See also *Sun Microsystems, Inc
v Microsoft Corp*, 87 F Supp 992 (N D Cal 2000) (Microsoft's unauthorized distribution of incompatible implementations of Sun's Java Technology threatens to undermine Sun's goal of cross-plat-
form and cross-implementation compatibility); *Decca Navigation Systems* [1990] 4 CMLR 627 (the
EU Commission found an abuse of a dominant position when competing products were made incompatible by changing a signal for navigation equipment at short notice).

the Software Directive contains some important balancing elements. According to section 6 of the directive, copyright protection is excluded for elements and acts that are necessary in order to achieve interoperability.[160] Also the directive relating to industrial designs excludes from design protection elements that are technically necessary in order to make compatible products.[161]

4.170   In the US, a similar outcome is usually achieved through fair-use limitation of the copyright laws or through the doctrine of copyright misuse. The fair-use defence was successfully used in the game cartridge cases. In order to manufacture game cartridges for products manufactured by companies such as Nintendo, Sega and Sony, a company needs to copy particular bits or 'keys'. The courts have usually held that such copying is fair use.[162] The misuse defence has been used successfully against infringement claims when the rights holder has tried to limit the efforts of a competitor to achieve interoperability, eg through reverse-engineering the rights holder's product in order to gain access to the bit-by-bit information of the interface.[163]

4.171   Apart from these 'technically necessary' elements, there may be a number of commercially necessary elements that need to be copied in order successfully to sell the product to the customer. It is typical that a particular product can technically be used with other products without copying this element but for some reason such an alternative is not commercially attractive.[164] A typical justification for intervention in such cases is customer lock-in. The cost for customers to change their practices may be so high that they are not likely to buy a competing product even when such product could be commercially superior.[165]

4.172   In the US, this reasoning was used in *Lotus v Borland*.[166] A particular menu

---

[160] The Council Directive for the Legal Protection of Computer Programs (OJ L 122/42), § 6.

[161] Directive 98/71/EC of the European Parliament and of the Council of 13 October 1998 on the legal protection of designs, OJ L 289, 28/10/1998, p 0028–0035, Art 7.1: A design right shall not subsist in features of appearance of a product which are solely dictated by its technical function.

[162] *Sony Computer Entertainment, Inc v Connectix Corp* (9th Cir 2000); *Sega Enters Ltd v Accolade, Inc*, 977 F 2d 1510 (9th Cir 1993); *Atari Games Corp v Nintendo of Am, Inc*, 975 F 2d 832 (Fed Cir 1992).

[163] *Lasercomb America, Inc v Reynolds*, 911 F 2d 970 (4th Cir 1990) (establishing the modern version of the misuse defence).

[164] It is sometimes suggested that spare parts need to have more similarity with the original product whereas for accessories or enhancements the limited technical compatibility is enough. Schovsbo, n 143 above, 28 (discussing protection through industrial designs). See also Directive 98/71/EC of the European Parliament and of the Council of 13 October 1998 on the legal protection of designs, OJ L 289, 28/10/1998, p 0028–0035, Art 7.2: A design right shall not subsist in features of appearance of a product which must necessarily be reproduced in their exact form and dimensions in order to permit the product in which the design is incorporated or to which it is applied to be mechanically connected to or placed in, around or against another product so that either product may perform its function.

[165] W A Sheramata, 'Barriers to Innovation: A Monopoly, Network Externalities, and the Speed of Innovation' [1997] Anti-trust Bulletin, 937, 955.

[166] *Lotus Development Corp v Borland Intern*, 49 F 3d 807 (1st Cir 1995), aff'd, 116 S Ct 804 (1996), reh'g denied, 116 S Ct 1062 (1996).

command structure used in Lotus 1-2-3, popular spreadsheet software, was held to be an uncopyrightable method of operation. *Lotus v Borland* reflects one possible way to solve the issues involving compatibility: internalization of the issue into intellectual property laws by explaining that a particular element be excluded from protection. In Europe, a similar issue has also been dealt with under competition laws. In *Dior v Evora*,[167] the European Court of Justice held that copyright protection in product packaging and the shape of the perfume bottle could not be used to object against the normal marketing of genuine products. Had the rights holder prevailed a parallel importer could not have sold products even though under trade mark laws the products could lawfully be distributed.

In general, the justification to rely on commercially necessary elements and the **4.173** justification to benefit from market power generated by success in the marketplace need to be balanced. There is no case law or doctrine suggesting that all elements that a competitor needs in order to sell a product to an existing user of a rights holder's product would be subject to critical scrutiny. Rather, the analysis calls for an evaluation of whether such element or the exercise of the protection is arbitrary and not justified.

In addition to technically and commercially necessary elements, a third party may **4.174** be prevented from selling compatible products because in order to do so the customer needs to run or play a rights holder's software, music file, DVD disk or any other work supplied by such third party. The customer may be prevented from doing this by restrictive contract terms that do not allow him to make a copy. Alternatively, the customer may be prevented from doing this by technical protection means, such as proprietary codes or 'patches' that make unauthorized products inoperable.

In Europe the justification for such practices would generally be subject to the **4.175** proportionality test of anti-trust laws established by the European Court of Justice.[168] In the US one would expect that the right of the rights holder is justified unless it is 'pretextual'[169] or a mere 'sham'[170] to exclude a competitor.[171] However, in *Alcatel v DGI*,[172] a US federal appeals court accepted a copyright misuse defence when a rights holder had licensed its operating systems software for use only in connection with equipment supplied by the rights holder. The case

---

[167] C-337/95 *Parfums Christian Dior SA v Evora BV* [1997] ECR I-6013.
[168] See ch 2, para 2.123–2.137 above for discussion.
[169] *Image Technical Services, Inc v Eastman Kodak Co*, 125 F 3d 1195, 1212 (9th Cir 1997).
[170] *Professional Real Estate Investors v Columbia Pictures Industries, Inc*, 508 US 49 (1993).
[171] Enforcement action by the movie industry against breaking the codes used in DVD disks fall in this category. See *Universal City Studios, Inc v Reimerdes*, 82 F Supp 2d 211(SDNY 2000). See also D McCullagh, 'DVD Battles: Copy Free or Die?' (2000) IP Worldwide 4-5, 38, 38. There were no DVD disks available at the time of the proceedings for Linux but only for Windows.
[172] *Alcatel USA, Inc v DGI Technologies, Inc*, 166 F 3d 772 (5th Cir 1999). See ch 4, para 4.16–4.18 above for further discussion of the case.

suggests licence restrictions and possibly also technical restrictions, eg technical protection means, that limit the equipment manufacturers' potential to supply compatible equipment for the end-user may sometimes make the copyright unenforceable under the doctrine of copyright misuse.[173]

4.176 As a summary, copyright laws provide more flexible and effective means to ensure compatibility than patent laws. Means available particularly in copyright laws have also been increasingly used, even though the proper limits of the US practice are yet to be formulated. As between Europe and the US, the Software Directive in Europe provided a well-functioning platform in the early 1990s. The EU Copyright Directive, limiting the possible ways to tailor flexible limitations to rights holders' exclusive rights, was a clear step backwards in this respect.[174] However, as indicated above, even the Software Directive only provides the solution to the most limited of compatibility issues: the issue of proprietary interface information. Any other issues are subject to anti-trust laws. The problem with anti-trust laws in general is that they are effective against unilateral conduct or enforcement of intellectual property rights only if it is possible to show market power in the relevant market. In Europe the spare part cases have created doctrines that allow the relevant market to be found in the products of a single producer. This may, if appropriately exercised, provide some new flexibility corresponding to the flexibility provided in the US by the intellectual property misuse doctrines.

4.177 Patent laws in general have not contained any similar exclusions or limitations that could effectively be used to maintain compatibility. However, interfaces in the communications industry are increasingly patented. The communications industry has developed some practices to solve the problems caused by increasing patenting activities. These practices are discussed in detail below in connection with standardization activities.[175]

Relevance of totality of circumstances

4.178 An obvious outcome of the identification of external effects is the notion that the intervention may be justified if the combined effect of various practices is harmful. This is not because any single practice would amount to the violation of laws but because the combination of practices has a harmful effect. Even though a single company is not required to make interoperable products, the same reasoning does not have to be valid in respect of architectural interoperability. A number

---

[173] Sheffner, n 152 above, 43–44. See also *Atari Games Corp v Nintendo of America, Inc,* 975 F 2d 832 (Fed Cir 1992).

[174] Directive 2001/29/EC of the European Parliament and of the Council of 22 May 2001 on the harmonization of certain aspects of copyright and related rights in the information society ([2001] OJ L 167/10), Art 5(2) (exclusive list of possible exceptions and limitations).

[175] See ch 6 below.

of independent but interoperable products form an architecture. Two products may lack interoperability without it having any significant impact on competition. If the products of one vertically or horizontally integrated manufacturer are interoperable with each other but they lack interoperability with the products of other manufacturers, there is lack of interoperability between architectures.

In the US the possibility to find a violation of anti-trust laws has been recognized **4.179** in a number of cases. In *Aspen Skiing*[176] the violation of the Sherman Act section 2 was found in the totality of practices. Such practices did not further the competition on merits and were unnecessarily restrictive. In *Union Carbide*[177] the court took the view that the various factual components should not be 'tightly compartmentalized'. The ruling against Microsoft in the US also discussed some elements of this reasoning.[178]

In Europe the European Court of Justice first discussed the issue of the combined **4.180** effect of various practices in *Brasserie de Haecht v Wilkin*.[179] The ECJ held that the effects of a practice have to be assessed in the context in which they occur and where they may have a cumulative effect on competition. In *Delimitis*[180] the court evaluated the effects of a single agreement together with other similar agreements. The combined effects of such contracts on the opportunities of competitors to gain access on the market were held to be anti-competitive.

In *Magill*[181] the ECJ based its findings leading to an abuse of a dominant posi- **4.181** tion on a number of circumstances. It was relevant that none of these circumstances involved restrictive contract practices but that the television broadcasters unilaterally imposed all. Consequently, after *Magill* there was some uncertainty on the issue of whether *Magill* was as decided because of cumulative effects of circumstances or based on an individual practice to refuse to license underlying copyrights to weekly television listings. In *Oscar Bronner*[182] the ECJ confirmed that the totality of circumstances led the court to find abuse in *Magill*. The mere refusal to license does not amount to an abuse.

---

[176] *Aspen Skiing Co v Aspen Highlands Skiing Corp*, 472 US 585 (1985).

[177] *Continental Ore Co v Union Carbide & Carpon Corp*, 370 US 690 (1962).

[178] Microsoft was very carefully, and according to some views sometimes aggressively, making strategic use of its intellectual property rights by maximizing its effect on the behaviour of others. *United States v Microsoft Corp*, 87 F Supp 2d 30, 44 (US Dist 2000) ('Viewing Microsoft's conduct as a whole also reinforces the conviction that it was predacious'), rev'd *United States v Microsoft Corp*, 253 F 3d 34, 78 (DC Cir 2001) (no specific acts identified as a basis for course of conduct liability).

[179] *Brasserie de Haecht v Wilkin* [1968] CMLR 26.

[180] *Delimitis v Henninger Bräu* [1992] 5 CMLR 210 (restrictive beer supply agreements held to violate Art 85(1) of EC Treaty).

[181] *Radio Telefís Éireann (RTÉ) and Independent Television Publications Ltd (ITP) v Commission* ('*Magill*') [1995] 4 CMLR 718.

[182] Case C-7/97 *Oscar Bronner GmbH & Co KG v Mediaprint Zeitungs- und Zeitschriftenverlag GmbH & Co KG*.

4.182 In the network economy, the lack of compatibility between architectures has an increasing importance even though interoperability between individual products does not necessarily have any particular significance. This is because a lack of architectural compatibility may allow a dominant position on the market for one product to be extended, or leveraged, to other markets. Consequently, architectural interoperability may have significant importance as a safeguard for effective competition because it makes leveraging more difficult.

5

FRAGMENTATION PROBLEM

Fragmentation and success of new products

The problem of external effects and the concept of rebuttable entitlements can **5.01** further be illustrated by introducing the fragmentation problem. Why do the biggest manufacturers in the industry never adopt some perfectly brilliant ideas? Why is it so difficult for any independent inventor or small company to find its way to the technology manager of major companies? Why do innovative concepts, such as the software operating system Linux, suddenly gain popularity?

Some high-tech marketing theories rely on product life cycle theories to explain **5.02** the challenge.[1] The majority of purchasers are presumed to be sceptical, relying on proof that the new product will truly increase their profits or provide other benefits. In order to be successful it is necessary to be first successful in the early markets consisting of 'early adopters', those who adopt new technologies quickly.[2] Some economists also explain this success to be the consequence of positive feedback in industries that have network effects.[3] In order to win a significant share among the sceptical majority of purchasers, a complete product and the support of the industry is required.

---

[1] G A Moore, *Crossing the Chasm—Marketing and Selling High-Tech Products to Mainstream Customers* (New York, 1991), G A Moore, *Inside the Tornado—Marketing Strategies from Silicon Valley's Cutting Edge* (New York, 1995). See also S George, 'Assessing Future Markets for New Technologies', in Wharton on *Managing Emerging Technologies* (New York, 2000), 127, 130 (perceived advantages, risks, barriers to adoption, opportunities to learn and try); E Mansfield, *Technological Change. An Introduction to a Vital Era of Modern Economics* (New York, 1971), 93–94 (listing the following factors as having an impact on innovators: (1) size of the firm (big firms have advantages), (2) expectations of profit, (3) rate of growth, (4) the firm's profit level, (5) the age of the firm's management personnel, (6) liquidity of the firm, and (7) the firm's profit trend. See also C M Christensen, *The Innovator's Dilemma—When New Technologies Cause Great Firms to Fail* (Boston 1997), 165 (suggesting that at some point new technical performance may exceed market demand and that opens markets for new simplified solutions).

[2] Early adopters and innovators who are more enthusiastic about any new technologies even in the testing phase. See Moore, n 1 above, 12–13; Moore, n 1 above, 24–26.

[3] W E Cohen, 'Competition and Foreclosure in the Context of Installed Base and Compatibility Effects' (1996) 64 Anti-trust Law Journal, 535, 541, M Katz and C Shapiro, 'Technology Adoption in the Presence of Network Externalities' (1986) 94 Journal of Political Economy, 822, 830–833.

5.03   A summary of the biggest success stories in US industry helps to associate these theories with intellectual property rights: aeroplanes, cars, personal computers, music, films and the Internet. These are the industries that have enabled the production of complete products by creating viable licensing platforms and thereby avoided the negative effects caused by the fragmentation of intellectual property rights.[4] In many other industries, and especially Japanese companies, the problem of fragmented intellectual property rights is understood and they have contracted away the fragmentation.[5]

5.04   Until very recently, despite the evidence of the above-mentioned success stories US policy appears to have favoured fragmentation and supported proprietary concepts. This policy has been based on the idea that it is more important to encourage innovation. It has been presumed that fragmentation will be solved through private negotiations between individual parties. Proprietary concepts have sometimes been a solution to the fragmentation problem but other kinds of problems of monopoly behaviour have later emerged.[6]

5.05   This author suggests that intellectual property rights strategies and public policies may have a significant effect on the failure or success of new product concepts. This author also suggests that the control of fragmentation of intellectual property rights may partially be used as an underlying explanation for this phenomenon. The technical initiatives that successfully control fragmentation are potentially successful technologies. Furthermore, the companies that solve fragmentation more effectively than their competitors have the greater potential for success. Consequently, companies in the communications industry compete fiercely to control the costs caused by fragmentation.

Fragmentation problem introduced

5.06   If there were no patent or copyright systems, any new innovations or works

---

[4] Between 1917 and 1975 the aircraft industry had a pooling arrangement for aircraft patents, see G Bittlingmayer 'Property Rights, Progress, and the Aircraft Patent Agreement' (1988) 31 Journal of Law and Economics, for description and analysis; RCA, AT&T and IBM were all at their times persuaded to the benefits of cross-licensing, see P C Grindley and D J Teece, 'Managing Intellectual Capital: Licensing and Cross-Licensing in Semi-conductors and Electronics' (1997) 39(2) California Management Review, 8 (discussing cross-licensing in the radio, telephone, computer and semiconductor industries).

[5] Some commentators suggest also that this may be due to weak and narrow patents granted in Japan. See P A David, 'Intellectual Property Institutions and the Panda's Thumb: Patents, Copyrights and Trade Secrets in Economic Theory and History, in Global Dimensions of Intellectual Property Rights in Science and Technology' (National Research Council, Washington DC, 1993), 55; J A Ordover, 'A Patent System for Both Diffusion and Exclusion,' (1991) 5 Journal of Economic Perspectives, 43.

[6] See J Farrell, 'Standardisation and Intellectual Property' (1989) 30 Jurimetrics Journal, 35, 42 (intellectual property may tend to obstruct *de facto* standardization, destroying network benefits and fragmenting the market).

would be in the public domain. This new information available to anyone free of charge is sometimes also identified as a positive externality or social gains of innovation and creativity. It is an externality because those who consume it have not created or paid for it.

The information made available free of charge is available for anyone to copy. It **5.07** does not normally make sense to invest in creation of information if it is not possible to gain any return for the investment. In order to invest, there is a need to have a limited exclusivity protecting the investment.[7] Without these systems, information would be treated as any public property available for anyone: it would be overused in the sense that it had no particular value to any single company. Such overuse would then lead to the slower creation of new innovations and works.[8] In traditional property theory, this is referred to as the tragedy of the commons. According to this theory, common property is less valuable to anyone as a consequence of such overuse.[9]

Therefore, according to the traditional wisdom, the incentive to innovate is one **5.08** of the key drivers in any anti-trust or competition law enforcement. Until recent years, this has led enforcement agencies and courts to condemn or at least limit any arrangements that could substantially affect the incentives of a single firm to innovate. However, this approach is unlikely to provide any solutions to the following problem.

The problem of anti-commons in the communications industry

In early 2000 the Japanese standardization organization ARIB received initial **5.09** information from different patent owners who claim to own patents relating to the third-generation wireless communication standards UMTS.[10] This initial inquiry revealed some thirty to forty potential patent holders. As some commentators have estimated that royalty rates as high as 2% would be paid in the communications industry, the use of such royalty rates by each patent owner would cause the business to be unattractive to any company. Still, for any single company, the

---

[7] J A Schumpeter, *Capitalism, Socialism, and Democracy* (3rd edn, New York 1950) 88; J W Schlicher, *Patent Law: Legal and Economics Principles* (1999) 2–4; Katz–Shapiro, n 3 above, 825 (in the absence of property rights, new networks are not likely to attract 'sponsors' that support their adoption).

[8] The merits of this argument have been subject to widespread debate and economic research. It is also sometimes argued that public funding could also produce new innovation and works, as is done in several countries. Also network effects may change the concept. See K Kelly, *New Rules for the New Economy: 10 Radical Strategies for a Connected World* (Viking, 1998) 55–56 (suggesting that the more a resource is used the more demand there is for it).

[9] M A Heller, 'The Tragedy of the Anticommons: Property in the Transition from Marx to Markets' (1998) 111 Harvard Law Review, 621, 623–624.

[10] Universal Mobile Telecommunications System.

decision to reduce its royalty rates is likely to depend on each firm's estimation of what others do. A single firm is not likely to reduce its royalty demands unless it sees any viable business reasons for doing so. This means that the supply of products compatible with third-generation cellular standards may potentially be reduced because of the inability of some manufacturers to clear the fragmented patent rights at a reasonable cost.[11]

5.10   Heller identifies the connection between fragmented property rights and reduced supply or the 'underuse' as the problem of 'anti-commons'.[12] Anti-commons are properties in which no single entity controls a large enough bundle of rights that would enable it alone to make the product. If Japanese third-generation cellular patents are anti-commons property, the third-generation cellular market is likely to emerge only if the owners of various exclusive rights can agree with each other on the use of the property. If there are a large number of patent owners, the transaction costs will increase.[13] However, transaction costs are not likely to be the most critical factor. Most companies have professional licensing teams and, unlike in the music industry, the group of rights holders is likely to be stable.

5.11   Even if transaction costs were not substantial, the more fundamental issue is the cumulative royalty costs any manufacturers may face. Fragmentation has a tendency to lead to underuse because several patent owners potentially price their licences too high.[14] The economic model to explain this is not the one that explains the interest of every party to manufacture the standardized product. Rather, the model would be the one that explains how people behave when they are given the right to veto everyone else's activities. How would one price such a right? Is such right the core of the patent right or should the entitlement of the patent owner for this type of circumstances be modified? This author argues that the current policy choices in both intellectual property and anti-trust law unnecessarily support fragmentation and the consequent underuse in the network economy.

---

[11] Since in addition to technically necessary patents leading manufacturers have several hundreds of other patented innovations implemented into their products, the problem of imitation of entire products is seldom discussed as a serious concern. Rather, the inability of new entrants to access the market is increasingly a concern. See R Bekkers and I Liotard, 'European Standards for Mobile Communications: The Tense Relationship between Standards and Intellectual Property Rights', [1999] EIPR 110, 124.

[12] Heller, n 10 above, 624 (using the empty storefronts of Moscow as an example of fragmented property rights leading to the underuse of property); M A Heller, 'The Boundaries of Private Property' (1999) 108 Yale Law Journal, 1163, 1166–1167 (discussing various ways to prevent fragmentation).

[13] H Demsetz, 'Towards a Theory of Property Rights' (1967) 57 American Economic Review, 347, 357 (an increase in the number of owners leads to an increase in the cost of internalizing any effects such ownership may have).

[14] The traditional wisdom effectively used in the 1980s and 1990s suggested that any price may be charged for using the invention to attract capital to make more inventions. See eg J W Schlicher, 'If Economic Welfare is the Goal, Will Economic Analysis Redefine Patent Law' (1992) 4 Journal of Proprietary Rights no. 6, 12, 16. See Bekkers–Liotard, n 12 above, 126 (suggesting high cumulative licensing costs as a potential barrier to entry).

Fragmentation is a problem in any field where new property rights are created.[15] In the intellectual property field, this problem is likely to emerge in the multimedia industry, in business process and software patenting and in any industry which is based on system architecture and combinations of different technologies or works, in brief: the network economy.[16]

The creation of licensing platforms does not necessarily solve the issue of frag- **5.12** mentation. A company may still face the problem that the combined cost of acquiring the licences for such a platform may be excessive. Further, any licensing platforms reduce the competition between companies on sourcing markets: the sourcing costs would be controlled by the licensing platform. In addition, and especially in the US, patentees are increasingly unwilling to join any such platforms, often under pressure from their equity owners to maximize their licensing revenues. This is also reflected by the growing idea that convergence of the communications industry would open up almost unlimited markets for licensing revenue. Even though this idea may well be viable, the risk of fragmentation may significantly limit any growth of such markets.

In the field of tangible property, the law has in every jurisdiction solved the prob- **5.13** lem of fragmentation. When rights have been granted to real property, the minimum useful size of the property has been regulated. In modern days, zoning requirements have effectively taken this role. Also, when buying a computer, the laws controlling the sale of goods and consumer protection usually provide some kind of presumptions that the computer has all the functional elements necessary for the normal use of such machine. In the intellectual property field, there are no safeguards available to avoid fragmentation.[17] Rather, there is an increasing tendency to award property rights to new types of inventions and works without any significant quality criteria.

Heller has identified the problem of fragmentation in the following way.[18]   **5.14**

---

[15] Heller, n 10 above, 625.

[16] Thurow has illustrated this issue by the following example. A physician is granted a patent for the invention covering his finding of a relationship between an elevated level of a particular human hormone and a congenital birth defect. The invention is commercially useful only if used along with two methods developed later. The physician is suing every laboratory using his invention and asking royalties that would double the price of the product. L C Thurow, 'Needed: A New System of Intellectual Property Rights' (1997) Harvard Business Review, 95, 95–96. Should the physician be granted a patent? Should he be able fully to benefit from the value created by the combination of all three necessary features? See also M Levin, P J Nordell, P Sundberg (eds), *Upphovsrätt i Millenietid* (Stockholm, 1999), 201 (discussing the fragmentation problem in multimedia industry); M Salokannel, *Ownership of Rights in Audiovisual Productions*, (The Hague, 1997), 164–165; G Karnell, 'Den odägliga upphovsrätten' (1997) NIR, 370; H Bjelke, 'Den utålelige opphavsretten-ja, hva, så' (1997) NIR 384 (targeting low requirement of originality as a reason for increased pressure against rights holders).

[17] The traditional concept of inventive step (or non-obviousness) in patent law and originality in copyright law have largely lost their significance in this respect.

[18] M A Heller, 'The Boundaries of Private Property' (1999) 108 Yale Law Journal, 621, 1198.

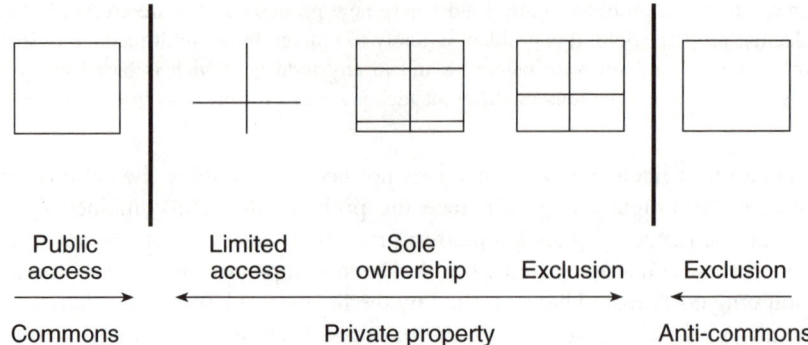

Public access	Limited access	Sole ownership	Exclusion	Exclusion
Commons		Private property		Anti-commons

5.15 The increasingly popular view is that new information, innovations and works are most effectively created by granting inventors and authors property rights to their inventions and works. When software developers invest in the development of new useful software it may be justified to grant copyright protection to the software code. As a consequence of the development starting in the 1970s, copyright protection was extended to cover computer codes. Computer codes were therefore largely transferred from common property into private property. The creation of this new property right was justified mostly as a response to the socially detrimental risk of imitation. Typically for any new property rights, the right was created without any need to compensate the public for this loss of open access.[19]

5.16 In the 1980s it was seen that (1) new useful features in any communications equipment were increasingly implemented by using software, and (2) the actual computer code was increasingly written by code generators. Instead of allowing these new features to become open-access solutions in the public domain, patent protection was extended to cover software features in a series of cases.

5.17 At the same time the original idea of each software product containing a functional set of proprietary features started to lose ground. Sole ownership of rights was primarily based on the idea of functionally independent proprietary elements. The vast majority of relevant legal and economic literature still focuses on this idealistic formulation of functionally independent features. In reality, software products increasingly combine elements from previous solutions. In addition, protection is increasingly granted to solutions that are not independent from other features. The industry is moving into the world of limited access where the functional product is increasingly subject to the exclusive rights of others. In this

---

[19] Heller, n 19 above, 1195 (the government may destroy open-access rights of use without compensating the general public); J M Buchanan and Y J Yoon, 'Symmetric Tragedies: Commons and Anticommons' (2000) 43 Journal of Law and Economics, 1, 3 (suggesting that the problems involving fragmentation and common property are symmetric—too much exclusivity reduces the value of the combination the same way as too little exclusivity does).

continuum of increasingly fragmented rights to exclude, the cost of producing a functionally complete product is increasing if one allocates a cost of infringement risk to each potential third-party exclusive right.

The software industry is responding to this development by actively protecting **5.18** their businesses through cross-licensing and distribution of risk through contractual indemnity provisions. Also contract terms that involve the assignment of all rights to the results of the development work against the payment of development costs have a partial consequence of reducing fragmentation.

The increasing cost of infringement risk, potentially increasing licensing costs **5.19** and transaction costs are likely to have several long-term influences:

(1) only those companies that can effectively carry the increased risk will prevail in competition; and
(2) because of increased demands, access to the market of functionally complete software products becomes increasingly difficult and thereby potentially limits the supply of such products.[20]

The potential delays in acquiring all the necessary licences has led to an increasing number of licensing transactions being made after the product has been introduced to the market place.[21]

Therefore, it is understandable that the industry is generally opposing the creation **5.20** of new additional rights in the form of utility models or petty patents.[22] This is primarily due to the notion that while new forms of property rights for software solutions may increase the supply of such solutions, increasing fragmentation is likely to cause the supply of complete functional products to decrease or their price to increase. This author argues that *increasing fragmentation of intellectual property rights has a negative external effect: that of higher costs and potentially lower output of functionally complete products.*

In this book it is recognized that a certain amount of fragmentation is evident in **5.21** the network economy and should not be a concern to any courts of law or policymakers. Until fragmentation increases to a particular level companies are likely

---

[20] S L Parente and E C Prescott, 'Barriers to Technology Adoption and Development' (1994) 102 Journal of Political Economy, 298, 1231 (discussing the problems that increasing numbers of strong property rights potentially cause for developing countries). This book suggests a new type of competition between companies: who can solve the fragmentation problem at the lowest cost.

[21] This potential development is affected by doctrines defining damages for infringement. Potentially, uncertainty as to the amount of damages is likely to encourage licensing. The potentially unnoticed effect of clear rules defining damages for infringement at a substantial level is likely to have an effect on the licensing market.

[22] Utility models are generally granted for inventions that do not fulfil the criteria of patentability because they do not have the required non-obviousness or inventive step. However, they still clearly differ from previously known solutions and, thus, are granted a protection with a more limited term, usually six to ten years.

to bargain away the problem of fragmentation. Also, the increasing costs and risks caused by fragmentation of rights could well be lower than the expected increase in profits caused by other (positive) externalities. However, in the increasing fragmentation of rights, there is a point where the incremental costs caused by fragmentation are higher than the consequently increased revenue. At that point outside intervention is appropriate.

Incremental costs for manufacturer of complete product, including costs caused by fragmentation	>	Incremental increase in revenue from complete product

5.22   The problem is that fragmentation affects different companies in different ways. The market leader may be able to benefit from the largest economies of scale and highest network externalities. Therefore, fragmentation is likely firstly to affect companies other than the market leader. To a certain extent the market leader may even benefit from fragmentation since competitors may be forced to allocate funds from their product development and marketing budgets to licensing payments. This may cause oligopolistic polarization in the industry. Smaller companies either leave the industry or merge with others. This author argues that fragmentation of intellectual property rights is one of the structural reasons for this development—the results of which merger control laws try to control after the development has already taken place.

5.23   In order to minimize the structural changes caused by the fragmentation of rights, one should intervene when average incremental costs of the industry exceed the average incremental revenue. One possible indication is the average net operating profit of the industry. If typical licensing costs of functionally complete products exceed the average net operating profit of the industry, the fragmentation is likely to have detrimental effects on the long-term structure of the market of functionally complete products.

5.24   A more practical approach is the notion that intellectual property rights lose their relative value as fragmentation increases. If fragmentation continues, the value approaches zero. Even though this is not supported by current intellectual property case law, it has some support in the general taking laws. In the US the taking case of *Loretto* provides a useful example. The issue before the court was whether a cable TV company could attach a cable box in the building. The court held that 'whether the installation is a taking does not depend on whether the volume of space it occupies is bigger than a breadbox'. This may be interpreted to establish a rule that even if fragmentation increases there is no limit where property would lose its meaning.[23] Heller does not agree with that interpretation.[24] Relying on the fact that in *Loretto* the court established the value of the takings right at one dollar[25] and in *Phillips* in the minimum amount, the property right effectively lost value as a consequence of fragmentation.

This author disagrees with Heller's argument that increasing fragmentation would mean the loss of character as privately owned property. The value of intellectual property may rather, as a consequence of fragmentation in specific circumstances, be close to zero. It is also possible that the rights holder loses its entitlement under specific circumstances because there is no longer any justification for such an entitlement.[26] In other circumstances where fragmentation is not as pronounced, the value of the same rights may be substantial. This conclusion supports the conclusion of rebuttable entitlements introduced in Chapter 3, paras 3.106–3.111 above.

5.25

---

[23] See *Phillips v Washington Legal Foundation*, 118 S Ct 1925 (1998) (holding that clients have property rights to the interest earned on lawyers' trust accounts even though the amount may be minimal).

[24] Heller, n 19 above, 1206. See also Heller, n 19 above, 1222 (arguing that anti-commons property should lose its private property attributes).

[25] *Loretto v Group W Cable,* 522 NYS 2d 543, 546 (App Div 1987).

[26] See J Dowell, 'Bytes and Pieces: Fragmented Copies, Licensing, and Fair Use in a Digital World' (1998) 86 California Law Review, 843, 843 (suggesting that fragmented pieces of digital works could be fair use); R H Stern, 'Scope of Protection Problems with Patents and Copyrights on Methods of Doing Business' (1999) 10 Fordham Intellectual Property, Media & Entertainment Law Journal, 105, 154 (suggesting a new doctrine in patent laws similar to scènes à faire in the US copyright law excluding from patentable scope some basic business practices); R P Merges, 'The End of Friction? Property Rights and Contract in the "Newtonian" World of On-line Commerce' (1997) 12 Berkeley Technology Law Journal, 115, 130 (suggesting that rather than reasoning fair use being justified only because it is costly to collect licence fees from consumers, the fair use doctrine could be justified as a solution to fragmentation: a rule establishing redistribution of entitlements in *de minimis* cases).

EXTERNAL EFFECTS OF INTELLECTUAL PROPERTY RIGHTS IN TECHNOLOGY ADOPTION

Tipping of scale

Network industries may involve tipping, a point at which the joint existence of **6.01** two incompatible products may be unstable, with the possible consequence that a single product and standard will dominate.[1] Therefore, the control of third-party behaviour through external effects to support tipping is potentially an effective strategy in the network economy. Traditional industries where tipping has occurred are FM versus AM radio, colour versus black-and-white television, VHS versus Beta in videocassette recorders and typewriter keyboards. In marketing language, these industries have experienced a paradigm shift with new technologies successfully replacing old technologies on the majority market.

Tipping can occur very rapidly. If firms are competing on the basis of innovation **6.02** and if network effects make it likely that the better product will win the battle to dominate a market, then the competitive process can be beneficial.[2] To the extent that tipping maximizes the size of the network, it does create consumer benefits. However, tipping also increases the leverage of the winning technology. The developer of such technology gains not only in proportion to the value of its

---

[1] N Rubinfeld, 'Competition, Innovation, and Anti-trust Enforcement in Dynamic Network Industries', Speech before Software Publishers Association Meeting (1988), 9; M A Lemley and D McGowan, 'Legal Implications of Network Economic Effects,' (1998) 86 California Law Review, 469, 515; M L Katz and C Shapiro, 'System Competition and Network Effects' (1994) 8 Journal of Economic Perspectives, 93, 105–106; W A Sheramata, 'Barriers to Innovation: A Monopoly, Network Externalities, and the Speed of Innovation' [1997] Anti-trust Bulletin, 937, 958–959; W A Sheramata, 'New Issues in Competition Policy Raised by Information Technology Industries' (1998) 43 Anti-trust Bulletin, 547, 581 (network effects can cause it to take a long time for markets to correct any failure); T F Cotter, 'Pragmatism, Economics and the Droit Moral' (1997) 76 North Carolina Law Review, 1, 237.

[2] K Kelly, *New Rules for the New Economy: 10 Radical Strategies for a Connected World* (Viking, 1998), 34 (suggesting that in the network economy the tipping point is significantly lower than in traditional industries because of low fixed costs, insignificant marginal costs and rapid distribution).

contribution but also in proportion to the value of the network.[3] With tipping, exclusionary practices that deny access to the network effects from the competing technology can be particularly effective.

6.03   Economists suggest that since the initial advantage in the network market is important, it would be beneficial for companies to use aggressively promotional strategies,[4] such as penetration pricing,[5] establishment of a reputation and consumer beliefs through advertising[6] and early visible investment in complementary products markets.[7]

6.04   Intellectual property rights may effectively be used to facilitate tipping. In general, tipping may be influenced by using multiple leveraging practices (as identified in Chapter 3, para 3.35–3.40) at the same time. In particular, it may be possible to make parallel use of technical solutions, contract practices and enforcement of intellectual property rights. It may also be possible to address customers, competitors, authorities, suppliers and users simultaneously. Finally, it may be possible to use practices that affect behaviour in the market for a particular product but may also target competing technologies or market those technologies that are interrelated with the primary target market.

6.05   There is a general presumption among anti-trust and competition law agencies that in network industries, especially those in which tipping is a real possibility, allegations of anti-competitive behaviour need to be treated quickly and seriously.[8] Once the market has tipped it may be difficult or even undesirable to undo any anti-competitive effects that have arisen (eg to switch locked-in users to another standard or to impose compatibility requirements that are otherwise not in effect).[9] The challenge for anti-trust law is to distinguish legitimate pro-competitive innovation strategies that harm competitors simply because they are successful from those that are motivated by predatory reasons.

---

[3] Lemley and McGowan, n 1 above, 515.

[4] Katz–Shapiro, n 1 above, 107; C Shapiro and H R Varian, *Information Rules—A Strategic Guide to the Network Economy* (Boston, 1999), 270–272.

[5] Microsoft and Netscape have distributed their Internet browsers royalty-free.

[6] In this respect, famous trade marks may serve as effective indicators to attract majority customers.

[7] In connection with the introduction of new WAP phones in 1999–2000, several cellular phone manufacturers, such as Nokia, announced cooperation agreements with entities providing content tailored to be accessible by WAP phones.

[8] J Farrell and M L Katz, 'The Effects of Anti-trust and Intellectual Property Law on Compatibility and Innovation' (1998) Anti-trust Bulletin, 609, 610–611; Rubinfeld, n 1 above, 14–15. See, however, S J Liebowitz and S E Margolis, 'Should Technology Choice be a Concern of Anti-trust Policy' (1996) 9 Harvard Journal of Law and Technology, 283, 317 (intervention justified only if market is deficient at making choices).

[9] C Shapiro, 'Exclusivity in Network Industries' (1999) 7 George Mason Law Review, 673, 675 (switching costs for new technologies are high); R T Nimmer, 'Standards, Antitrust and Intellectual Property' (1995) 414 PLI/PAT 797, II.B.2.

Standardization is an increasingly popular and effective way of creating markets **6.06**
for information technology products and services. The reasoning is simple:
customers (typically the majority of the customers known to be sceptical about
new technologies) are reluctant to choose between competing new technologies
since those making purchasing decisions want to avoid making the wrong decisions. If they make the wrong choice they may end up using a second-tier technology for which services, spare parts and new versions are not readily available
or are more expensive than for some competing technologies.[10] Furthermore, it
may turn out to be that even for the early majority—those who buy new products
if they are convinced that the new product provides them concrete benefits—the
targeted benefit of increasing efficiency is not likely to happen unless the technology is adopted throughout the industry. Only if the technology is adopted
throughout the industry are the network benefits going to be maximized.[11]

Standardization is also a potentially effective way of controlling fragmentation of **6.07**
intellectual property rights. Without standardization, there is likely to be an
increasing number of different interests and rights that make the manufacturing
of complete systems increasingly difficult and costly.

Therefore, as a strategic approach, standardization is a likely pro-competitive **6.08**
alternative in the network economy even for a single company. From the viewpoint of a typical customer or the user of the technology, standardization is likely
to reduce risk, to increase output and quality and to lead to lower prices than without standardization. From the viewpoint of a manufacturing company that does
not possess the necessary market power in order to force the market to accept its
own proprietary solution, active engagement in standardization is also likely to
reduce the risk of investing in development of minority technologies which never
gain acceptance among the sceptical majority purchasers. In simple terms, standardization is an outstanding method to gain the acceptance of that market.[12]

For intellectual property owners and users, standardization practices provide **6.09**
numerous possibilities and benefits but also provide pitfalls and alternatives

---

[10] P S Menell, 'An Epitaph for Traditional Copyright Protection of Network Features of Computer
Software' [1998] Anti-trust Bulletin, 651, 664.

[11] R J Kauffman et al, 'Opening the Black Box of Network Externalities in Network Adoption'
(2000) 11 Information Systems Research, 61, 77.

[12] M L Katz and C Shapiro, 'Network Externalities, Competition, and Compatibility' (1985) 75
American Economic Review, 424, 436 (any privately profitable industry-wide standard is desirable).
See also R T Nimmer, 'Standards, Anti-trust and Intellectual Property' (1995) 414 PLI/PAT 797:
Standards, 2A, listing the following benefits of standardization: increased price competition,
increased compatibility, increased number of vendors and increased network effects. As potential
detriments of standardization, Nimmer lists potential loss in variety in different systems, lock-in
effects and decrease in research going beyond the standard; J Farrell and G Saloner, 'Converters,
Compatibility and the Control of Interfaces' (1992) 40 Journal of Industrial Economics, 9, 9–10 (identifying that standardization may involve high costs and delays because of slow process); J J Anton and
D A Yao, 'Standard-setting Consortia, Anti-trust and High Technology Industries' (1995) 64 Anti-
trust Law Journal, 247, 249.

affecting the behaviour of other companies. The interface between intellectual property rights and standards is also a good example of the conflict between different balancing theories.

Technology adoption re-examined: standardization

6.10 A single company has various alternatives to drive or support standardization.[13] *Public standardization* is driven by governments[14] or official standardization organizations such as ETSI,[15] ARIB,[16] ANSI[17] or ITU.[18] These organizations are typically closely related to government organizations or they have a broad representation from the relevant industry. *Semi-public standardization* is driven by private standardization consortia such as IETF,[19] SDMI,[20] WAP Forum[21] or Bluetooth Consortium.[22] Semi-public organizations do not benefit from the official status of the official standardization organizations but they are open for any interested parties to join. Their success is usually due to their ability to attract the majority of the relevant industry to participate in the standardization work.[23]

6.11 The third alternative is *semi-private standardization* by a handful of companies who think they have the technical knowledge and the combined power to agree on a certain solution and have it adopted throughout the industry. The fourth

---

[13] For commentaries, see Lemley and McGowan, n 1 above, 515–523; J Farrell, 'Standardisation and Intellectual Property' (1989) 30 Jurimetrics Journal, 35, 39; Shapiro–Varian, n 4 above, 273; R Bekkers and I Liotard, 'European Standards for Mobile Communications: The Tense Relationship between Standards and Intellectual Property Rights' [1999] EIPR, 110, 113.

[14] Governments have traditionally intervened in standards setting. Recently, in the Western world, intervention has been limited primarily to the fields of public safety issues, such as electronic interference, product safety or sometimes also interconnectivity or broadcasting technology. As some commentators have remarked, governmental standardization may open certain interfaces but it does not mean royalty-free use of the standards. Furthermore, government organizations are also subject to suggestions and lobbying of private companies. See Lemley and McGowan, n 1 above, 542–543; Farrell, n 13 above, 39.

[15] European Telecommunications Standardization Institute is an organization that establishes telecommunication standards for Europe.

[16] Association of Radio Industries and Businesses establishes telecommunication standards for Japan.

[17] American National Standardization Institute establishes standards for the US.

[18] International Telecommunications Union establishes telecommunication standards globally.

[19] Internet Engineering Task Force is an organization of private entities engaged in specifying the technical solutions for the Internet backbone technology.

[20] Strategic Digital Music Initiative is a consortium of private companies engaged in specifying the technical protection methods to be used to prevent unauthorized copying and distribution of digital music files.

[21] Wireless Application Protocol Forum is an entity of private companies engaged in defining the technical specifications for accessing all kinds of services by using a cellular phone.

[22] Bluetooth Consortium is an entity of private organizations engaged in defining the technical specifications for low-intensity wireless data transmission technologies enabling home and office appliances to communicate with each other without any wires.

[23] Even though some successful initiatives have started from initiatives of small groups.

alternative is to drive *private standards* that are often also called *de facto standards* because there is no formal standardization procedure. *De facto* standards are created because on the market the majority of the companies adopt a certain technical solution. Some of the typical examples of proprietary *de facto* standards are QWERTY keyboards for typewriters and computers and IBM compatible PCs.[24]

Standardization may be public or private depending on whether everyone has **6.12** access to participate in standardization procedures. Even private standards may be partially public depending on whether the results of such standardization are made available to anyone or whether the access is limited to particular entities.[25]

Standards are sometimes categorized as being either *open* or *proprietary*. There is a general misunderstanding that this would reflect the need to acquire licences in order to be able to manufacture or use the standardized product.[26] This presumption is usually incorrect. Patent rights may even cover open standards. Therefore, the distinction between open and proprietary standards normally refers to the standardized products that are either available for anyone to manufacture (open) or that only the owner of the proprietary rights can manufacture (proprietary). Apart from this principal difference on the issue whether licences are openly available, the distinction does not identify the underlying rules relating to intellectual property rights.[27]

Intellectual property rights related to standards are important because as a conse- **6.13** quence of standardization they may derive market power that they did not have before.[28] There are various practices that are used as a strategy to maximize the impact of intellectual property rights.[29] These practices are of interest from a practical strategy perspective and from a broader policy perspective. Patent rights

---

[24] Large buyers may force *de facto* standards by announcing their preferred technologies, or a single company may create a *de facto* standard if others follow the initial selection. See J Farrell, 'Standardization and Intellectual Property' (1989) 30 Jurimetrics Journal, 39–40 (citing pre-1984 AT&T as an example).

[25] For private standardization it is increasingly typical to gather an early group of 'members', which can even be a single company, to draft the specification for a particular technical solution. After the specification has been drafted, the results are made open for a forum of 'adopters' that by joining the forum get simultaneous access to the specification. See analysis of standardization activities also in Commission Notice on the applicability of Art 81 of the EC Treaty on horizontal co-operation agreements, Section 6 (2001 C 3/02), [2001] OJ C3/2, 2001.

[26] See Nimmer, n 12 above: Standards, IIIA.

[27] The standards containing proprietary technologies are usually referred to as 'sponsored' standards. Farrell, n 13 above, 42–43. Some commentators recognizing the importance of network effects and standardization surprisingly argue that open standards would normally be the outcome of some external impact, eg market demand or governmental rules, and not the initial market penetration strategy of the company, see Lemley and McGowan, n 1 above, 599 n 499, suggesting that IBM was driven to 'open' the PC market as was Matsushita driven to 'open' the VHS VCR market.

[28] Anton–Yao, n 12 above, 261.

[29] See discussion in Bekkers–Liotard, n 13 above, 117 (listing a number of practices without separating between pro-competitive and potentially anti-competitive practices). One needs to always recognize that normal competition and normal uses of intellectual property rights may lead to wealth transfers and consequently the abilities of single companies to compete may be significantly different. Such differences should normally not be of any concern.

have been the main category of intellectual property rights that have had an impact on standardization. This is because patent laws do not contain provisions that would allow third parties to make standardized products without a licence from the patent owner.[30] The concept of essential patents is of key importance because standardization organizations frequently impose rules on their members. Typically, such rules require licensing on 'fair, reasonable and non-discriminatory terms'[31] of any essential patents but not of any other patents.

A patent is technically necessary or essential if 'it is not possible on technical (but not commercial) grounds, taking into account normal technical practice and the state of the art generally available at the time of standardization, to make, sell, lease, otherwise dispose of, repair, use or operate equipment or methods which comply with a standard without infringing that IPR. For the avoidance of doubt in exceptional cases where a standard can only be implemented by technical solutions, all of which are infringements of IPRs, all such IPRs shall be considered essential.'[32] The concept makes a distinction between technically and commercially necessary patents.[33]

6.14   In copyright laws, various methods have been developed to solve the issue of proprietary rights especially with respect to interfaces.[34] Interfaces are functional elements that serve a particular functional purpose. The law is not necessarily uniform in this respect and may differ from country to country. There is also some vagueness built into the law.[35]

---

[30] See Farrell, n 13 above, 44 (intellectual property owners may help standardization through licensing but they may also hope that standardization will happen without any licensing).

[31] ETSI IPR Policy, Art 6 ('irrevocable licences on fair, reasonable and non-discriminatory terms and conditions'); ISO/IEC Policy on IPR, Annex A.2 (b) ('on reasonable and non-discriminatory terms and conditions'); ANSI Patent Policy 1.2.11.1 (b) ('under reasonable terms and conditions that are demonstrably free of any unfair discrimination'); IETF IPR Policy, s 10.3.2 (C) ('openly specified, reasonable, non-discriminatory terms').

[32] ETSI IPR Policy, Art 15 (leaving unsolved the issue whether a patent is covered by the rules if one of several alternative solutions is not covered by any patents; see also ANSI Patent Policy, s 1.2.11.1 ('any invention the use of which would be required for compliance with the proposed American National Standard'); IETF IPR Policy, s 10.3 (intellectual property rights 'with respect to' specification). The fact that a patent is essential or technically necessary does not usually have any reflection as to the superiority of the technical solution covered by such patent. The solution may just be one solution chosen from many solutions into standards specification. This may happen because such technical solution may be the easiest to integrate into the system of other parallel technical solutions, or the majority of the members of the standardization organization may otherwise have supported the solution. Therefore, such patent does not usually have any of the characteristics of patents that are traditionally called 'basic' or 'pioneering'.

[33] A patent covering a solution that is commercially superior but not the only technical alternative to implement the standard specification is not a technically necessary patent. The standard specification may dictate the use of a solution a+b+c. The solution consisting of a+b1+c is not technically necessary if it is technically possible to implement a+b+c also by a solution consisting of a+b2+c. If the solution a+b1+c is commercially superior, eg because it is 30% less expensive to manufacture, the patent covering such solution is generally referred to as a *commercially necessary patent*.

[34] For discussion on compatibility, see ch 4 above.

[35] See Farrell, n 13 above, 47–48 (questioning the social value of protecting arbitrary solutions that become valuable because standardization limits users' choices). See also *Secure Services Technology, Inc v Time & Space Processing Inc*, 722 F Supp 1354 (E D Va 1989) (no protected expression when details of the program were dictated by a standard).

The European Union directive on the protection of computer programs, Article 6, contains detailed rules in respect of use of information acquired through reverse engineering for the purpose of interoperability. Article 1(2) excludes interface specifications from copyright protection.[36]

Functional elements of the computer program are not likely to be protected by **6.15** copyright if only *de minimis* copying takes place. Case law and commentators support this.[37] Therefore, the treatment of copyrights covering standardized computer programs is relevant only if the standardization extends to non-functional elements of such programs. This is unlikely since there is no need for standardization for other than functional elements.[38]

Even though there are rather established practices for treating intellectual prop- **6.16** erty rights in standardization, there is no uniform view with respect to the primary drivers for policy decisions. There are several alternatives. Firstly, encouragement may be provided for innovation and consequently immunity granted for the rights holder. This favours rules that encourage patenting of contributions before they are submitted to the standardization process, acceptance of patented technologies into standards[39] and the reliance on private bargaining as a solution to solve licensing issues.

In 1990 the European Commission published a Green Paper on Standardization recognizing the importance of proper intellectual property rules. Consequently, ETSI drafted its intellectual property rules. However, the first draft received severe criticism primarily from the US since the rules contained an obligation to grant licences whenever a patented solution was adopted into the standard.[40] In the consequent discussion, some other controversial elements, such as geographical scope, monetary compensation and maximum

---

[36] Council Directive 91/250 of 14 May 1991 on the Legal Protection of Computer Programs (OJ L 122 [1991]); T C Vinje, 'The Final Word on *Magill*' (1995) NIR, 156, 259 (limited bit-by-bit copying of interfaces not likely to constitute any copyright infringement); the Finnish Copyright Council 1995:5 (copyright protection of standards subject to case-by-case study). See also *Sony Computer Entertainment, Inc v Connectix Corp*, 9th Cir 2000 (copies made and used by defendant during course of its reverse engineering were a protected fair use, necessary to permit defendant to make its non-infringing system function with plaintiff's system).

[37] *Practice Management Info Corp v AMA*, 121 F 3d 516 (9th Cir 1997) (enforcement of copyright against competitor constituted copyright misuse when rights holder had submitted its medical reference work to federal agency on condition that the agency would not use any other reference system); P S Menell, 'An Epitaph for Traditional Copyright Protection of Network Features of Computer Software' [1998] Anti-trust Bulletin, 651, 652–654.

[38] Software copyrights in standardization are a typical example of the tension between different balancing theories. There is a tendency under property theories to support the extension of private property rights and the immunity of the rights holder. Anti-trust theory supports interoperability and recognizes the need to limit the scope of exclusive rights in order to achieve standardization.

[39] ANSI Patent Policy, s 1.2.11: 'There is no objection in principle to drafting proposed American National Standard in terms that include the use of a patented item, if it is considered that technical reasons justify this approach.' ISO/IEC IPR Policy: 'If, in exceptional cases, technical reasons justify such a step, there is no objection in principle to preparing an International Standard in terms which include the use of items covered by patents, even if the terms are such that there are no alternative means of compliance.'

[40] See for an overview of the discussion D Good, '1992 and Product Standards: A Conflict with

royalty rates, were also removed from the policy. An express term stating the non-existence of any obligation to make patent searches was added.

As an obvious consequence of this discussion, the US Justice Department adopted in its International Antitrust Guidelines examples making it clear that if a foreign trade association refused to adopt any US company technology in industry standards merely because of its origin, the US Justice Department would have jurisdiction.[41] The application of this potential jurisdiction is obviously rather limited since any modern communications standard is not likely to be based on any proprietary technologies but rather on a combination of innovations from various parties.[42]

6.17   Secondly, competition between technologies may be protected. This means that public policy tries to prevent too early final choices during the standardization process. This policy has three main implementations. The adoption of multiple technological alternatives may be supported relying on competition in the market place to cause the final choice between competing alternatives to be made.

Concerted actions have been a focus for this policy choice. From the policy perspective the treatment of the unilateral action is different and does not normally raise any particular concerns.[43]

Concerted actions in standardization have resulted in comment and analysis[44] and a number of concerns and proposals have been expressed. In the US, the law in this field is based on several principles. Primarily, exclusion from a private group may be seen as a horizontal group boycott or concerted refusal to deal with competitors. In *Northwest Wholesale*[45] the US Supreme Court found an illegal joint refusal to deal when the plaintiff was denied access from a wholesale purchase co-operative. The court first discussed

Intellectual Property Rights' [1991] II EIPR 398, 398–403 (expressing concerns of *de facto* compulsory licensing); D Good, 'How Far Should IPR Rights have to Give Way to Standardisation: The Policy Positions of ETSI and the EC' [1992] 9 EIPR 295, 295–297 (questioning whether the IPR policy encourages innovation); R Tuckett, 'Access to Public Standards: Interoperability Revisited' [1992] 12 EIPR 423, 423–427 (arguing the pro-competitive target of ETSI IPR Policy); Bekkers–Liotard, n 13 above, 120–122; Nimmer, n 12 above.

   [41]   DOJ International Antitrust Guidelines, Example E.

   [42]   Sometimes, obviously because of publicity purposes, some companies or individuals claim to be the inventors of particular standardized technologies. Even though they may have developed some parts of such standardized technology, the claims are often grossly exaggerated and based on traditional (no more up-to-date) view of the communications industry using the 'serial model of innovation' instead of the 'circular model of innovation'. See discussion of these models in ch 1.

   [43]   However, see *Allied Tube & Conduit Corp v Indian Head, Inc*, 486 US 492 (1988) (a dominant company opposing a standard may abuse its market power). Id, 500 (agreement on a product standard is, after all, implicitly an agreement not to manufacture, distribute or purchase certain types of products). In the network economy, this view may be challenged on the grounds that most standards are combinations of different elements and not a single technology against another technology.

   [44]   Lemley–McGowan, n 1 above, 517; W E Cohen, 'Competition and Foreclosure in the Context of Installed Base and Compatibility Effects' (1996) 64 Anti-trust Law Journal, 535, 557; M A Lemley, 'Anti-trust and the Internet Standardisation Problem' (1996) 28 Connecticut Law Review, 1041; C Bellamy and G Child, *European Community Law of Competition* (P M Roth ed) (London, 2001), 194; J Temple-Lang, 'European Community Antitrust Law—Innovation Markets and High Technology Industries'. Speech before Fordham Corporate Law Institute, 17 October 1996.

   [45]   *Northwest Wholesale Stationers v Pacific Stationery & Printing Co*, 47 US 284 (1985). See similarly in Europe in *IGR*, Eleventh Report of Competition Policy 1981, point 94 (German manu-

in detail the importance of membership to effective competition and the dominant posses-sion of the member firms, and found *per se* violation without detailed inquiry as to the competitive effects of such violation.

In *Silver v New York Stock Exchange*[46] the US Supreme Court refused to find any joint refusal to deal, primarily because NYSE was already subject to extensive regulation by the Securities and Exchange Commission (SEC).

Another possibility is to consider the standards-setting organization to be an essential facility. However, this approach is not generally favoured by any of the commentators.[47]

Even in light of the case law, not all standardization groups are necessarily open to all.[48] The issue seems, even in light of *Northwest Wholesale*, to depend on the joint market power of the participating companies. Furthermore, commentators seem to share the view that there must be open access to the standard as such but not necessarily to the standards-setting activity.[49] Any reasons for opening the standards-setting activity or excluding a particular company should also be taken into account, such as exclusionary conduct, free-riding or unwillingness to accept reasonable monetary obligations as a condition of membership.[50]

It may also be allowed for patent owners to 'opt out' if the final standardization **6.18** specification is not satisfactory to them.

A typical rule of a standardization organization requires any member to identify at a given time whether it is willing to license its technically necessary intellectual property rights covering the final technical specification.[51] Accordingly, if someone refuses to license, the same rules usually state that the standard cannot in that case be adopted. This formulation is clear: it requires that every member expressly consent to the licensing of technically necessary intellectual property rights as a condition to the adoption of the standard.

The most influential and powerful form of leveraging technically necessary intel- **6.19** lectual property rights in connection with standardization is to refuse to license them

---

facturers denying patent licences for non-members); *Video Cassette Recorders* [1978] CMLR 160 (German manufacturers all agreeing to support a VCR standard sponsored by the Dutch manufacturer Philips); *IAZ v Commission* [1972] CMLR D130 (Belgian resellers agreed that they would only sell certified equipment when certification was available only for domestic manufacturers or distributors).

[46] 37 US 341 (1963).
[47] See eg Lemley–McGowan, n 1 above, 519 (referring to the disputed nature of the doctrine).
[48] 64 F 3d 1130 (8th Cir 1995).
[49] Bellamy–Child, n 45 above, 196.
[50] Some commentators have suggested that the activities of a standardization organization should not be subject to any anti-trust or competition law concerns if they fulfil the following requirements: (1) in general, standards developers are free to act on any reasonably persuasive and credible infor-mation; (2) the quality and amount of information possessed by the organization may affect the deter-mination of their decision; (3) mere speculation is not sufficient justification against costly modifications; (4) a formal record of the available technical basis is not necessary; (5) the mere fact that some experts may disagree with the technical merits of the standard is not a sufficient cause to condemn the process used; (6) the technical basis must be present at the time of the decision-making; (7) the use of balanced committees and other consensus procedures alone do not guarantee adequate technical basis. See Nimmer, n 12 above (referring to the list prepared by Phoebe Morse).
[51] ETSI IPR Policy, Art 6; ANSI Patent Policy, s 1.2.11.1; ISO/IEF IPR Policy, Annex A.2 (b); IETF IPR Policy, s 10.3.3.

to anyone. In addition, the refusal to license in connection with standardization almost always indicates leveraging of intellectual property rights to gain other related or unrelated business benefits.

6.20   As an economic background, a manufacturing company that intends to participate in the market for standardized products is not likely to refuse to license its intellectual property rights. If it were to refuse to license, the other companies also with technically necessary intellectual property rights would probably refuse to license their rights to that company. That would make it impossible for anybody to manufacture the standardized product.

6.21   Similarly, a company that intends to provide technology for manufacturing companies, to use the standardized products, and/or to license its technically necessary intellectual property rights is not likely to refuse to license its technically necessary intellectual property rights. If it were to do so, it would lose the benefits of the emerging market for the standardized product, the underlying technologies and the income from licensing.

6.22   Consequently, the refusal to license is a viable strategy for a company only if it opposes the standard. There may be a reason for opposing standardization because it has proprietary products that would compete with the standardized product. There may also be the goal of modifying the standard in order to increase the strength of its portfolio of technically necessary intellectual property rights. Still another possibility is that a company refusing to license in connection with a standard wishes to delay the emergence of the standard in order to obtain more time for it to develop standardized products.

6.23   The refusal of a particular company to grant licences for other companies under its technically necessary patents is likely to have extensive consequences. In practice, such refusal to license is likely to make it impossible for the standard to emerge or at least delay its adoption until such patent has expired or an alternative solution has been defined. The implications of a refusal to license and the respective regulations were discussed in more detail in Chapter 4, para 4.80–4.103. In respect of standardization, it seems likely that it is necessary to distinguish between the justified 'opt-out' and the leveraging of intellectual property rights in order to achieve benefits in related but separate markets.[52]

6.24   Finally, early identification and disclosure of patents may be required in reliance that such disclosure will encourage competitors to develop technical alternatives for patented technologies.

6.25   In the few published cases in the field it has been established that a company may not mislead other companies to believe that a company does not have intellectual

---

[52] So far, there is no reported case law to confirm whether a licensing market or a component market would be separate from the market of complete standardized products in the sense justifying the rebuttal of the presumption of the unilateral refusal to license.

property rights covering a standard or that such rights would be licensed royalty-free.[53] In *Wang v Mitsubishi*[54] Wang developed during 1982–1983 memory modules known as 'single in-line memory modules' or SIMMs and applied for a patent for the related invention. Mitsubishi engaged in co-operation with Wang. The co-operation involved design of prototypes at the cost of Mitsubishi and co-operation before the Joint Electronic Device Council (JEDEC) that was designing the standard. Wang never informed Mitsubishi about its patent applications. After the standard was adopted, Mitsubishi engaged in mass production. Wang sued Mitsubishi for patent infringement in 1992. The court held that Wang was estopped from suing Mitsubishi under the equitable theory of implied licence. In particular, the court found that implied licences are rare but the entire course of conduct between the parties led Mitsubishi to infer consent to manufacture and sell the patented products.

In *Dell*[55] Dell became a member of Video Electronics Standards Association **6.26** (VESA) in 1992. At the same time VESA initiated the creation of a standard for VL-bus.[56] Dell's representative participated in the standardization work and the VL-bus was standardized in late 1992. Dell voted among others to approve the standard. As part of the approval, Dell's representative signed a statement that according to his best knowledge the proposal 'does not infringe any trade marks, copyrights or patents' of Dell.[57] After the standard became successful, Dell contacted some manufacturers of standardized products claiming that they infringed Dell's patent that Dell had acquired in 1991. After the complaint, the Federal Trade Commission initiated investigation and filed the complaint based on section 5 of the Federal Trade Commission Act.[58]

---

[53] These cases reflect the idea that the potentiality of exclusive rights should be disclosed. In the absence of any further case law, it is difficult to draw any further conclusions. In particular, there is nothing in these cases that would suggest that the enforceability of intellectual property rights would somehow be reduced if the respective companies had properly disclosed their intention to collect royalties. The underlying idea is that if intellectual property rights are properly disclosed, competitors have the incentive to develop and propose competing solutions.

[54] *Wang Laboratories, Inc v Mitsubishi Electronics America, Inc*, 103 F 3d 1571 (Fed Cir 1997).

[55] *In the matter of Dell Computer Corporation*, 121 FTC 616 (FTC Consent Order 1996). See also *Potter Instrument Co v STC*, 641 F 2d 190 (4th Cir 1981) (patentee's representative had participated in the standardization meeting but did not indicate that the patentee's patent may cover the implementation of the standard. On the ground of laches, the patentee could not claim past damages for its patents after waiting for six years. 'Equity will rarely, if ever permit one to waive by acquiescence its alleged patent rights for a long period of time and attempt to assert them after they have been adopted as the industry standard.'); *Stambler v Diebold, Inc*, 11 USPQ2d 1709 (EDNY 1988), aff'd (Fed Cir, 17 May 1989) (patentee was estopped from enforcing its patent against manufacturers of ATM machines after its delay to enforce its patent until ATM machines developed into an industry standard was intentionally misleading).

[56] Like other computer buses, VL-bus carries information and instructions between a computer's central processing unit and its peripheral units, such as hard drives, display terminals or a modem.

[57] 121 FTC 616, 617.

[58] The Act § 5 provides that 'Unfair methods of competition in or affecting commerce, and unfair or deceptive acts or practices in or affecting commerce, are declared unlawful'.

6.27 The complaint claimed that Dell's activity created four harmful effects: (1) the industry acceptance of the standard was delayed because some computer manufacturers delayed their use of the design standard until the patent issue was clarified; (2) systems utilizing the VL-bus design standard were avoided due to concerns that patent issues would affect the VL-bus' success as an industry standard; (3) uncertainty concerning the acceptance of the VL-bus design standard raised the costs of implementing the VL-bus design as well as the costs of developing competing bus designs; and (4) willingness to participate in industry standard-setting efforts had been chilled.[59] In the resulting consent decree, Dell was prohibited from enforcing the respective US patent against any company for such company's use of VESAs standard for VL-buses.

6.28 Sometimes, the policy of encouraging the development of alternative solutions may threaten the entire existence of the standard as a widespread solution since other participants have a strong incentive in investing in alternative technologies.[60] In addition, early identification of essential patents may encourage misuse of patent declarations because of the obvious importance of such declarations for investors and competitors.[61]

6.29 According to the third main policy choice, standardization may be supported as a pro-competitive alternative and support initiatives that aim to minimize any effects intellectual property rights may have on the adoption of it. Anti-trust immunity may be provided to royalty-free licensing initiatives[62] or the creation of patent pools and other mechanisms that are aimed at controlling the fragmentation of intellectual property rights may be supported. In addition to fragmentation, patent pools sometimes try to solve the problem caused by the fact that inventions may be rewarded by an amount more than their social value would justify.[63]

---

[59] 121 FTC 616, 618. In respect of private *de facto* standards, see also *Stryker Corp v Zimmer, Inc,* 741 F Supp 509 (DNJ 1990) (patentee was estopped from enforcing its patent after it had for years misled the industry to believe that there was no problem with its patent).

[60] Nimmer, n 12 above, III.A.

[61] This relates to the importance of perceptions involving future technologies. So far, only a 'sham litigation', the bad faith claim of a patent against a defendant, may have been an anti-trust law violation. See *Professional Real Estate Investors v Columbia Pictures Industries, Inc,* 508 US 49 (1993).

[62] In the 1970s and 1980s, during the development of the Scandinavian analog mobile telephony standards, NMT, the development was based on local standardization rules that did not allow the adoption of patented features into standards. At that time, it was thought that such rules would allow the operators to benefit from the relatively low entry barrier of new competing manufacturers while still encouraging the participating manufacturers to innovate. The merits of such approach are still supported by some. For participating manufacturers, the policy certainly did not impede their growth and innovation. However, the policy may have delayed the beginning of large-scale patenting activities in the participating companies, thus forcing them to compete by using other means than the leverage of their intellectual property rights portfolios. In the recent discussion, other than merely voluntary royalty-free licensing is seen to discourage innovation. See Lemley and McGowan, n 1 above, 603; see also ANSI Patent Policy, s 1.2.11; IETF IPR Policy, s 10.1 (intention is to benefit the Internet community and the public at large, while respecting the legitimate rights of others).

[63] Farrell, n 13 above, 46. A strong patent pool or collecting society may also increase the collec-

There are a number of initiatives to control fragmentation through voluntary   **6.30**
pooling.[64] While pooling may effectively solve the fragmentation problem, it
may also have anti-competitive effects. The most obvious anti-competitive effect
is that pooling eliminates price competition on the technology sourcing market.[65]
Another critical element is exclusivity: whether licences may only be obtained
from the pool or collecting society.

Finally, intervention can occur into licensing practices that are aimed at making   **6.31**
use of the market power of an essential patent. The primary reason behind this
policy choice is the fact that developers of the standardized technology, irrespective of the method of standardization, may have a strong interest in enforcing
their intellectual property rights covering the standardized technology, charging
the highest possible royalty and maintaining control over exploitation of their
rights.[66]

The requirement to grant licences on fair, reasonable and indiscriminatory terms   **6.32**
aims to minimize the use of licensing terms for leveraging. The rule leaves the
determination of exact terms for the parties to decide. This case-by-case determination allows parties to a particular licensing transaction to find their own interpretation of 'fair and reasonable'. There has been little guidance for the parties as
to the concrete terms one can or cannot use in such bilateral licensing transactions.[67] Case law and commentaries are also vague in this respect.

tive market power of individual rights holders. In that sense, the real effect of pooling arrangements
should be carefully evaluated in particular cases.

[64] The best-known examples are collecting societies in the music industry. See *Broadcast Music,
Inc v Columbia Broadcasting System, Inc*, 441 US 1 (1979) (authorizing non-exclusive collecting
societies). In the communications industry, MPEG-LA has frequently been cited as the leading exam-
ple, see *DOJ Business Review Letter* of 26 June 1997; H Ozaki and H Kato, 'MPEG 2 Patent Portfolio
License—Patent Pooling of Technical Standards of Picture Compression' (1998) 48 Intellectual
Property Control, 329. Other fairly recent public examples are DVD pool, see *DOJ Business Review
Letter* of 10 June 1999 (approving establishment of DVD patent pool) and Digital Compact Cassette
(DCC) pool, see *Philips International BV and Matsushita Electric Industrial Company Ltd* [1993] 4
CMLR 286. An initiative to create a licensing platform for cellular technologies implementing third-
generation cellular standards, 3G Patent Platform ('3GPP'), has also emerged.

[65] S C Carlson, 'Patent Pools and the Anti-trust Dilemma' (1999) 16 Yale Journal on Regulation,
359, 383. See also *Philips Electronics NV v Ingman Ltd*, High Court, Chancery Division, Patents
Court, 13 May 1998 [1998] 2 CMLR 1185 (dispute over allegedly extensive royalties collected by
Philips/Sony for CD patents—no violation of Art 85 or 86).

[66] This strategy would not necessarily undermine any single rights holder since the value of the
network will increase as the number of users increases, resulting in increased revenues to such
company, even though not necessarily increased relative royalty rates. This is because market size and
market share affect the revenue of a single company. By multiplying the size of the market for standardized products even if one's own market share is decreasing will lead to the best overall outcome.
Consequently, even a modest share of the market may justify high revenues as compared to high
market share in a smaller market. See Nimmer, n 9 above, III.A.2; M L Katz and C Shapiro, 'Network
Externalities, Competition, and Compatibility' (1985) 75 American Economic Review, 424, 439 (even
the market of loosely enforced and narrowly applied patents and copyrights leads to a perfectly
competitive market of standardized products).

[67] S D Anderman, *EC Competition Law and Intellectual Property Rights* (Oxford 1998), 214–220

6.33 The determination of the concept of 'fair and reasonable' is closely tied to national contract theories. Therefore, it is always subject to some national interpretation. This is important since the interpretation of the rules of standardization organizations is not the same as the interpretation of anti-trust or competition law rules. When someone makes a public promise to the standardization organization to use 'fair and reasonable' terms, such promise may be a binding promise made to the potential licensees. The treatment of such promise depends on the concepts in local contract laws.[68]

6.34 In connection with standardization, the term 'fair and reasonable' is usually understood as a reference to the economic reality.[69] Generally, a licence is fair and reasonable if the terms would be acceptable in arm's-length negotiations.[70] The first possible interpretation of 'arm's-length negotiations' connects 'fair and reasonable' with the rationality of the request. The requested licensing terms are reasonable if they are not irrational. The licensing terms are unreasonable and not within the rules of the standardization organization if they are irrational.[71] The following chart illustrates this.

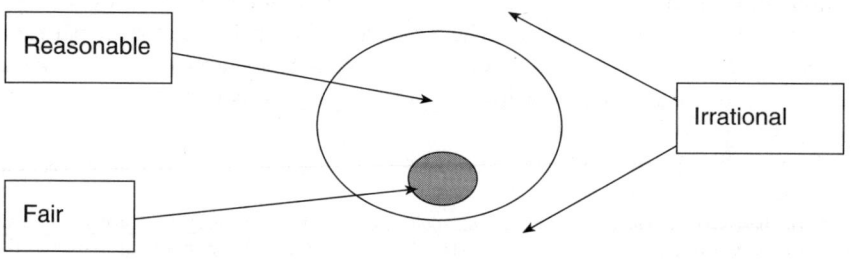

6.35 In order to determine rationality, it is usually asked whether a rational licensee would accept the proposed terms. The rationality of a decision may be determined by various ways.

(suggesting that royalty for essential IPR should be more than just incremental cost but rights holder should not benefit from 'the full appropriation value of the right in the secondary market'). It is clear that a fair and reasonable royalty rate does not usually reflect the production costs. P Kuoppamäki, *Kilpailuoikeudon perusteet* (Vantoa, 2000), 171.

[68] This book does not discuss the national law in any detail but such discussion would be appropriate research of its own. This book aims only to illustrate some economic models to explain the concept.

[69] See discussion in ch 4, paras 4.98–4.123 in respect of extensive royalties and incentives of parties to refrain from asking extensive royalties. See also ch 5, paras 5.01–5.25 for the problem of fragmentation and its relation to standardized products.

[70] 'Arm's length' means that a transaction is 'negotiated by unrelated parties, each acting in his or her own self interest'. See *Black's Law Dictionary*, 7th edn, 1999.

[71] J A Franco, 'Limiting the Anticompetitive Prerogative of Patent Owners: Predatory Standards in Patent Licensing' (1983) 92 Yale Law Journal, 831, 849 (suggesting that the right to set the royalty level is qualified—one may not use royalty level to expand one's market power).

One method of evaluating rationality is to ask whether the licensee, if it accepts **6.36** the required terms, still can effectively compete with other manufacturers. The method emphasizes *competitive rationality*. Competitive rationality may be difficult to estimate. It is most appropriately used whenever a manufacturing entity requires specific licensing terms from its competitors. Another method is to try to determine whether the licensee, if it accepts the proposed terms, still has an incentive to innovate and whether its cost structure after paying the required licence fees would be substantially worse than that of the licensor.

The terms may be considered rational, if the licensee, if it accepts the proposed licens- **6.37** ing terms, still can make a profitable business. This method emphasizes *profitability rationality*. This reasoning has been used frequently when evaluating damages in patent infringement cases. In determining the rationality of licensing terms, this analysis is to a certain extent different from that of patent infringement cases.

Firstly, the rationality of a decision has to be determined at the time of the decision, **6.38** and without the hindsight of actual profitability. Secondly, it must be presumed that a licensee has available all the information that a reasonable licensee would need in order to evaluate its profitability. This would primarily involve the information needed also to acquire other licences, the operating profits expected in the business and other elements relevant for the typical revenue and cost structure. Thirdly, an element of business risk needs to be taken into account. It can be estimated that any business requires some initial investments that will not be recouped unless a certain market share or sales volume is achieved.

The terms can be identified as reasonable if the majority of the potential licensees **6.39** accept them. Licensing terms are reasonable if independent parties willingly agree to them in arm's-length negotiations. Therefore, the number of existing licensees is frequently used to support the argument that particular terms are 'fair and reasonable'. This can be illustrated in the following manner:

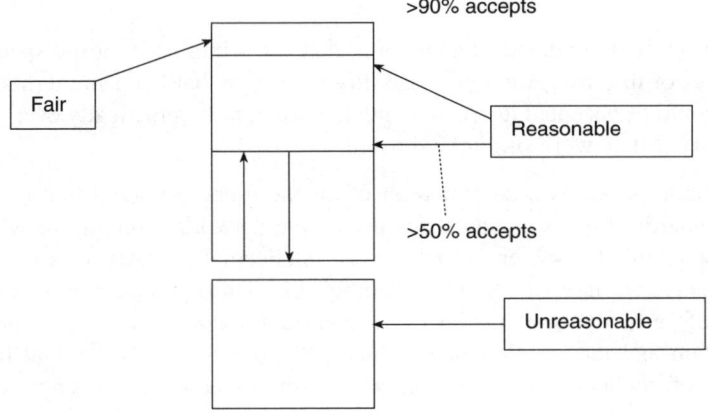

6.40 A licence request is generally reasonable if the majority of licensees have accepted it. If the majority of licensees cannot accept the proposed licence terms, this may indicate that the request is unreasonable. However, the request is fair only if all similarly situated licensees can accept it. The deficiency of this theory is that it does not take into account the market power a licensee of technically necessary intellectual property rights has. The 'willingness' of the parties may have been due to the fact that in order to be able to manufacture standardized products they need a licence. It may be argued that it is up to the voluntary decision of a party to enter the market of standardized products. In that sense, it is necessary to distinguish the relevant market in which a company is voluntarily acting from a related market in which a company is forced to act as a consequence. This may be called a kind of lock-in effect.

6.41 It may be possible to distinguish between (1) the market for standardized products, (2) the market for components, raw materials and component technologies for standardized products, and (3) technically necessary intellectual property rights. If a company is entering the market for standardized products, it may face the fact that its freedom to choose within (2) and (3) is limited.

6.42 Consequently, the willingness of other licensees to accept certain licensing terms does not necessarily reflect their acceptance of such terms in arm's-length negotiations. It may also reflect the market power of the licensor in implementing such terms. Furthermore, the acceptance by a number of licensees does not necessarily reflect that they have had all the necessary information available when making such decisions.

6.43 The number of licensees does not reflect the fact whether the market shares of such licensees constitute a majority of the market. The majority should usually be estimated as the majority of the relevant market, not the number of licensees. Furthermore, instead of determining the 'market acceptance' by the number of licensees, a typical rate requested by other similarly situated licensors could be defined.

6.44 Fairness is usually determined as something that takes into account the specific circumstances of the case. Another possibility is to state that licensing terms are fair if they could be accepted in arm's length negotiations by practically everyone in the industry if they were similarly situated.

6.45 A typical public policy is a combination of all these choices identified in this chapter. Standardization is a typical feature of the network economy to which normative economic theory, or formal uses of intellectual property, or anti-trust law doctrines are not likely to be directly applicable. This is because of the close interaction of particular activities. Strong patent enforcement is likely to delay standardization and the creation of new market opportunities. Rules that limit enforcement of intellectual property rights are likely to reduce the incentives for innovative activities and in the long run reduce the number of potential promoters for new technologies. Consequently, the optimum policy would balance different traditions and economic theories in order to achieve an appropriate allocation of rights and resources.

This author favours intervention only into misuses that threaten the entire adop- **6.46** tion of a standardized technology or the creation of a competitive supply market for standardized products. Earlier in this book, rebuttable entitlements and properly tailored misuse doctrines have been favoured as proper solutions in addition to selected direct anti-trust enforcement.

CONCLUSIONS

This book is based on the presumption that intellectual property rights are valu- **7.01**
able because they can be used to affect the way in which other companies behave
and allocate their resources. This ability or opportunity to influence others is
increasingly replacing the traditional 'reward' as the primary business justification for investment in intellectual property rights. In the network economy the
activities of single companies always affect the value other companies derive
from the same network.[1] Consequently, the business environment offers increasingly possibilities to influence others.

'Strong' patents or copyrights can be distinguished from 'weak' patents and copy- **7.02**
rights by the amount of influence that they allow the rights holder potentially to
have over the activities of other companies. The strength of such influence may
be controlled through business practices. A successful intellectual property strategy in the communications industry optimizes the influence of intellectual property rights on one's own activities and on the activities of other parties. An
optimum influence is one that maximizes the value from the combination of
market size and the company's market share.

Chapter 2 described and analysed the legal tradition in the field. The analysis **7.03**
revealed that there are several parallel and competing doctrines. However, such
competing doctrines are not entirely mutually exclusive. Rather, several of them
provide useful explanations for practical decision-making. One of the key arguments in this book is that in order to achieve a balanced outcome, none of these
doctrines should be applied in its purest form by excluding the teaching of all
other doctrines. This applies particularly to traditional theories which stress the
need for effective anti-trust enforcement and the popular property theories which
stress private bargaining.

The arguments and conclusions of this book are a consequence of the methodol- **7.04**
ogy chosen in Chapter 1, paras 1.33–1.56. That choice of methodology was based
on Scandinavian legal tradition but its application is not limited to the
Scandinavian doctrine. The key elements of this methodology are:

(1) Legal conclusions may be based on arguments other than legal doctrines
    alone.

---

[1] C Shapiro and H R Varian, *Information Rules—A Strategic Guide to the Network Economy*
(Boston, 1999), 198–199.

(2) Economic arguments are important but at the level of legal or political decision-making other arguments are also relevant, eg distribution of wealth among the affected parties.

(3) Legal doctrines, such as the scope of copyright and patent rights or conclusions reached from the 'reproduction right' or 'exclusive right to manufacture', should be applied in new circumstances only after careful analysis taking into account effects such an application may cause to third parties.

7.05   Chapters 3 and 4 considered the application to selected issues of the results or conclusions reached in Chapter 2. In particular, the emerging network economy and increasingly complex value creation within the network economy were identified as issues requiring some novel approaches.

7.06   Chapter 3, paras 3.43–3.49 3 identified the first main conclusion and theoretical frameworks of this book. It identified practices that can be used to control the effects of a company's intellectual property portfolio. A company's success is increasingly dependent on its ability to optimize the combined effects of various practices. When should it use proprietary and when should it use open practices? Is it better for the company to have entirely open systems and no proprietary elements or is it better to have some (minimum) openness and a number of proprietary features? How can it minimize the effects of practices used by competitors?

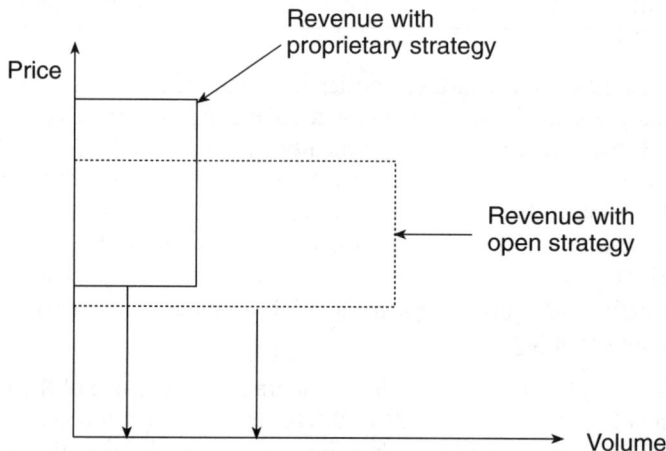

Open versus proprietary features. It is difficult to establish whether the company should choose open or proprietary strategies. The size of the box identifies the revenue potential.

7.07   In this book the author is not suggesting any one solution to this difficult question. It is important to recognize that the question is not black and white. The company may have full interoperability and proprietary user interfaces at the

Target group	Enforcement	Contract	Technical design
Consumers	Litigate against individual consumers hacking copy protection (yes/no)	Allow play-back on multiple devices (yes/no)	Use copy protection (yes/no)
Users (radio stations, bars, record producers, Internet sites)	Distinguish between geographic territories and litigate against users outside the territory (yes/no)	1. Allow sublicensing of end-user copying (yes/no) 2. Ask for the commitment to pay the same royalty as to the highest competitor (yes/no)	Use copyright to force users to acquire particular technology (yes/no)
Equipment manufacturers	Ask for levies (yes/no)	Require use of particular technical protection (yes/no)	Use technical protection to force new purchase of content whenever new equipment is purchased (yes/no)
Technology suppliers (eg CD printing technology, DVD, DRM)	Minimize outgoing royalty (yes/no)	Require access to IPR portfolio of technology provider to support own enforcement (yes/no)	Commit to exclusive use of particular technical solution against favourable treatment (yes/no)
Competitors (other music publishers/ collecting societies)	1. Litigate against counterfeiters (yes/no) 2. Agree on joint enforcement (yes/no)	Facilitate uniform licence fees in licence agreements (yes/no)	Drive uniform technical approach, and share information (yes/no)
Intermediaries (eg record shops, Internet radio streaming services)	Ask for separate royalties for public performance (yes/no)	Grant only territorial licences (yes/no)	Use copyright to force users to acquire particular technology (yes/no)
Composers	A composer always needs to deal with the collecting society in his home country (yes/no)	Exclusive licences to all future works are required (yes/no)	New technical formats are licensed separately (yes/no)

Example. A simple strategy form reveals that music publishers and collecting societies have at least 23 different issues and 46 alternative strategic choices to make when establishing an IPR strategy. The most appropriate strategy may vary for each case.

same time. It may also be forced to keep its product proprietary, because otherwise it would be exposed to too many intellectual property rights of other parties. The cost of licences for such fragmented rights would decrease the profitability of the activity. The identification of various practices and their impact on the strategic planning of intellectual property owners is the first key conclusion of this book. The potential to use the external effects of intellectual property rights strategically to influence the behaviour of others ('leveraging') has not previously been discussed in the organized way it has been considered here. The example on the previous page from the music industry illustrates the complexity of the issue.

7.08   The legal doctrines controlling the strategic uses of intellectual property rights are still underdeveloped. This is mainly because intellectual property laws are designed to deal with issues involving simple traditional value chains and the 'serial model' of innovation.[2] For years, public policy has been focused on expanding the protection of rights holders. The greater the share of the total social benefit derived by society from innovation or creation that is passed to the rights holder, the more inventors and authors are presumed to create. The exclusive property right has been favoured as a means to increase the rights holder's share and to encourage rights holders. This element of reward has frequently been balanced with 'public interest' to favour free competition, freedom of speech and dissemination of inventions. In recent years, the balance has frequently been tipped in favour of the rights holder.

7.09   The second main conclusion of this book is that in addition to the anonymous public interest, the effects of the strategic use of intellectual property rights on particular markets or even on individual companies should increasingly be taken into account. The targets for particular practices are identifiable and the effects of particular practices are apparent on particular markets. The increasing challenge is that a particular practice may have an impact on several entities and on several markets. Therefore, the balancing of competing interests is becoming increasingly necessary. The right of the intellectual property owner to use a particular practice may need to give way to the interest of another entity whose activities are affected by the rights holder's exclusive rights. Therefore, any entitlement provided by intellectual property laws should be rebuttable depending upon the balance of interests against the rights holder.

7.10   Existing legal doctrines have recognized the necessity sometimes to adjust the initial selection of entitlements. For instance, public policy has not favoured practices that have their primary effects on remote markets. Consequently, in the US there has been developed an intellectual property misuse doctrine that limits any practices that have their primary effects beyond the scope of the patent or copyright grant. In Europe the concept of specific subject matter of protection has been used to intervene in any practices that are beyond such specific subject matter. Even though frequently criticized, the doctrines reflect the idea that patents and copyright should not be used to influence activities that are not covered by such rights.

---

[2] See ch 1 and 3, para 3.10.

These traditional doctrines do not respond satisfactorily if a particular practice is **7.11** within the scope of the grant or specific subject matter but has also an impact on remote markets. This book provides several examples of such effects. These examples include: (1) the effects on the allocation of advertising revenue between different electronic media potentially caused by discriminatory music licensing terms, (2) the effects of compatibility or the lack of it, (3) the effects of licence programmes that collect additional licence fees from the customers of the licensee, (4) the effects of the fixed exhaustion doctrine whenever innovation is produced on different levels of the value chain, and (5) the effects of the increasing fragmentation of exclusive rights on the market for complete products. Whenever it is possible to identify the effects on separate or remote markets, there is a need to balance different competing interests so that all interests may be provided with protection simultaneously. The challenge for intellectual property policy is to find an appropriate method for balancing these interests and the most suitable legal structure for applying that method. The first challenge involves the test itself: how entitlements should be divided. The second challenge involves a policy issue: should the resulting rule be implemented as part of intellectual property or anti-trust laws?

An examination of the laws of the US and the European Union has revealed that **7.12** there is no uniform test or legal structure to solve these issues. Even within the US and Europe respectively, various tests and legal doctrines are used. The result was not surprising. Laws in both areas have evolved over a number of years and this particular problem has really only become a major issue relatively recently.

One may start with the universal presumption that a particular practice should not **7.13** be accepted if the gravity of the harm outweighs the utility of the rights holder's conduct. Cost-benefit theories have analysed this starting point at considerable length. However, this author suggests that legislators, judges and anti-trust enforcement agencies should consider not only the interest of the rights holder and the public interest in general, but also the interest of the entity harmed by a particular practice and the related public interest in that. Any practice should be approved only if it is justified when compared with any competing interests.

The effects of compatibility or the lack of compatibility have generally received **7.14** the most attention. Public policy has generally favoured compatibility at the cost of the rights holder's exclusive rights. However, there is a fundamental difference between copyright laws and patent laws. In both the US and Europe it has been concluded that copyright laws might not be used to support incompatibility. The outcome of the balance has either been implemented in copyright statutes or adopted as part of the doctrine. Patent laws do not contain any similar provisions that would allow the balance to be 'internalized' into the legislation or doctrine itself. Consequently, the necessary balance can generally be achieved only through private negotiations or through anti-trust enforcement.

7.15 Other external effects have not received the same attention. In principle, the doctrines do not favour contract terms that extend the effects of intellectual property protection to other markets. However, if a particular limitation has a justified effect of controlling the use of the intellectual property rights and a side effect on the market of other products, then public policy has been vague.

7.16 In Europe the Block Exemption for Technology Transfer Agreements provides an indication of the balance between competing interests. In the US the *IP Guidelines* provide a similar indication. Some practices are *per se* illegal, while others are subject to a 'rule of reason' analysis that takes into account all relevant circumstances and justifications. The problem with the Block Exemption or the *IP Guidelines* is that they focus on restrictions on competition on the same primary market that the exclusive right covers. They do not consider any practices that have either harmful effects on other markets or positive effects on other markets even though possibly restricting competition in the primary market.

7.17 Unilateral conduct, such as enforcement of intellectual rights or proprietary product designs, benefits from the broadest immunity under anti-trust laws. Anti-trust laws both in Europe and in the US may be used for intervention in unilateral conduct only if the rights holder has market power. This favours 'internalization' of the balance into intellectual property laws whenever a particular practice might have harmful effects irrespective of market power. Another possibility is to favour internalization whenever one presumes that the definition of a limited relevant market would lead to the finding of market power in the majority of cases.

7.18 In Europe the acceptability of unilateral conduct is determined by using the proportionality test. Under that test it is asked whether a particular practice is justified. Practices that are within the specific subject matter for protection are presumed to be justified and it takes a strong argument and evidence to rebut that presumption. In the US the courts ask whether the practice is a mere 'sham' or 'pretextual'. In particular, the 'sham' rule provides effective anti-trust immunity for most enforcement actions, since it allows intervention only for actions that do not have any reasonable likelihood of success. The 'pretextual' test invites courts to evaluate whether the unilateral action is primarily used to promote other interests than the protection of exclusive rights.

7.19 This author does not suggest any single solution for all practices involving external effects. Rather, a general balancing of interests is always appropriate. As discussed above, the so-called 'internalization' of the balance has some traditional basis especially in the field of copyright. The problem is that TRIPS, Article 13 effectively restricts the 'internalization' of any new limitations or balancing factors into copyright laws. In Europe the Copyright Directive of 2001 also imposes considerable restrictions on national legislators. In this sense the US intellectual property laws, with built-in doctrines of copyright fair use or intellectual property misuse, provide more flexibility. This author suggests that the introduction of the general 'misuse' concept into intellectual property laws in Europe could be appropriate. The concept of misuse could be tailored in Europe to deny enforcement of intellectual property rights for practices that have their primary effect on activities that are not covered by such intellectual property rights or that are otherwise unjustified. Practices that have their impact mostly on imitations would not be affected by the doctrine. The 'misuse' doctrine would allow a flexible balancing within intellectual property laws.

Fragmentation of intellectual property rights is an increasing challenge for any **7.20** manufacturer of complete communication products that combine technologies from various sources. Any producer of multimedia products is likely to face the same challenge. This author suggests that present intellectual property or anti-trust doctrines do not deal satisfactorily with the potentially extensive royalty costs such fragmentation may cause. Two solutions are suggested for this grow-ing problem. Firstly, the courts should accept that the value of any single right potentially decreases as fragmentation increases. Secondly, contract practices, such as grant-back clauses, aimed at solving fragmentation should be treated differently from practices abusing licensees or customers. This author does not favour the pooling of intellectual property rights as a solution to fragmentation because any pooling has the side effect of eliminating competition between companies when they try to control fragmentation.

Finally, intellectual property rights have an important role in the communications **7.21** industry. Patents undoubtedly encourage companies to invest in innovation and to identify and record their innovations. Copyright encourages content production and software development. This author does not challenge the basic need of a well-functioning and effective intellectual property protection system. However, in the increasingly complex web of rights, the leverage of any single rights holder should be restricted to opposing imitations. Any impacts beyond that primary 'core' of intellectual property protection should be subject to balancing against the competing interests.

BIBLIOGRAPHY

MONOGRAPHS AND LAW REVIEW ARTICLES

Aarnio, Aulis: On the legal reasoning. Turku 1977. (Aarnio)

Ackermann, Thomas: Art 85 Abs. 1 EGV und die Rule of Reason. Bonn 1997.

Adelman, Martin J.: The New World of Patents Created by the Courts of Appeals for the Federal Circuit. 20 University of Michigan J.L. Ref. 979–1006 (1987).

Addanki, Sumanth and Anderson, Kent: The Relevant Market in Intellectual Property Antitrust: An Economists' Overview. 414 PLI/Pat 557 (1995).

Anderman, Steven D.: EC Competition Law and Intellectual Property Rights. Oxford 1998.

Anthony, Sheila F.: Antitrust and Intellectual Property Law: From Adversaries to Partners. 28 AIPLA Quarterly Journal 1–38 (2000).

Anton, James J. and Yao, Dennis A.: Standard-setting Consortia, Antitrust, and High Technology Industries. 64 Antitrust Law Journal 247–265 (1995).

Aoki, Keith: 'Intellectual Property and Sovereignty: Notes Toward a Cultural Geography of Authorship'. 48 Stanford Law Review 1293–1355 (1996). (Aoki 1996)

Areeda, Philip E.: Antitrust Law. An Analysis of Antitrust Principles and their Application. Volume IX (Boston 1991).

Areeda, Philip E. and Hovenkamp, Herbert: Antitrust Law. An Analysis of Antitrust Principles and Their Application. Volume I. Revised Edition (1997).

Areeda, Philip E., Hovenkamp, Herbert and Solow, John: *Antitrust Law. An Analysis of Antitrust Principles and Their Application.* Volume IIA (Boston 1995).

Areeda, Philip E. and Hovenkamp, Herbert: Antitrust Law. An Analysis of Antitrust Principles and Their Application. Volume III. Revised Edition (Boston 1996).

Areeda, Philip E., Elhauge, Einer and Hovenkamp, Herbert: Antitrust Law. An Analysis of Antitrust Principles and Their Application. Volume X (Boston 1996).

Areeda, Philip E. and Kaplow, Louis: Antitrust Analysis. Problems, Text, Cases. Boston 1988.

Aro, Pirkko-Liisa: Ennakkokäyttöoikeus patentinhaltijan yksinoikeuden rajoituksena. Vammala 1972.

Ayres, Ian–Klemperer, Paul: Limiting Patentees' Market Power without Reducing Innovation Incentives: The Perverse Benefits of Uncertainty and Non-injunctive Remedies. 97 Michigan Law Review 985–1032 (1999).

Ayyar, R.V. Vaidyanatha: Interest or Right? The Process and Politics of a Diplomatic Conference on Copyright. 1 Journal of World Intellectual Property 3–35 (1998).

Baird, Douglas G.: Common Law Intellectual Property and the Legacy of International News Service *v* Associated Press. 50 University of Chicago Law Review 411–429 (1983).

Baker, Jonathan B.: Fringe Firms and Incentives to Innovate. 63 Antitrust Law Journal 622–641 (1995).

Balto, David A.: Network and Exclusivity: Antitrust Analysis to Promote Network Competition. 7 George Mason Law Review 523–576 (1999).

Balto, David A. and Pitofsky, Robert: Antitrust and High-Tech Industries: The New Challenge. 43 Antitrust Bulletin 583–607 (1998).

Barker, Ernest: Introduction to Social Contract. Essays by Locke, Hume and Rousseau. Oxford 1947.

Barlow, John Perry: The Next Economy of Ideas, Wired Magazine, October 2000, 240–252.

Barnett, Otto Raymond: Patent Property and the Anti-Monopoly Laws. Indianapolis 1943.

Baumol, William J. and Ordover, Janusz A.: Antitrust: Source of Dynamic and Static Inefficiencies, in Jorde, T.–Teece, D., Antitrust, Innovation, and Competitiveness, 82–97. New York 1992.

Baxter, William F.: Legal Restrictions on Exploitation of the Patent Monopoly: An Economic Analysis. 76 Yale Law Journal 267–370 (1966).

Beier, Friedrich-Karl: Exclusive Rights, Statutory Licenses and Compulsory Licenses in Patent and Utility Model Law. 30 IIC 251–275 (1999).

Beier, Friedrich-Karl: The Significance of the Patent System for Technical, Economic and Social Progress. 11 IIC 563–584 (1980).

Bekkers, Rudi and Liotard, Isabelle: European Standards for Mobile Communications: The Tense Relationship between Standards and Intellectual Property Rights. [1999] EIPR 110–126.

Bellamy, Christopher and Child, Graham: European Community Law of Competition. 5th ed. (P.M. Roth, ed.). London 2001.

Bergström, Svante: Uteslutande rätt att förfoga över verket. Uppsala 1954. (Bergström)

Bernitz, Ulf: Marknadsrätt. Stockholm 1969.

Bernitz, Ulf, Svensk: Marknadsrätt. Stockholm 1991.

Bernitz, Ulf, Karnell, Gunnar, Pehrson, Lars and Sandgren, Claes: Immaterialrätt. 7th ed. Stockholm 1998.

Besen, Stanley M.–Farrel, Joseph: Choosing How to Compete: Strategies and Tactics in Standardisation. 8 Journal of Economic Perspectives 117–131 (1994).

Besen, Stanley M. and Raskind, Leo J.: An Introduction to the Law and Economics of Intellectual Property. 5 Journal of Economic Perspectives 1–25 (1991).

Bittlingmayer, George: Property Rights, Progress, and the Aircraft Patent Agreement. 31 Journal of Law and Economics 227–248 (1988).

Bjelke, Harald: Den utålelige opphavsretten—ja, hva så. NIR 1997 384–394.

Blok, Peter: Patentrettens konsumptionsprincip—patentmonopol og fri konkurrence i national ret og faellesmarkedsret. Copenhagen 1974.

Bork, Robert H.: The Antitrust Paradox. Chicago 1978 (Rev. ed. 1993).

Bowman, Ward S.: Patent and Antitrust Law. A Legal and Economic Appraisal. Chicago 1973.

Brennan, Timothy J.: Copyright, Property, and the Right to Deny. 68 Chicago–Kent Law Review 675–714 (1993).

Brennan, Timothy J.: Taxing Home Audio Taping. Economic Analysis Group Discussion Paper 86-6. US Department of Justice, Antitrust division 1986.

Breyer, Stephen: The Uneasy Case for Copyright: A Study of Copyright in Books, Photocopies, and Computer Programs. 84 Harvard Law Review 281–351 (1970).

Brinson, Dianne J.: Proof of Economic Power in a Sherman Act Tying Case: Should Economic Power be Presumed When the Tying Product is Patented or Copyrighted? 48 Lousiana Law Review 29–85 (1987).

Bruun, Niklas: Immateriaalioikeus ja määräävän markkina-aseman väärinkäyttö EU:ssa Magillin jälkeen, in Juhlajulkaisu Roschier-Holmberg & Waselius 60v., 40–51. Jyväskylä 1995.

Bruun, Niklas: The Role of the Patent System in the Protection of Intellectual Property. NIR 1992 205–215.

Buchanan, James M. and Yoon, Yong J.: Symmetric Tragedies: Commons and Anticommons. 43 Journal of Law and Economics 1–13 (2000).

Calabresi, Guido and Melamed, A. Douglas: Property Rules, Liability Rules, and Inalienability: One View of the Cathedral. 85 Harvard Law Review 1089–1128 (1972).

Calabresi, Guido: Transaction Costs, Resource Allocation and Liability Rules—a Comment. 11 Journal of Law and Economics 67–73 (1968).

Carlson, Steven C.: Patent Pools and the Antitrust Dilemma. 16 Yale Journal on Regulation 359–399 (1999).

Chafee, Zecharias Jr.: Reflections on the Law of Copyright 1–2. 45 Columbia Law Review 503–529, 719–738 (1945).

Cheung, Steven N.S.: Property Rights and Invention. 8 Research in Law and Economics 5–18 (1986).

Chisum, Donald S.: Foreign Activity: Its Effect on Patentability Under United States Law. 11 IIC 26–48 (1980).

Chisum, Donald D. and Jacobs, Michael A.: Understanding Intellectual Property Law. New York 1992 (rep. 1999).

Christensen, Clayton M.: The Innovator's Dilemma—When New Technologies Cause Great Firms to Fail. Boston 1997.

Coase, R.H.: The Firm, the Market and the Law. Chicago 1988.

Coase, R.H.: The Problem of Social Cost. 3 Journal of Law and Economics 1–45 (1960).

Cohen, William E.: Competition and Foreclosure in the Context of Installed Base and Compatibility Effects. 64 Antitrust Law Journal 535–569 (1996).

Cooter, Robert—Ulen Thomas: Law and Economics. Glenview 1988.

Cornish, W.M.: Intellectual Property: Patents, Copyrights, Trademarks and Allied Rights. 4th ed. London 1999.

Copinger and Skone James on Copyright. 12th ed. London 1980.

Cotter, Thomas A.: Intellectual Property and the Essential Facilities Doctrine. [1999] Antitrust Bulletin 211–250.

Cotter, Thomas F.: Pragmatism, Economics and the Droit Moral. 76 North Carolina Law Review 1–96 (1997).

David, Paul A.: Intellectual Property Institutions and the Panda's Thumb: Patents, Copyrights and Trade Secrets in Economic Theory and History, in Global Dimensions of Intellectual Property Rights in Science and Technology (by National Research Council) 19–61. Washington D.C. 1993.

Davies, Gillian: Copyright and the Public Interest. IIC Studies Vol. 14. Munich 1994.

Davies, Gillian and Hung, Michele E.: Music and Video Private Copying. Sweet & Maxwell 1993.

Day, George S.: Assessing Future Markets for New Technologies, in Wharton on Managing Emerging Technologies (Day–Schoemaker–Gunther eds.), 127–149. New York 2000.

Demaret, Paul: Patent, Territorial Restrictions, and EEC Law. A Legal and Economic Analysis. IIC Studies Vol. 2. Weinheim 1978.

Demsetz, Harold: Towards A Theory of Property Rights. 57 American Economic Review 347–359 (1967).

Domeij, Bengt: Läkemedelspatent. Stockholm 1998.

Douros, Timothy J.: Lending the Federal Circuit a Hand: An Economic Interpretation of the Doctrine of Equivalents. 10 High Tech Law Journal 321–354 (1995).

Dowell, Jonathan: Bytes and Pieces: Fragmented Copies, Licensing, and Fair Use in a Digital World. 86 California Law Review 843–877 (1998).

The Economics of Intellectual Property Rights for Design. Bureau of Industrial Economics, Occasional Paper 27. Canberra 1995.

Eklöf, Dan: Konkurrensbegränsningsrätt och immaterialrättlig konventionsreglering. NIR 1998, 391–405.

Esala, Päivi and Manni-Loukola, Sirkka: Tekijänoikeuden merkitys Suomen kansantaloudessa vuonna 1988. Helsinki 1991.

Farrell, Joseph: Standardization and Intellectual Property. 30 Jurimetrics Journal 35–50 (1989).

Farrell, Joseph and Katz, Michael L.: The Effects of Antitrust and Intellectual Property Law on Compatibility and Innovation. [1998] Antitrust Bulletin 609–650.

Farrell, Joseph and Saloner, Garth: Converters, Compatibility, and the Control of Interfaces. 40 Journal of Industrial Economics 9–35 (1992).

Federal Trade Commission Staff: Anticipating the 21st Century: Competition Policy in the New High-Tech, Global Marketplace. Volumes I–II, 1996.

Feldman, Robin Cooper: Defensive Leveraging in Antitrust. 87 Georgetown Law Journal 2079–2115 (1999).

Fellmeth, Aaron Xavier: Copyright Misuse and the Limits of the Intellectual Property Monopoly. 6 Journal of Intellectual Property Law 1 (1998).

Fikentscher, Wolfgang: Urhebervertragsrecht und Kartellrecht, in Urhebervertragsrecht, Festgabe für Gerhard Schricker (Beier–Götting–Lehmann–Moufang, eds.). München 1995.

Fitzgerald, D.: 'Magill Revisited. Tiercé Ladbroke SA v The Commission' [1998] 4 EIPR 154.

Franco, Joseph A.: Limiting the Anticompetitive Prerogative of Patent Owners: Predatory Standards in Patent Licensing. 92 Yale Law Journal 831–860 (1983). (Franco)

Gerber, David J.: Rethinking the Monopolist's Duty to Deal: A Legal and Economic Critique of the Doctrine of 'Essential Facilities'. 74 Virginia Law Review 1069–1113 (1988).

Gifford, Daniel J.: The Damaging Impact of the Eastman Kodak Precedent Upon Product Competition: Antitrust Law in Need of Correction. 72 Washington University Law Quarterly 1507–1535 (1994).

Ginsburg, Jane C.: Authors and Users in Copyright. 45 Journal of the Copyright Society in the USA, 1–20 (1997).

Ginsburg, Jane: Copyright and Intermediate Users' Rights, in Festskrift till Gunnar Karnell, 227–235. Stockholm 1999.

Glazer, K. and Lipsky, A.: Unilateral Refusals to Deal under Section 2 of the Sherman Act [1995] 63 Antitrust Law Journal 749.

Godenhielm, Berndt: Om patenträtten in konkurrensrättsligt hänseende, in Uppsatser i immaterialrätt, 25–32. Lund 1983.

Godenhielm, Berndt: Patentskyddets omfattning i europeisk och nordisk rätt. Helsinki 1994.

Godenhielm, Berndt: Verksbegreppet inom upphovsrätten, in Uppsatser i immaterialrätt, 101. Lund 1983.

Goldstein, Paul: International Copyright—Principles, Law, and Practice. Oxford University Press 2001.

Good, Diana: 1992 and Product Standards: A Conflict with Intellectual Property Rights. 11 EIPR 398–403 (1991).

Good, Diana: How Far Should IPR Rights Have To Give Way To Standardization: The Policy Positions Of ETSI And the EC. 9 EIPR 295–297 (1992).

Gordon, Wendy J.: A Property Right in Self-Expression: Equality and Individualism in the Natural Law of Intellectual Property. 102 Yale Law Journal 1533–1609 (1993).

Gordon, Wendy J.: Assertive Modesty: An Economics of Intangibles. 94 Columbia Law Review 2579–2593 (1994).

Gordon, Wendy J.: Fair Use as Market Failure: A Structural and Economic Analysis of the Betamax Case and its Predecessors. 82 Columbia Law Review 1600–1657 (1982).

Gotts, Ilene Knable and Fogt, Howard W.: Clinton Administration Expresses More Than Intellectual Curiosity in Antitrust Issues Raised by Intellectual Property Licensing. 22 AIPLA Quarterly Journal 1 (1994).

Govaere, Inge: The Use and Abuse of Intellectual Property Rights in E.C. Law. London 1996.

Grady, Mark F. and Alexander, Jay I.: Patent Law and Rent Dissipation. 78 Virginia Law Review 305–350 (1992).

Haarmann, Pirkko-Liisa: Tekijänoikeus & lähioikeudet. Helsinki 1999.

Grindley, Peter C. and Teece, David J.: Managing Intellectual Capital: Licensing and Cross-Licensing in Semiconductors and Electronics, 39 (2) California Management Review 8–41 (1997).

Hamilton, Walton H.: Property—According to Locke. 41 Yale Law Journal 864–880 (1932).

Handler, Milton-Blake, Harlan M., Pitofsky, Robert and Goldschmid, Harvey J.: Patents and Antitrust. Mineola 1983.

Hanisee, J. Miles: An Economic View of Innovation and Property Right Protection in the Expanded Regulatory State. 21 Pepperdine Law Review 127–163 (1994).

Hannah, Ramsey: Misusing Antitrust: The Search for Functional Copyright Misuse Standard. 46 Stanford Law Review 401 (1994).

Harenko, Kristiina: Copyright Question in the Digital Environment. Helsinki 1999.

Heinemann, Andreas: Antitrust Laws of Intellectual Property in the TRIPs Agreement of the World Trade Organization, in From GATT to TRIPs (Friedrich-Karl Beier and Gerhard Schricker, eds.) 239–247. IIC Studies Vol. 18. Munich 1996.

Heinemann, Andreas: Immaterialgüterschutz in der Wettbewerbsordnung. Eine grund-lagorientierte Untersuchung zum Kartellrecht des geistiges Eigentums. German Habilitationsmanuscript (in print). Munich 2000.

Helin, Markku: Immateriaalioikeuksien kohteesta. Lakimies 1978, 645 ss.

Helin, Markku: Lainoppi ja metafysiikka. Vammala 1988.

Heller, Michael A.: The Boundaries of Private Property. 108 Yale Law Journal 1163–1223 (1999).

Heller, Michael A.: The Tragedy of the Anticommons: Property in the Transition from Marx to Markets. 111 Harvard Law Review 621–688 (1998).

Heller, Walter P. and Starret, David A.: On the Nature of Externalities, in Theory and Measurement of Economic Externalities (ed. Steven A. Y. Lin), 9–22. London 1976.

Hemmo, Mika: Vahingonkorvauksen sovittelu ja moderni vahingonkorvausoikeus. Helsinki 1998.

Holmes, William C.: Intellectual Property and Antitrust Law. West Group 2000 (looseleaf).

Hsieh, Charles C.: Professional Real Estate: The Line Between Patent and Antitrust. 7 Harvard Journal of Law & Technology 173–186 (1993).

Die Internet-Ökonomie. Strategien für die digitale Wirtschaft. European Communication Council Report (by Axel Zerdick, Arnold Picot, Klaus Schrape, Alexander Artope, Klaus Goldhammer, Ulrich T. Lange, Eckart Vierkant, Esteban López-Excopar, Roger Silverstone). Berlin 1999.

Jacob, Robin: Objectionable Narrowness of Claim, in Principles of Patent Law (by Chisum–Ward–Schwartz–Newman–Kieff) 974–976 (1998).

Jorde, Thomas M. and Teece, David J.: Innovation Cooperation and Antitrust, in Antitrust, Innovation, and Competitiveness 47–81 (Thomas M. Jorde and David J. Teece eds.). New York 1992.

Jorde, Thomas M. and Teece, David J.: Rule of Reason Analysis of Horizontal Arrangements: Agreements Designed to Advance Innovation and Commercialize Technology. 61 Antitrust Law Journal 579 (1993).

Kant, Immanuel: Von der Unrechtmässigkeit des Büchernachdrucks, in VIII Kant's gesammelte Schriften 77–87 (Herausgegeben von Königlich Preuischen Akademie der Wissenschaft). Berlin 1912.

Kaplow, Louis: Extension of Monopoly Power Through Leverage. 85 Columbia Law Review 515–556 (1985).

Kaplow, Louis: The Patent Antitrust Intersection: A Reappraisal. 97 Harvard Law Review 1815–1892 (1984).

Karnell, Gunnar: Den odägliga upphovsrätten. NIR 1997, 370–383.

Karnell, Gunnar: Rättskydd för exemplarframställning, offentligt framförande, visning och spridning vid elektronisk exploatering, in Digitalisering och upphovsrätt (Gunnar Karnell, ed.). Stockholm 1993.

Karnell, Gunnar: Vidarespridning av utgivna verksexamplar, särskilt om vidareförsäljning, uthyrning och utlåning av videogram: Skall vi leva med nordisk rättsolikhet? NIR 1984, 265–278 (reprinted in Karnell om upphovsrätt, 221–232. Stockholm 1990).

Katz, Michael L. and Shapiro, Carl: Network Externalities, Competition, and Compatibility. 75 American Economic Review 424–440 (1985).

Katz, Michael L. and Shapiro, Carl: Product Introduction with Network Externalities. 40 Journal of Industrial Economics 55–83 (1992).

Katz, Michael L. and Shapiro, Carl: System Competition and Network Effects. 8 Journal of Economic Perspectives 93–115 (1994).

Katz, Michael and Shapiro, Carl: Technology Adoption in the Presence of Network Externalities. 94 Journal of Political Economy 822–841 (1986).

Katz, Ronald S. and Safer, Adam J.: Copyright Misuse: Inconsistent Cases From the 1990s, and Simple Formula for the 21st Century. 17 No. 4 Computer Law 3–7 (2000).

Kauffman, Michael H.: Image Technical Services, Inc. v Eastman Kodak Co.: Taking One Step Forward and Two Steps Back in Reconciling Intellectual Property Rights and Antitrust Liability. 34 Wake Forest Law Review 471–529 (1999).

Kauffman, Robert J., McAndrews, James and Wang, Yu-Ming: Opening the 'Black Box' of Network Externalities in Network Adoption. 11 Information Systems Research 61–82 (2000).

Kelly, Kevin: New Rules for the New Economy: 10 Radical Strategies for a Connected World. Viking 1998.

Kitch, Edmund W.: Patents: Monopolies or Property Rights? 8 Research in Law and Economics 31–49 (1986).

Kitch, Edmund W.: The Nature and Function of the Patent System. The Journal of Law and Economics 265–290 (1977).

Kivimäki, T.M.: Tekijänoikeus. Porvoo 1948.

Kivimäki, T.M.: Uudet tekijänoikeus- ja valokuvauslait. Porvoo 1966.

Knoph, Ragnar: Åndsretten. Oslo 1936.

Koktvedgaard, Mogens: Konkurrencepraegede immetrialretspositioner. Copenhagen 1965.

Koktvedgaard, Mogens: Laerebog in immaterialrett. Copenhagen 1999.

Koktvedgaard, Mogens and Levin, Marianne: Lärobok i immaterialrätt. 6th ed. Helsingborg 2000.

Kolstad, Olav: Fra konkurrenspolitikk till konkurrancerett. Oslo 1998.

Korah, Valentine: Patents and Antitrust, in Strategic Issues of Industrial Property Management (Cottier, Widmer and Schindler eds.) 46–87. Oxford 1999.

Korah, Valentine: Technology Transfer Agreements and the EC Competition Rules. Oxford 1996.

Krattenmaker, Thomas G.: Monopoly Power and Market Power in Antitrust Law, in Revitalizing Antitrust in Its Second Century (Harry First et. al. eds.) (1991).

Krattenmaker, Thomas G. and Salop, Steven C.: Anticompetitive Exclusion: Raising Rivals' Costs to Achieve Power over Price. 96 Yale Law Journal 209 (1986).

Kretzer, Martin: Immanentztheorien im Kartellrecht. Methodische Fehlentwicklungen im Wirtschaftsrecht. Kehl 1992.

Kuoppamäki, Petri: Kilpailuoikeuden perusteet. Vantaa 2000.

Kuoppamäki, Petri: Määräävän markkina-aseman väärinkäyttö ja fuusiovalvonta EY.n kilpailuoikeudessa. Helsinki 1992.

Kur, Annette: The 'Presentation Right'—Time to Create a New Limitation in Copyright Law? 31 IIC 308–318 (2000). (Kur 2000)

Kurlantzick, Lewis and Pennino, Jacqueline E.: The Audio Home Recording Act of 1992 and the Formation of Copyright Policy. 45 Journal of the Copyright Society of the USA 497–545 (1998).

Laddie, Hugh, Prescott, Peter and Vitoria, Mary: The Modern Law of Copyright and Designs (3rd ed. London 2000).

Lande, Robert B. and Sobin, Sturgis M.: Reverse Engineering of Computer Software: The Antitrust Issues. 9 Harvard Journal of Law and Technology 237–281 (1996).

Lande, Robert H.: Wealth Transfer As the Original And Primary Concern of the Antitrust: The Efficiency Interpretation Challenged. 34 Hastings Law Journal 67–151 (1982).

Landes, William M. and Posner, Richard A.: An Economic Analysis of Copyright Law. 18 Journal of Legal Studies 325–363 (1989).

Leaffer, Marshall: Understanding Copyright Law. 3rd edn, New York 1999.

Lehmann, Michael: The Theory of Property Rights and the Protection of Intellectual and Industrial Property. 16 IIC No. 5, 525–540 (1985).

Lehmann, Michael: TRIPs, the Berne Convention, and Legal Hybrids. 94 Columbia Law Review 2621–2629 (1994).

Leivo, Kirsi and Leivo, Timo: Euroopan yhteisön kilpailuoikeus. Helsinki 1997.

Lemley, Mark A: Antitrust and the Internet Standardization Problem. 28 Connecticut Law Review 1041–1094 (1996). (Lemley 1996)

Lemley, Mark A.: Beyond Preemption: The Law and Policy of Intellectual Property Licensing. 87 California Law Review 111–172 (1999).

Lemley, Mark A.: The Economic Irrationality of the Patent Misuse Doctrine. 78 California Law Review 1599–1632 (1990).

Lemley, Mark A.: The Economics of Improvement in Intellectual Property Law. 75 Texas Law Review 989–1084 (1997).

Lemley, Mark A. and McGowan, David: Legal Implications of Network Economic Effects. 86 California Law Review 469–611 (1998).

Lessig, Lawrence: Code and Other Laws of Cyberspace. New York 1999.

Lessig, Lawrence: Reclaiming a Commons. Keynote Address at the Berkman Center's 'Building a Digital Commons' (May 29, 1999).

Levin, Marianne: Formskydd. Helsingborg 1984.

Levin, Marianne: Immaterialrätten. Stockholm 1999.

Levin Marianne, Nordell, Per Jonas and Sundberg, Pia (eds.): Upphovsrätt i millenietid. Stockholm 1999.

Lewis, Tracy R. and Yao, Dennis A.: Some Reflections on the Antitrust Treatment of Intellectual Property. 63 Antitrust Law Journal 603–619 (1995).

Liebowitz, S.J. and Margolis, Stephen E.: Are Network Externalities a New Source of Market Failure? 17 Research in Law and Economics 1–22 (1995).

Liebowitz, S.J. and Margolis, Stephen E.: Network Externality: An Uncommon Tragedy. 8 Journal of Economic Perspectives 133–150 (1994).

Liebowitz, S.J. and Margolis, Stephen E.: Should Technology Choice Be a Concern of Antitrust Policy. 9 Harvard Journal of Law and Technology 283–318 (1996).

Lipsky, Abbott B. Jr. and Sidak, Gregory J.: Essential Facilities. 51 Stanford Law Review 1187–1248 (1999).

Locke, John: An Essay Concerning the True Original Extent and End of Civil Government, in Social Contract: Essayes by Locke, Hume and Rousseau with an introduction by Sir Ernest Barker. Oxford 1947.

Lopatka, John E. and Page, William H.: Antitrust on Internet Time: Microsoft and the Law and Economics of Exclusion. 7 Supreme Court Economic Review 157–231 (1999).

Lund, Torben: Ophavsretsloven. Copenhagen 1961.

Machlup, Fritz: An Economic Review of the Patent System. Study No. 15, Sub-Committee of the Judiciary of the US Senate. Washington 1958.

Mackaay, Ejan: Legal Hybrids: Beyond Property and Monopoly? 94 Columbia Law Review 2630–2643 (1994).

Mandich, Giulio: Venetian Patents (1450–1550). 30 Journal of the Patent Office Society 166–224 (1948).

Mansfield, Edwin: Intellectual Property, Innovation and Economic Growth, in Intellectual Property Rights in Science, Technology, and Economic Performance (Rushing, F.W. and Brown, B.B. eds.) 17–30. Boulder 1990.

Mansfield, Edwin: Technological Change. An Introduction to a Vital Era of Modern Economics. New York 1971.

Markey, Howard T.: Special Problems in Patent Cases. 57 Journal of the Patent Office Society 675–695 (1975).

McCullagh, Declan: DVD Battles: Copy Free or Die? IP Worldwide 4–5/2000, 38–43.

Meinhardt, Marcel: Die Beschränkung nationaler Immaterialgüterrechte durch Art. 86 EG-Vertrag. Bern 1998.

Melamed, A. Douglas: Network Industries and Antitrust. Speech before the Federalist Society (April 10, 1999).

Menell, Peter S.: An Analysis of the Scope of Copyright Protection for Application Programs. 41 Stanford Law Review 1045–1103 (1989).

Menell, Peter S.: The Challenges of Reforming Intellectual Property Protection for Computer Software. 94 Columbia Law Review 2644–2654 (1994).

Menell, Peter S.: An Epitaph for Traditional Copyright Protection of Network Features of Computer Software. [1998] Antitrust Bulletin 651–713.

Menell, Peter S.: Tailoring the Legal Protection of Computer Software. 39 Stanford Law Review 1329–1372 (1987).

Mentula, Arttu, Pokela, Hannu and Saraste, Tuomas: Määräävän markkina-aseman väärinkäyttö kilpailuoikeudessa. Helsinki 1998.

Merges, Robert P.: Commercial Success and Patent Standards: Economic Perspectives on Innovation. 76 California Law Review 805–876 (1988).

Merges, Robert P.: Contracting into Liability Rules: Intellectual Property Rights and Collective Rights Organizations. 84 California Law Review 1293–1393 (1996).

Merges, Robert P.: The Economic Impact of Intellectual Property Rights: An Overview and Guide. 19 Journal of Cultural Economics 103–117 (1995).

Merges, Robert P.: The End of Friction? Property Rights and Contract in the 'Newtonian' World of On-Line Commerce. 12 Berkeley Technology Law Journal 115–136 (1997).

Merges, Robert P.: Of Property Rules, Coase, and Intellectual Property. 94 Columbia Law Review 2655–2673 (1994).

Merges, Robert P. and Nelson, Robert P.: On the Complex Economics of Patent Scope. 90 Columbia Law Review 839–916 (1990).

Merges, Robert P. and Reynolds, Glen Harlan: The Proper Scope of the Copyright and Patent Power. 37 Harvard Journal on Legislation 45–68 (2000).

Meiners, Roger E. and Staaf, Robert J.: Patents, Copyrights, and Trademarks: Property or Monopoly? 13 Harvard Journal of Law & Public Policy 911–947.

Moore, Geoffrey A.: Crossing the Chasm—Marketing and Selling High-Tech Products to Mainstream Customers. New York 1991 (1st paperback edn, 1995).

Moore, Geoffrey A.: Inside the Tornado—Marketing Strategies from Silicon Valley's Cutting Edge. New York 1995.

Nelson, Richard R.: Intellectual Property Protection for Cumulative Systems Technology. 94 Columbia Law Review 2674–2677 (1994).

Nimmer, David, Brown, Elliot and Frischling, Gary N.: The Metamorphosis of Contract into Expand. 87 California Law Review 19–77 (1999).

Nimmer, Raymond T.: Standards, Antitrust and Intellectual Property. 414 PLI/PAT 797 (1995).

Nimmer, Raymond T. and Santhanam, Murali: The Concept of Misuse in Copyright and Trademark Law: Searching for a Concept of Restraint. 524 PLI/PAT. 397 (1998).

Nordell, Per Jonas: Vad är en stark upphovsrätt? In festskrift till Gunnar Karnell, 513–522. Stockholm 1999.

Nordell, Per Jonas: Rätten till det visuella. Stockholm 1997.

Nordemann, Wilhelm: A Right to Control or Merely to Payment?—Towards a Logical Copyright System. 11 IIC 49–54 (1980).

Nordhaus, Raymond C.: Patent-Antitrust Law. 2nd rev. ed. Chicago 1972.

Nordhaus, William D.: Invention, Growth, and Welfare: A Theoretical Treatment of Technological Change. Cambridge, Mass. 1969.

Novos, Ian E. and Waldman, Michael: The Effects of Increased Copyright Protection: An Analytical Approach. 92 Journal of Political Economy 236–248 (1984).

Nyberg, Hanna: Missbruk av dominerande ställning i EG-rätten och patent. Åbo 1999.

OECD Report: Competition Policy and Intellectual Property Rights. Paris 1989.

Oesch, Rainer: Oikeus valokuvaan. Jyväskylä 1993.

Olsson, Henry: Copyright. Svensk och internationell upphovsrätt. 7th ed. Stockholm 1998.

Ordover, Janusz A.: A Patent System for Both Diffusion and Exclusion. 5 Journal of Economic Perspectives 43–60 (1991).

O'Rourke, Maureen: Striking a Delicate Balance: Intellectual Property, Antitrust, Contract, and Standardization in the Computer Industry. 12 Harvard Journal of Law & Technology 1–41 (1998).

Ozaki, Hideo and Kato, Hisashi: MPEG2 Patent Portfolio License-Patent Pooling of Technical Standards of Picture Compression. 48 Intellectual Property Control 329 (1998).

Page, William H. and Lopatka, John E.: The Dubious Search for Integration in the Microsoft Trial. 31 Connecticut Law Review 1251–1274 (1999).

Parente, Stephen L. and Prescott, Edward C.: Barriers to Technology Adoption and Development. 102 Journal of Political Economy 298–321 (1994).

Parente, Stephen L. and Prescott, Edward C.: Monopoly Rights: A Barrier to Riches. 89 American Economic Review 1216–1233 (1999).

Pehrson, Lars: Förhållandet mellan immaterialrätten och konkurrensbegränsningsrätten inom EG, EES och Sverige, in Vennebog til Mogens Koktvedgaard, 385–401. Stockholm 1993.

Pitofsky, Robert: Challenges of the New Economy: Issues at the Intersection of Antitrust and Intellectual Property. Speech at American Antitrust Institute Conference on an Agenda for Antitrust in the 21st Century (2000).

Polinsky, A. Mitchell: An Introduction to Law and Economics. Boston and Toronto 1989.

Posner, Richard A.: Antitrust Law, an Economic Perspective. Chicago and London 1976.

Posner, Richard A.: Economic Analysis of Law. New York 1998.

Prosi, Gerhard: Patents and Externalities. Zeitschrift für Nationalökonomie 31 (1971), 63–80.

Quaedvlieg, Antoon: Copyright's Orbit Round Private, Commercial and Economic Law— The Copyright System and the Place of the User. 29 IIC 420–438 (1998).

Rahnasto, Ilkka: Scope of IP Protection—Application of Abstraction Theory, in Ånd og rett (Festskrift til Birger Stuevold Lassen), 825–829. Oslo 1997.

Reichman, J.H.: Legal Hybrids Between the Patent and Copyright Paradigms. 94 Columbia Law Review 2432–2558 (1994).

Reichman, J.H. and Samuelson, Pamela: Intellectual Property Rights in Data? 50 Vanderbilt University Law Review 51–166 (1997).

Rissanen, Kirsti: Kilpailu ja tavaramerkit. Kilpailunrajoituslain soveltaminen tavaramerkin yksilöimiin järjestelyihin. Vammala 1978.

Rivette, Kevin G. and Kline, David: Rembrandts in the Attic—Unlocking the Hidden Value of Patents. Boston 2000.

Rognstad, Ole-Andreas: Spredning av verkseksemplar. Oslo 1999.

Rosen, Jan: Förlagsrätt. Stockholm 1981.

Rubinfeld, Nataniel: Competition, Innovation, and Antitrust Enforcement in Dynamic Network Industries. Speech before Software Publishers Association meeting (1998).

Saarenheimo, Tuomas: Studies on Market Structure and Technological Innovation. Helsinki 1994.

Sack, Rolf: Der markenrechtliche Erschöpfungsgrundsatz in deutschen und europäischen Recht. Wettbewerb und Recht und Praxis 1998, 549–576.

Salokannel, Marjut: Ownership of Rights in Audiovisual Productions. The Hague 1997.

Samuelson, Paul A. and Nordhaus, William D.: Economics. 12th edn, New York 1985.

Samuelson, Pamela: Challenges for the World Intellectual Property Organization and the Trade-related Aspects of Intellectual Property Rights Council in Regulating Intellectual Property Rights in the Information Age. [1999] EIPR 578–591.

Samuelson, Pamela: Digitisation: Comments for Panel Session, in the Boundaries of Copyright, Its Proper Limitations and Exceptions (Libby Baulch, Michael Green and Mary Wyburn eds), 76–83. Australian Copyright Council 1999.

Samuelson, Pamela: Information as Property: Do Ruckelhaus and Carpenter Signal a Changing Direction in Intellectual Property Law. 38 Catholic University Law Review 365–400 (1989).

Samuelson, Pamela: The US Digital Agenda at WIPO. 37 Virginia Journal of International Law 369–439 (1997).

Samuelson, Pamela, Davis, Randall, Kabor, Mitchell D. and Reichmann, J.H.: A Manifesto Concerning the Legal Protection of Computer Programs. 94 Columbia Law Review 2308–2431 (1994).

Sandgren, Claes: Patentlicenser. Studier i licensavtal angående patent, patentansökningar och know-how med särskild hänsyn till amerikansk och tysk rätt. Stockholm 1974.

Sarraute, Raymond: Current Theories on the Moral Right of Authors and Artists Under French Law. 16 American Journal of Comparative Law 465–506 (1968).

Scherer, F.M.: The Economic Effects of Compulsory Licensing. New York University Monograph Series in Finance and Economics 1977-2 (1977).

Scherer, F.M.: Industrial Market Structure and Economic Performance. Chicago 1980.

Scherer, F.M.: Innovation and Growth. Schumpeterian Perspectives. Cambridge, Massachusetts 1984.

Schlicher, John W.: If Economic Welfare Is the Goal, Will Economic Analysis Redefine Patent Law. 4 Journal of Proprietary Rights no. 6, 12–19 (1992).

Schlicher, John W.: Patent Law: Legal and Economic Principles. 1999 (looseleaf).

Schonning, Peter: Ophavsretten—mellem kulturpolitik og handelspolitik. Århus 1994.

Schovsbo, Jens: Graensefladesporsmål mellem immaterialretten og konkurrenceretten. Copenhagen 1996.

Schovsbo, Jens: Markedsforing af parallelimporterede markevarer. UfR 1998, 16–21.

Schovsbo, Jens: 'Ophavsrettens monopolprobleme', in Ånd og rett, Festskift till Birger Stuevold Lassen, 921–946. Oslo 1997.

Schovsbo, Jens: Som skabt for hinanden—Immaterial- og konkurrenceretlig beskyttelse af kompatible produkter. NIR 1997, 16–47. Published also in English, 'As If Made for Each Other—Intellectual Property Rights and Protection of Compatible Products', 29 IIC 510–534 (1998).

Schricker, Gerhard and Katzenberger, Paul: Die urherberrechtliche Leerkassetten-vergütung. GRUR 1985, 87–111.

Schumpeter, Joseph A.: Capitalism, Socialism and Democracy. 3rd ed. New York 1950.

Scotchmer, Suzanne: Standing on the Shoulders of Giants: Cumulative Research and the Patent Law. 5 Journal of Economic Perspectives 29–41 (1991).

Schumann, Jochen: Grundzüge der Microeconomischen Theorie. Berlin 1984.

Segerstrom, Paul S.: Innovation, Imitation, and Economic Growth. 99 Journal of Political Economy 807–827 (1991).

Shapiro, Carl: Exclusivity in Network Industries. 7 George Mason Law Review 673–682 (1999).

Shapiro, Carl and Varian, Hal R.: Information Rules—A Strategic Guide to the Network Economy. Boston 1999.

Sheffner, Ben: Alcatel USA, Inc. v DGI Technologies, Inc. 15 Berkley Technology Law Journal 25–47 (2000).

Sheramata, Willow A.: Barriers to Innovation: A Monopoly, Network Externalities, and the Speed of Innovation. [1997] Antitrust Bulletin 937–972.

Sheramata, Willow A.: 'New' Issues in Competition Policy Raised by Information Technology Industries. 43 Antitrust Bulletin 547–581 (1998).

Sherman, Brad and Bently, Lionel: The Making of Modern Intellectual Property Law. The British Experience, 1760–1911. Cambridge 1999.

Sherwin, Emily: Two- and Three-Dimensional Property Rights. 27 Arizona State Law Journal 1075–1102 (1997).

Sherwood, Robert M.: Intellectual Property and Economic Development. Boulder 1990.

Silverstein, David: Patents, Science and Innovation: Historical Linkages and Implications for Global Technological Competitiveness. 17 Rutgers Computer & Technology Law Journal 261–319 (1991).

Sinkfield, Richard H. and Houser, Terry L.: Patent Misuse and Antitrust. 572 PLI/Pat 383–430 (1999).

Stern, Richard H.: Refusals to License Intellectual Property Rights and Monopoly 'Leverage'. [1998] EIPR 390–395.

Stern, Richard H.: Scope-of-Protection Problems with Patents and Copyrights on Methods of Doing Business. 10 Fordham Intellectual Property, Media & Entertainment Law Journal 105–158 (1999).

Stigler, George: United States v Loew's, Inc.: A Note on Block Booking. 1963 Supreme Court Review 152, 152–153 (1963).

Stocking, George W. and Watkins, Myron W.: Monopoly and Free Enterprise. New York 1991.

Strömholm, Stig: A Short History of Legal Thinking in the West. Lund 1985.

Strömholm, Stig: Upphovsrättens verksbegrepp. Stockholm 1970.

Sullivan, Lawrence A. and Jones, Ann I.: Monopoly Conduct, Especially Leveraging Power from One Product or Market to Another, in Jorde, T.–Teece, D., Antitrust, Innovation, and Competitiveness, 165–184. New York 1992.

Swygert, Michael J. and Yanes, Katherine Earle: A Primer on the Coase Theorem: Making Law in a World of Zero Transaction Costs. 11 Depaul Business Journal 1–42 (1998).

Takalo, Tuomas: Essays on the Economics of Intellectual Property Rights. Helsinki 1999.

Taylor, C.T. and Silberston, Z.A.: The Economic Impact of the Patent System. A Study of the British Experience. Cambridge 1973.

Temple Lang, John: European Community Antitrust Law—Innovation Markets and High

Technology Industries. Speech before Fordham Corporate Law Institute. 17 October, 1996.

Thomson, William E. Jr. and Chu, Margaret Y.: Overstepping the Bounds: Copyright Misuse. 15 No. 11 Computer Law 1 (1998).

Thurow, Lester C.: Needed: A New System of Intellectual Property Rights. Harvard Business Review 1997, 95–103.

Timonen, Pekka: Määräysvalta, hinta ja markkinavoima. Helsinki 1997.

Tom, Willard K. and Newberg, Joshua A.: Antitrust and Intellectual Property: From Separate Spheres to Unified Field. 66 Antitrust 167–229 (1997).

Torvalds, Linus and Diamond, David: Just for Fun—Menestystarina. Keuruu 2001.

Towse, Ruth: Copyright as an Economic Incentive. 17 Copyright Reporter 15–25 (1999).

Tuckett, Roger: Access to Public Standards: Interoperability Revisited. 12 EIPR 423–427 (1992).

Turner, Donald F.: The Durability, Relevance, and Future of American Antitrust Policy. 75 California Law Review 797–815 (1987).

Turner, Donald F.: The Patent System and Competitive Policy. 44 New York University Law Review 450–476 (1969).

Turner, Julie S.: The Nonmanufacturing Patent Owner: Toward a Theory of Efficient Infringement. 179 California Law Review 179–210 (1998).

Tye, William B.: Market Imperfections, Equity, and Efficiency. 37 Antitrust Bulletin 1–34 (1992).

Vinje, Thomas C.: Die EG-Richtlinie zum Schutz von Computerprogrammen und die Frage der Interoperabilität. GRUR Int. 1992, 250–260.

Vinje, Thomas C.: The Final Word on Magill. NIR 1995, 156–168.

Virtanen, Pertti: Määräävän markkina-aseman kontrollointi. Jyväskylä 2001.

Webb, Jere M. and Locke, Lawrence A.: Intellectual Property Misuse: Development in the Misuse Doctrine. 4 Harvard Journal of Law & Technology 257–267 (1991).

Weinstein, Roy–Huang, Shane: Valuing Patents and Intangible Assets in the Semiconductor Industry. 19 The Licensing Journal 2:8–13 (1999).

White, James A.D.: Misuse or Fair Use: That Is the Software Copyright Question. 12 Berkeley Technology Law Journal 251–310 (1997).

OFFICIAL SOURCES

Betenkning angående nordisk patentlovgivning NU 1963:6.

ETSI Intellectual Property Rights Policy, version of April 5, 2000.

Förslag till lag om upphovsmannarätt till litterära och konstnärliga verk. Helsinki 1953.

ISO/IEC Policy on IPR (1994).

Green Paper—Copyright and Related Rights in the Information Society, COM(95) 382 final.

Intellectual Property and the National Information Infrastructure. Information Infrastructure Task Force 1994.

The Internet Standards Process. Revision 3, April 1996 (by S. Bradner, Harvard University).

Procedures for the Development of American National Standards, April 1998.

Regeringens proposition 1981/82: 165 med förslag till Konkurrenslag.

Tekijänoikeudet tietoyhteiskunnassa. Opetusministeriön työryhmien muistioita 1995:13. Helsinki 1995.

Tekijänoikeuskomitean III osamietintö. Helsinki 1987.

Via satellit och kabel. SOU 1984: 5.

INDEX

Please note that IPRs stand for Intellectual Property Rights